Ecotourism:
Impacts, Potentials and Possibilities

Ecotourism:
Impacts, Potentials and Possibilities

Stephen Wearing and John Neil

OXFORD   AUCKLAND   BOSTON   JOHANNESBURG   MELBOURNE   NEW DELHI

Butterworth-Heinemann
Linacre House, Jordan Hill, Oxford OX2 8DP
225 Wildwood Avenue, Woburn, MA 01801-2041
A division of Reed Educational and Professional Publishing Ltd

℞ A member of the Reed Elsevier plc group

First published 1999
Reprinted 2000

British Library Cataloguing in Publication Data
A catalogue record for this book is available from the British Library

Library of Congress Cataloguing in Publication Data
A catalogue record for this book is available on request

ISBN 0 7506 4137 1

Composition by Genesis Typesetting, Laser Quay, Rochester, Kent
Printed and bound in Great Britain

Contents

Foreword

Ecotourism, the idea that nature based tourism could contribute social and environmental benefits, burst into public consciousness in the late 1980s and became virtually a phenomenon in the 1990s. In many countries, it became a substantial focus of debate, generating numerous conferences, new courses and challenging policy development at all levels of government, the tourist industry and the environment movement.

It is not too difficult to explain the extraordinary rise of interest. The publication of the Brundtland Report, *Our Common Future*, in 1987 by the United Nations Commission on Environment and Development was the catalyst which saw a major world-wide rise in environmental consciousness. It focused on the greatest dilemma of life on earth – in a world of over 5 billion people how do you meet the needs and demands of humans without destroying the very ecological fabric of the planet which underpins all life and human well being? The report identified the concept of sustainable development as the answer.

While conceptually there was broad agreement, it was not easy to find clean, green industries which were truly environmentally benign or had positive outcomes over the long haul. This was especially true in developing countries where nature had its strongholds, but where short-term economic drivers often saw natural lands and wildlife disappearing fast to satisfy both the needs of survival and resource industries. Scientists and environmentalists could see that there was little hope of saving these lands unless they could generate income from their natural state to meet the needs of their people. Ecotourism appeared to offer a sustainable development option for countries, regions and local communities, which would provide an incentive to retain and manage their wild lands and wildlife and hence the crucial biodiversity of life. It could be an alternative to rapacious, resource extraction of logging and mining. It could earn the desperately sought foreign currency and bring in revenues to properly manage protected areas.

A crucial component of the concept is that affected local communities need to be recipients of such benefits if this incentive is to work. However, beyond simply being an incentive to keep forests alive and keep dynamite fishing away from reefs, many saw that such tourism could actually foster an environmental ethic through both the experience and good interpretation. Most people who have swum on a coral reef would want that reef to remain protected for all time.

Ecotourism also appeared to hold promise to ameliorate another dilemma of our age. The twentieth century has seen the tragic and rapid demise of the rich cultural heritage of the world's indigenous people by the relentless pressure of modern industrialized society. Environmentalists viewed this as both a human and ecological tragedy as 'the wisdom of the elders' seemed doomed to disappear. Ironically, as the diversity and integrity of native cultures and natural places were increasingly under threat, the world's educated and environmentally aware travellers sought contact with them. Low key tourism appeared to offer an economic return to such communities for conserving and celebrating their cultures.

Overall therefore the ecotourism concept was to some degree the right idea at the right time. Tourism interests were looking for areas where their country had a competitive advantage and new angles to market their countries or regions. Environmentalists were looking for reasons why governments should conserve land, as well as examples of green industries and an alternative to the rapacious model of mass tourism. Indigenous and rural communities were looking for alternatives to destructive industries, new employment opportunities, particularly ones that could enhance their communities. Governments were looking for economic development, income from their protected area assets and lower costs in land management.

However, in the decade of ecotourism we have found that these benefits are not always easy to deliver. Undoubtedly there are forests still standing, rivers still clean and wildlife alive because of ecotourism. But we have also seen ecotourism as the thin end of the wedge in allowing for development in protected areas and fragile environments. Spreading benefits to local communities is also fraught with problems and often inadequate to offset the appeal of short-term but more lucrative extractive industries. Tourism is after all an industry frequently locked into the dynamic of short-term profit before long-term social, cultural or ecological sustainability.

This broad-reaching and comprehensive book gives an excellent coverage of this important issue. It asks all the key questions about whether ecotourism can ultimately deliver on its undoubted promise. In fact the book itself may assist in the process of ecotourism realizing its potential benefits as its wide ranging chapters identify many of the key issues practitioners and policy makers need to consider and identify many of the pitfalls.

I certainly commend the call in the introduction for the need to get the frameworks right, ecotourism is unlikely to succeed unless many of the key components such as an adequate protected area system, sound regulation and adequate funding of good management are available.

Penelope Figgis AM

About the authors

Dr Stephen Wearing's background is in environmental and tourism planning and management. He has an undergraduate and masters degree in town planning. He has worked in both local and state government and consulted internationally in the area or ecotourism. His work in establishing the Santa Elena Ecotourism Rainforest Reserve in Costa Rica saw him receive an award from the Costa Rican Government and this work also forms the core of his PhD. Stephen's research focuses on the social sciences in natural resource management including community development, community-based tourism, ecotourism, gender and leisure theory, outdoor education, guiding and interpretation management, environmentalism and sociology of tourism. He is a Senior Lecturer in the School of Leisure and Tourism Studies, Faculty of Business at the University of Technology, Sydney where he teaches in a number of these areas.

John Neil is a freelance researcher, writer and teacher across a range of subjects including community development, ecology, poststructuralism, continental philosophy and textuality. He is currently completing a PhD at the University of Sydney and is a research officer and tutor at the University of Technology, Sydney.

Acknowledgements

We have many people to thank for this book:

To Penny Figgis, for providing the motivation to begin this book by choosing to put her family first. We thank her for her inspiration and for providing case study material and her Foreword. She has also contributed the second case study in Chapter 7, 'Issues in protected area policy in Australia'. It is an infinitely better book for her contribution.

Thanks to Paula Drayton and Isabel Sebastian for their research and editorial comment and just for being fun to be around.

To Julie for the support.

To Geraldene.

Thanks also to Penny Davidson for all her comments and her contribution to Chapter 10; her insights added great depth.

Finally, thanks to all those students who have contributed to the development of the ideas in the numerous workshops in ecotourism and protected area management – their enthusiasm and creativity created the basis for the book; to Barbara Almond in particular for work done that contributed to Chapter 5; to Joanne McLean and Nikki Phillips for their ideas; and to Mark Jackson for the index.

S.W.
J.N.

Introduction

Ecotourism? A simple enough word but a complex and often contradictory concept. A fashion, a fad? *Ecological travel is the 'next big thing'; the hippest way to travel is to backpack off the beaten track to experience 'nature' up close and personal (with all the luxuries of home included).*

A tourism industry marketing exercise that effectively packages 'nature' for affluent urban dwellers to 'experience' a romantic world now lost to us moderns? *Lush rainforests, arid deserts, the polar caps – these are the 'hottest' destinations (while they last).*

Or a way for environmentalism to enter the mainstream in the 1990s after losing its impetus in an economic rationalist world? *Conservation issues are now at the forefront of public opinion. The decline of natural rainforests, loss of endangered species, global warming and land degradation have galvanized public support for conservation.*

But can we even speak of 'nature' in a world that has less of it than ever before in human history? Western society is indifferent if not downright hostile to the existence of wilderness except where its value can be quantified as a resource or as a spectacle, a tourist attraction. Does a suicidal society need nature to justify its travel? Is it an escape, an excuse, or simply a distraction? Or is it something more profound?

Whatever the origins, nature is calling and we are responding in droves. And ecotourists are leading the charge. But getting 'off the beaten track' often means that the track soon becomes a road, even a highway. And the beautiful wild spaces sought after by ecotourists often are extremely fragile and sensitive to human impact, however 'lightly we tread'. One thing however is certain, the increasing global interest and expo-nential growth in ecotourism cannot simply be explained as another in a long line of recreational trends. Instead it reflects a fundamental shift in the way human beings view and engage with nature.

We have begun with a lot of questions and no easy answers yet in sight. Where would you dare start? Well, why not the word itself – *ecotourism*? Within this word exist two seemingly contra-dictory meanings. Let's take the most obvious: *tourism*. Tourism is currently the world's largest industry. World tourism grew by 260% between 1970 and 1990 and world-wide international arrivals are predicted to reach between 637 and 956 million by the year 2000[1] (World Tourism Organisation, 1990). The projected growth in travel and tourism is expected to be between 2% and 4.5% per year. A growth rate of 4.5% for example would see world travel and tourism increase to around 600 million international arrivals (over 50% increase). This would contrib-ute to the creation of up to 55 million jobs by the end of the 1990s (WTTC, 1992).

Tourism has a gross throughput of more than US\$3.5 trillion per year, employing around 127

---

[1] World-wide international arrivals have increased from 25 282 000 in 1950 to 476 000 000 (WTO, 1990, 1993).

million people world-wide, accounting in 1993 for over 7% of the world's capital investment (WTTC, 1995). It is currently estimated that tourism will generate:

- 10.9% of world GDP, or $3.4 trillion;
- over 11.4% of the world's capital investment;
- over $665 billion to total tax payments world-wide (WTTC, 1995).

For these reasons alone tourism is valued highly by many countries and often holds a very prominent position in development strategies. It is actively promoted and industry bodies are courted by governments due to its potential to significantly bolster foreign exchange and domestic employment.

Increases in leisure time, the growth in real income, mobility, technological improvements in communications and international transportation, and demographic changes in the West all have led to the strong global demand for tourism.[2] This growth has significant implications for developing countries. Revenues received from tourism receipts now account for more than 10% of the value in 47 developing countries and more than 50% of the comparable amount received from export revenues in 17 countries (Healy, 1989: 4). Relatively cheap air travel puts the entire planet within reach of the modern-day tourist – half of the people who holiday do so in the Third World.

And somewhere in this tourism 'explosion' lies ecotourism. 'Ecotourism' has evolved into a type of speciality travel, incorporating a diverse (and often bewildering) array of activities and tourism types, from birdwatching, scientific study, photography, diving, bushwalking, to regeneration of damaged ecosystems. It is a broad and loose garment this word 'ecotourism'. For some it is a subset of 'nature-based' tourism activities; for others it is a 'niche' market, a specific type of 'special interest tourism'. In a relatively short period of time it has caught the imagination of many local communities, governments and international environmental organizations. Estimates of ecotourism's growth are extremely variable at the present time, but range from anywhere between 10% and 30%[3] (Kallen, 1990; Vickland, 1989). Despite this variability, the tourism industry has wholly embraced ecotourism, even to the extent of the term 'ecotourism' becoming the buzz word of the late 1990s, and we are witness today to the plethora of tourism forms with the 'eco' prefix attached like some badge of honour.

In a multifaceted world something can mean anything depending on how the light strikes it. So let's narrow the prism and focus on the prefix – *eco* – from the word 'ecology' which itself is derived from the Greek word *oikos* meaning house or habitat. The environment that we humans inhabit is, at its most fundamental, our home, our dwelling, our life support. And despite the relative newness of the term, ecotourism's origins are deeply rooted in a form of philosophy and experience, and its philosophical heritage is embraced by conservationists and environmentalists alike. The environmental movement was born from the nature conservation movement, which recognized that nature is essential to human well-being. In recent years this conviction has been strengthened by the scientific understanding that biodiversity is essential to not only well-being, but to human survival. Many have also articulated the need for nature to be conserved regardless of any utility or value to humans but because nature has a right to exist and conversely the human species does not have the right to determine the fate of all other species (Nash, 1989).

But tourism involves travel away from our origin, from our individual homes, into dwellings that are not our own, but that may be

---

[2] According to one study a 10% increase in real income in developed countries leads to consumers increasing their foreign travel expenditures by 15 to 20% (Artis, in Goldfarb, 1989: 131).

[3] As we shall see, the diversity of tourism forms and controversies in classification partly explain the difficulties and variability in estimating the size of the ecotourism market.

constructed specifically for us, us tourists; to places that we tread upon which are a life support for 'others' both human and non-human. The world is a stage and we relentlessly strive to satisfy our desire, striding across the globe to experience these 'others' – cultures, nature, sights, sounds and smells – to see sights that are unusual, to explore the unknown, the alien, the 'magical'. The not-here.

This book embarks on its own journey, a journey in understanding that will, through the following pages, take us across the globe. We will be making stops along the way: visiting sites such as Costa Rica, Australia and Africa. The initial part of this journey takes place in Chapter 1, where we will discuss ecotourism's key principles. Fundamentally ecotourism involves travel to relatively undisturbed or protected natural areas, fostering understanding, appreciation and conservation of the flora, fauna, geology and ecosystems of an area. The fauna, geology and ecosystems of an area highlight the nature-based aspect of ecotourism. But ecotourism is not defined by this relationship alone. Biological and physical features are central to ecotourism and the conservation of natural areas and sustainable resource management is therefore essential to the planning, development and management of ecotourism. However, it also involves the notion that the activity of ecotourism must positively contribute to conservation in the destination area or host community. The understanding that ecotourism has the potential to create support for conservation objectives in both the host community and in the visitor alike, through establishing and sustaining links between the tourism industry, local communities, and protected areas will provide the basis for our journey, and leads us into understanding the central issues of conservation and sustainability of natural and social environments.

Chapter 2 places ecotourism within its historical context to connect it to the major philosophic and social currents that have contributed to its development. We focus here specifically on the human/nature relationship and the interaction between them as this will help us to understand the shift in the way nature is valued, both historically and philosophically, and how ecotourism fits into this change in values.

In our dominant market economies policy implications are predominantly defined by the interplay of government regulation and market forces. Chapter 3 examines why tourism is particularly attractive for governments, particularly in its potential for providing an alternative to traditional industry, such as forestry or mining. However, in many cases tourism has not lived up to its high expectations as its benefits are often circumscribed by the significant impacts tourism engenders upon ecosystems and local communities. Tourism is often promoted by government or industry without an overall strategy, without adequate attention to legislative frameworks, without consultation or inclusion of local communities and without effective protected area management plans. We will examine the key policy issues that relate to ecotourism, including a discussion of mechanisms to ensure that it does not exceed its sustainable base, in moving towards understanding the provision of infrastructure for development and the policy and institutional prerequisites for planning and managing ecotourism.

Nowhere are the conflicting views over ecotourism more evident than the current debate over the function and purpose of protected areas. It is a conflict over two primary orientations, 'preservation' versus 'use', and tourism in protected areas embodies precisely this dilemma. Such an opposition is illustrated and reinforced through accepted institutional arrangements in which tourism and conservation goals are pursued by independent organizations. The current focus of the debate on tourism in protected areas is the extension of a long controversy, a controversy that has existed since the conception of protected areas and equivalent reserves. The imperative for conservation advocates becomes *how* to conserve rather than whether or not to conserve. In this way ecotourism, as a sustainable development strategy, is increasingly being turned to as part of a political philosophy for protected area managers and conservation agencies as a means of providing practical outcomes in the struggle to provide a basis for continued protection for these areas.

Chapter 5 introduces the key elements of interpretation and education which further helps us to differentiate ecotourism from other forms of nature-based tourism. A focus on the dimensions of visitor experience reveals that the visitor is concerned not with simply looking at a setting or object, but with feeling and realizing some of its *value*. In this way, interpretation is oriented towards a visitor's cognitive and emotional state in order to raise awareness, enhance understanding and, hopefully, clarify or enlarge each participant's perspective and attitude. In this way, interpretation is essential to conservation goals and therefore central to ecotourism.

The tourism industry makes extensive use of natural assets – forests, reefs, beaches and parks, but what does it contribute to management of these assets? The provision of tourism infrastructure, and the costs of managing the impact of tourism on host communities, are often borne by the environment, the community itself and the government. Local communities are significantly vulnerable to the deleterious impacts of tourism development – particularly indigenous cultures – as they directly experience the sociocultural impacts of tourism. In many cases indigenous cultures are used extensively to promote destinations to overseas markets yet many indigenous people rightly feel that the tourism industry has a poor track record, in disregarding their legitimate interests and rights, and profiting from their cultural knowledge and heritage.

Chapter 6 explores ecotourism's relationship to local communities, particularly as an alternative form of development that is able to satisfy conservation and sustainability objectives. Features of the natural and cultural environment and supportive host communities are the foundations of a successful industry. Neglect of conservation and quality of life issues threatens the very basis of local populations and a viable and sustainable tourism industry.

Chapter 7 presents two case studies to give an operational context to what has been presented in the early chapters of the book. The first case study focuses on the local level in examining a small community-based ecotourism project in Costa Rica. The Santa Elena Rainforest Reserve (SERR) project demonstrates the critical problematic between development and the natural environment in attempting to foster economic self-sufficiency and natural resource conservation among a low-income community. It illustrates ecotourism's potential as an alternate strategy for development, particularly when the development process is actually led and controlled by the local community.

The second case focuses on the national level by examining the institutional arrangements in which ecotourism and conservation goals are pursued in relation to protected areas in Australia. The dominance of economic rationalist ideologies by government is inherently hostile to protected areas and has marginalized the role, and consequently the support for protected areas.

The global political agenda is increasingly being dominated by economic principles which serve actively to promote the ever-increasing consumption of resources in the West. Chapter 8 explores the relationship between ecotourism and one of the fundamental tools to enhance consumption, marketing. We examine the structure and nature of marketing in the tourism industry, focusing particularly on understanding and evaluating the connection between ecotourism and marketing – the issue of supply versus demand-driven marketing. Pivotal to understanding the marketing relationship to ecotourism are the implications for protected areas, conservation and local communities. Ecotourism marketing has been surrounded by much confusion and controversy as it attempts to take into account the dual objectives of protected areas and local communities on the one hand and those of the tourism industry on the other.

By analysing the market of ecotourism we find a new group of tourism clients, the ecotourists. In Chapter 9 we examine who they are and what they are demanding. We will explore the characteristics that differentiate ecotourists through an analysis of tourist motivation, demographic and psychographic characteristics, the needs of ecotourists, the images and attitudes ecotourists ascribe to a destination, and the influence of social, cultural and physical environments.

Ecotourism is a catalyst for change and this book will explore broad issues such as ecology, biodiversity, bioregionalism, economic rationalism, equity of access, approaches to management of protected areas, social policy, directions of the tourism industry and local communities. Central to all of these areas is the question of sustainability and its centrality to development. Sustainable development underpins questions of resource use, not only in providing income benefits to a region but also the preservation of social infrastructure and biosphere conservation. Chapter 10 discusses these issues in relation to ecotourism as a model for sustainable development.

But what of the future? Despite ecotourism's potential as a model for sustainable development we need to be aware of ecotourism's future direction. Frameworks are needed in which to evaluate ecotourism, mindful that economic ben-efits from tourism often create insufficient incentives for local communities to support conservation. Benefits are often offset in the eyes of the local communities by the intrusion of tourists, greater income inequality within and between local communities, increased pollution, sequestering of profits from outsiders and rising local prices.

Without continual questioning and evaluation we risk losing the impetus of change that ecotourism offers. Without adequate regulation of private sector activities and sound protected area management, ecotourism development may have adverse impacts on the resource base upon which it depends. However, a viable tourism practice needs to address the imperatives of the market. Alternative approaches in areas like research, management, marketing and planning can provide new answers to perennial questions that may keep ecotourism at the cutting edge of change in society.

In spite of the complexities of these issues, ecotourism is one of the few areas where the link between economic development and conservation of natural areas is clear and direct and we need to keep this at the forefront of our minds as we undertake our learning journey.

1

Departure – surveying the ground

Despite the conflicting interpretations and convenient deployment of the term 'ecotourism' within the tourism industry, one thing is certain – the increasing global interest and exponential growth in ecotourism cannot simply be explained as another in a long line of recreational trends. Instead it reflects a fundamental shift in the way human beings view and engage with nature.

This chapter will briefly trace the evolution of the ecotourism phenomenon and some of the definitional debates which have marked its evolution. Originally conceived as an alternative to the increasing threat posed to both the culture and the environment of destination areas by mass tourism, the original emphasis of ecotourism was on low key, unobtrusive tourism which had minimal impacts on natural ecosystems. However, the term 'alternative tourism' is interpreted by various authors in widely differing and sometimes openly contradictory ways. For some it is up-market package tours of rich people to exotic destinations, mostly wilderness areas, whereas others define it as rucksack wandering by young people with limited financial means (*cf.* Butler, 1990; Cohen, 1972).

For these reasons a definition of ecotourism, particularly as alternative tourism, is both contentious and difficult to determine with precision. For clarity, let's begin by unpacking the many elements that belong under the term 'ecotourism'. The term itself encompasses a wide range of elements and we will be covering each in detail throughout this book:

- a form of 'alternative tourism' opposed to mass tourism;
- a particular philosophical orientation towards nature;
- tourists characterized by particular motivations;
- touristic practices;
- a touristic product;
- levels of technology;
- solutions to planning;
- an approach to local, regional, national and international politics;
- a strategy for sustainable development.

The ecotourism alternative

The word 'alternative' logically implies its opposite. 'Alternative tourism' then is contrary to that which is seen as negative or detrimental about conventional tourism: it is characterized by its attempt at minimizing the perceived negative environmental and sociocultural impacts of people at leisure in the promotion of radically different approaches to conventional tourism.[1] Therefore the terminologies of alternative and mass tourism are mutually interdependent, each relying on a series of value-laden judgements that themselves structure the definitional content of the terms. In this way the concept of alternative tourism can itself be as broad and vague as its diametrical opposite, with many divergent leisure types being classified as alternative tourism, including adventure holidays, hiking holidays, or the solitary journeys undertaken by globe-trotters. Some authors even go so far as to suggest that anything other than mass tourism classifies as alternative tourism.

Dernoi (1988: 253) initially defined alternative tourism by accommodation type: 'In alternative tourism the "client" receives accommodation directly in, or at the home of, the host with, eventually, other services and facilities offered there.' However, he then went on to list a number of other features by which alternative tourism might be distinguished from 'mass tourism':

Simply stated, AT (alternative tourism)/CBT (community-based tourism) is a privately offered set of hospitality services (and features), extended to visitors, by individuals, families, or a local community. A prime aim of AT/CBT is to establish direct personal/cultural intercommunication and understanding between host and guest (Dernoi, 1988: 89).

Similarly, for the ECTWT (Ecumenical Coalition of Third World Tourism):

alternative tourism is a process which promotes a just form of travel between members of different communities. It seeks to achieve mutual understanding, solidarity and equality amongst participants (Holden, 1984: 15).

The stress here is on the facilitation and improvement of contacts between hosts and guests, especially through the organization of

well-prepared special interest tours, rather than on actual development of facilities.

Another body of literature dealing with tourism typologies gives greater attention to particular variations in terms of tourism classifications, often with a particular tourism form being placed in three or more categories. However, 'alternative tourism' rarely occurs specifically as one of the classes in the typology literature, which reflects the often disparate and very broad characteristics that it may encompass. Mieczkowski (1995) does identify 'alternative tourism' as a tourism type but only in its relation as one of two broad categories along a spectrum of tourism types. The first is conventional mass tourism (CMT), which has prevailed on the market for some time. The second broad category is that of alternative tourism (AT), a flexible generic category that contains a multiplicity of various forms that have one feature in common – they are alternatives to CMT. That is, they are not associated with mass large-scale tourism but are essentially small scale, low-density, dispersed in non-urban areas, and they cater to special interest groups of people with mainly above average education and with relatively high disposable incomes.

As to the specific forms of AT, Mieczkowski (1995) distinguishes such forms as cultural, educational, scientific, adventure and agri-tourism, with rural, ranch and farm subsets (see Figure 1.1). Significantly, there is some overlap with CMT but the main criterion of distinction is the scale and character of the impacts. Another overlap occurs between the various types of AT themselves. Cultural tourism, for example, is to a large extent educational and ecotourism is aligned with nature-based tourism. Thus Mieczkowski (1995) finds it difficult to place ecotourism in the context of AT because, while not coinciding directly with cultural tourism, it overlaps with the educational, scientific, adventure and agri-tourism forms.

Rather than entering into an increasingly complex debate over classifications of particular tourism forms as alternative, specific features are common to alternative tourism and we have

---

[1] Like 'alternative tourism', 'conventional tourism' itself has been designated by varying terms, the most prominent being conventional mass tourism (CMT: Mieczkowski, 1995) and mass tourism (MT: Butler, 1990).

identified here several of the key characteristics. Although not considered to be exhaustive, they are included here to provide the conceptual ideas and specific practices of forms of tourism that are in opposition to 'mass tourism'.

Features of alternative tourism

- The attempted preservation, protection and enhancement of the quality of the resource base which is fundamental to tourism itself.
- The fostering and active promotion of development, in relation to additional visitor attractions and infrastructure, with roots in the specific locale and developed in ways that complement local attributes.
- The endorsement of infrastructure, hence economic growth, when and where it improves local conditions and not where it is destructive or exceeds the carrying capacity of the natural environment or the limits of the social environment whereby the quality of community life is adversely affected (*cf.* Cox, 1985: 6–7; Yum, 1984).
- Tourism which attempts to minimize its impact upon the environment, is ecologically sound, and avoids the negative impacts of many large-scale tourism developments undertaken in areas that have not previously been developed (*cf.* Bilsen, 1987; Gonsalves, 1984; Saglio, 1979; Travis, 1985).
- An emphasis on not only ecological sustainability, but also cultural sustainability. That is, tourism which does not damage the culture of the host community, encouraging a respect for the cultural realities experienced by the tourists through education and organized 'encounters' (*cf.* Holden, 1984).

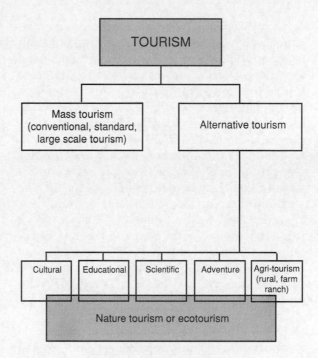

Figure 1.1 *The alternative tourism (after Mieczkowski, 1995: 459)*

Thus, in its most general sense, alternative tourism can be broadly defined as forms of tourism that set out to be consistent with natural, social and community values and which allow both hosts and guests to enjoy positive and worthwhile interaction and shared experiences.

Against the above broad characteristics we can begin to see ecotourism as a form of alternative tourism. In its simplest terms, ecotourism can be generally described as a low key, minimal impact, interpretative tourism where conservation, understanding and appreciation of the environment and cultures visited is sought. It is a specialist area of tourism, involving travel to natural areas, or areas where human presence is minimal, with the ecotourist involved in the ecotourism experience expressing an explicit motivation to satisfy the need for environmental, social and/or cultural education and awareness through visiting and experiencing the natural area.

Hector Ceballos-Lascurain is widely acknowledged as having first coined the term ecotourism itself. In 1981 Ceballos-Lascurian began using the Spanish term *turisimo ecologico* to designate forms of ecological tourism. This term then became shortened to *ecoturisimo* in 1983 and he used the word in discussions in his capacity as president of PRONATURA, a conservation Non-Government Organization (NGO) and director general of SEDUE, the Mexican Ministry of Urban Development and Ecology. At the time he was lobbying for the conservation of rainforest areas in the Mexican state of Chiapas and a primary strategy for maintaining the integrity of forest ecosystems involved the promotion of ecological tourism in the region. He emphasized that ecotourism could become a very important tool for conservation.

The first appearance of the word in the written form was in the March–April 1984 edition of *American Birds* as an advertisement for a tourist operation run by Ceballos-Lascurain. His definition as we now know it first appeared in the literature in 1987 in a paper entitled 'The future of ecoturismo' which was reprinted in the *Mexico Journal* of 27 January 1988 (Ceballos-Lascurain, n.d 2).

Ceballos-Lascurain identified ecotourism as a form of travel in which the natural environment is the primary focus and it is this element which provides us with a simple, yet core, starting point in understanding the ecotourism phenomenon; particularly as a specific form of alternative tourism. The centrality of the natural environment to ecotourism comprises two main facets:

- It involves travel to unspoilt natural environments.
- This travel is predominantly for experiencing the natural environment.

Ecotourism's focus on the natural environment has, in recent years, facilitated its evolution into a catchphrase that encompasses numerous tourism forms including *'nature tourism'*, *'wilderness tourism'*, *'low impact tourism'* and *'sustainable*

tourism' to name a few.[2] These diverse forms of tourism all focus on the natural environment to some extent and, although closely aligned and related to ecotourism, need to be distinguished from ecotourism as there are a number of dimensions to nature-based tourism. Most important for our concerns here is to what degree the tourist experience depends upon nature.

The nature of ecotourism

Nature-based tourism, according to the World Resources Institute, is growing by up to 30% whilst general tourism has increased at a rate of approximately 4% (Lindberg, 1991). While this increase may be slightly exaggerated, there can be no doubting the increasing trends in environmental concern allied with the historically prevalent trend of travel as a form of escape to nature, driven by 'the pressures of urban living [which] encourage people to seek solitude with nature' therefore increasing 'the numbers of visitors to national parks and other protected areas' (Ceballos-Lascurain, 1990: 1).

There are a number of dimensions to nature-based tourism. All forms of travel to natural areas are not necessarily ecotourism, but this provides a useful step in differentiating nature-based tourism from ecotourism and gives us a number of levels at which to distinguish the relationship between specific tourism activities and nature:

- those activities (experiences) that are dependent on nature;
- those activities (experiences) that are enhanced by nature;
- those activities (experiences) for which the natural setting is incidental.

---

[2] Other examples include green tourism (Jones, 1987) 'nature-oriented tourism' (Durst and Ingram, 1989), 'soft tourism' (Mader, 1988) and 'defensive tourism' (Krippendorf, 1982, 1987).

There are several classes of nature-based tourism, each utilizing a combination of these dimensions. Birdwatching for example is dependent on nature for 'satisfaction comes entirely from nature observations' (Valentine, 1991b: 477) and without the natural environment it would be difficult to carry out the activity. Similarly, camping is an activity/experience which is often enhanced by nature. Most people would prefer to camp in some type of bush or natural setting rather than on the side of a busy road. Therefore nature is an integral part of these experiences but not the fundamental motivation for them.

This is in contrast to non-specialist nature tourists whose interest may fundamentally lie in a desire to experience 'somewhere different from home'. These tourists 'may also have an interest in nature' but 'satisfaction comes mainly from the superficial interaction with nature and the sense of discovery associated with it' (Valentine, 1991b: 477). However, fundamental concerns of ecotourism include environmental degradation, impact on local communities, and the need for high quality tourism management for achievable sustainability. Clearly the overall definition of nature-based tourism is not totally appropriate in defining ecotourism.

Within this auspice we find 'low-impact tourism' (LIT), which is a specific form of tourism that enhances our understanding of ecotourism's nature base. Low-impact tourism focuses on establishing indigenous natural resource management through private sector incentives and investment in rural village-based tourism business infrastructure and on training villagers and rural area dwellers to take part in the tourism business. LIT is supply-driven (see Chapter 8), that is, it only takes on as many visitors as the cultural and physical environment can cope with. It is concerned explicitly with 'social impact, economic development and natural management of the supplier country and destination sites' (Lillywhite and Lillywhite, 1990: 90). Being supply-driven, LIT places control and regulation of tourism development into the hands of the destination country, rather than the travel and tour operators which are reliant on a demand-driven rationale. Thus, it is a fundamental consideration that LIT should not degrade the cultures they are involved with. Control by a destination country of tourism development requires a full and broad commitment. It requires regulations to protect the environment and the quality and integrity of the tourism experience, the establishment of carrying capacities, a large percentage of small operators as suppliers, value-added tourism and a sensitively developed infrastructure.

The goals of LIT then are to 'establish, coordinate and mutually support conservation and tourism policy, to fund parks development and management and foster indigenous natural or protected areas and to improve village standards in tour destination areas' (Lillywhite and Lillywhite, 1990: 92) and LIT's characteristics include:

- local management;
- the provision of a quality travel product and tourism experience;
- active valuation of culture;
- a training emphasis;
- a dependency on natural and cultural resources;
- the integration of development and conservation (Lillywhite and Lillywhite, 1990).

The principles of low-impact tourism are aligned strongly with ecotourism but, significantly, LIT has no specific location. Whether it be a remote rainforest village, or a specialized chocolate-making plant, its main focus is on the impact on the location of travel experiences. The important point to make here is that LIT does not necessarily take place in relatively undisturbed natural areas, while ecotourism generally does.

Sustainable tourism: conserving nature's base

The natural environment is central to ecotourism which has a focus on biological and physical features. The conservation of natural areas and sustainable resource management is therefore essential to the planning, development and management of ecotourism. Valentine (1991b) draws attention to the 'two-way interaction' between ecotourism and the environment upon which it depends, by suggesting that one characteristic of ecotourism is that it is both contributory to conservation as well as enjoyment of nature. That is, ecotourism involves a focus on nature as the primary motivation for travel, to further knowledge and awareness of nature. However, it also involves the notion that the activity of ecotourism must positively contribute to conservation in the destination area or host community. Planning for ecotourism is based on resource limitations as ecotourism opportunities will be lost if the resilience of an area and the ability of its communities to absorb impact are exceeded, or if its biodiversity and physical appearance are altered significantly.

Therefore an essential feature of ecotourism is sustainability – and sustainable development by implication – and we shall be dealing with these issues in detail in Chapter 3 and 4. Suffice it here to say that, despite the ambiguity surrounding it, the concept of sustainability is fundamental to the positioning of any tourist experience as alternative. The Bruntland Report[3] introduced the concept of sustainable development, defining it as: 'development that meets the needs of the present without compromising the ability of future generations to meet their own needs' (Mieczkowski, 1995: 457). Sustainability requires the establishment of baseline data from which change and rates of change can be measured (World Commission on Environment and Development, 1987; World Wide Fund for Nature, 1992). Environmentally sustainable tourism has come to be fundamentally identified with alternative tourism. Butler (1991) defines environmentally sustainable tourism as: a 'form of tourism that supports the ecological balance', suggesting 'a working definition of sustainable development in the context of tourism as: tourism which is developed and maintained in an area (community, environment) in such a manner and at such a scale that it remains viable over an indefinite period and does not degrade or alter the environment'.

Similarly, the World Tourism Organization guidelines concluded that:

Sustainable tourism can only take place if carrying capacities for key tourism sites are conducted and then rigorously implemented through a system of effective planning and operating controls. These studies and regulations will constitute the cornerstones of long term, local tourism management strategies and plans . . . it also requires acceptance of the concepts of validity and cooperation in its implementation from the tourism private sector, as well as the participation of local communities and tourists themselves. (WTO, 1990: 47)

Having minimal impacts implies that ecotours operate on a small scale thus requiring little specialized infrastructure and therefore not contributing to damaging the environment on which ecotourism (and all forms of tourism) depends. For, as Butler succinctly puts it: 'if ecotourism damages the natural resource then it isn't ecotourism' (Butler, 1992). Similarly Bragg (1990) states that 'ecotourism has by definition minimal environmental impact, since unspoiled natural environments are the attraction of this type of tourism'.

Fortunately, after much discussion at international conferences[4] conservationists and responsible tourism operators now believe that conservation is an essential part of any definition of ecotourism. As discussed previously in the

---

[3] The report of the World Commission on Environment and Development, also known as 'Our common future', Oxford: Oxford University Press, 1987.

[4] Chief among these were held in 1992: United Nations Earth Summit; International Union for Conservation of Nature and Natural Resources (IUCN); IV World Congress on National Parks and Protected Areas.

introduction, the 'eco' prefix is derived from the word 'ecology'. Thus, to be considered as ecotourism, an activity or experience must positively contribute to the environment: 'if the environment has not at least achieved a net benefit towards its sustainability and ecological integrity, then the activity is not ecotourism' (Butler, 1992). However, the 'environment' here refers not only to the natural environment – flora, fauna, landforms and atmospheric considerations – but also the social, economic, scientific, managerial and political elements. The Ecotourism Society agrees with this principle, stating that ecotourists 'must contribute to a sustainable future for the destinations they visit' (O'Neill, 1991).

Moving towards a definition

Ecotourism then includes four fundamental elements: Firstly, the notion of movement or travel from one location to another. This travel should be restricted to relatively undisturbed or protected natural areas as ecotourism's focus is fundamentally on experiencing natural areas. Protected or undisturbed natural areas offer the 'best guarantee for encountering sustained natural features and attractions' (Ceballos-Lascurain, 1990: 2).

This leads to the second component which must be included in a definition of ecotourism, that ecotourism is nature-based. Activities such as business travel, travel to cities, conventional beach holidays and sporting holidays cannot be considered as ecotourism as their focus is not primarily on an experience based on the natural environment of the area visited: 'Ecotourism is travel, often to developing countries, to relatively undisturbed natural areas for study, enjoyment or volunteer assistance that concerns itself with the flora, fauna, geology and ecosystems of an area – as well as the people (caretakers) who live nearby, their needs, their culture and the relationship to the land' (Swanson 1992: 2).

However, this does not mean that ecotourism is exclusively limited to relatively undisturbed natural areas. Ecotourism can rejuvenate nature as well. Rehabilitating degraded areas as a result of human activity can be classified as ecotourism as in this case there is a definite contribution to the environment and a direct benefit to the local community. There is an ethical impetus for tourists in travelling to these areas in volunteering their services to the environment. Common examples include oil spill clean-ups.

Thirdly, ecotourism is conservation-led. As an segment of the tourism industry, ecotourism has emerged as a result of 'increasing global concern for disappearing cultures and ecosystems' (Kutay, 1990: 34) and as a repudiation of 'inappropriate tourism development' which 'can degrade a protected area and have unanticipated economic, social or environmental effects on the surrounding lands' (Ceballos-Lascurain, 1990: 1). Ecotourism therefore aims to take small groups of people to natural or protected areas with a minimum impact on the physical, social and cultural environments. Further to the notion of conservation is the idea that ecotourism will 'contribute to a sustainable future' (O'Neill 1991: 25) for the destination it occurs in, in the form of economic returns or volunteer assistance. In this way, 'ecotourism has the potential to foster conservation of natural resources by increasing the awareness by people in the importance of the natural resources' (Swanson, 1992: 2) and for this reason, the notion of conservation must be included in a definition of ecotourism. Ecotourists are, as a general rule, more concerned with environmental impacts than mass tourists and as such ecotourism 'promotes a greater understanding and respect of cultures, heritage and the natural environment – and people usually protect what they respect' (Richardson, 1991: 244). In essence, ecotourism experiences are sustainable in respect both to the environment and local populations, their culture, needs and desires.

The fourth idea that must be included in a definition of ecotourism is that it has an educative role. The ecotourist generally express a strong desire to learn about nature on their trips (Eagles *et al.*, 1992). Therefore, a great emphasis is placed on nature appreciation, education and interpretation through the explanation of 'concepts, meaning and inter-relationships of natural phenomena' (McNeely and Thorsell, 1989: 37). Ecotourism's dependency on nature, as opposed to other forms of tourism where nature is incidental to the experience, includes the touristic motivation of satisfying an educational need which is derived from interactions with the natural environment.[5] Ecotourism operators may therefore be expected to provide an appropriate level of environmental and cultural interpretation, usually through the employment of appropriately qualified guides and the provision of environmental information both prior to and during the trip. This educative role refers not only to the tourists themselves but also to industry operators and local communities: 'The need to disseminate information to tourists on appropriate behaviour in fragile social and ecologic settings is increasingly being recognized as the responsibility of industry operators' (Blangy and Epler-Wood, 1992: 1). By their active participation, ecotourists are educated to appreciate the importance of natural and cultural conservation. Ecotourism attracts people who wish to interact with the environment and, in varying degrees, develop their knowledge, awareness and appreciation of it. Ecotourism can also provide local people the opportunity to learn about and use the area and attractions that tourists come to visit (Wallace, 1992). For the host community ecotourism may also stimulate renewed appreciation of the 'unique value of their own cultural traditions' as a result of the interest shown by tourists (Kutay, 1990: 40).

Ecotourism then is a vehicle for the enhancement of an understanding of environmental values, as well as an activity which has arisen due to a fundamental shift in the way nature is viewed by society.

Ecotourism travel essentials

- Ecotourism encourages an understanding of the impacts of tourism on the natural, cultural and human environments.
- Ecotourism ensures a fair distribution of benefits and costs.
- Ecotourism generates local employment, both directly in the tourism sector and in various support and resource management sectors.
- Ecotourism stimulates profitable domestic industries – hotels and other lodging facilities, restaurants and other food services, transportation systems, handicrafts and guide services.
- Ecotourism generates foreign exchange for the country and injects capital and new money into the local economy.
- Ecotourism diversifies the local economy, particularly in rural areas where agricultural employment may be sporadic or insufficient.
- Ecotourism seeks decision-making among all segments of the society, including local populations, so that tourism and other resource users can coexist. It incorporates planning and zoning which ensure tourism development appropriate to the carrying capacity of the ecosystem.
- Ecotourism stimulates improvements to local transportation, communications and other basic community infrastructures.
- Ecotourism creates recreational facilities which can be used by local communities as well as domestic and international visitors. It also encourages and helps pay for preservation of archaeological as well as domestic and international visitors. It also encourages and helps pay for preservation of archaeological sites, and historic buildings and districts.

---

[5] Consider for example a family on holiday in a resort in Hawaii. They each use the foreshore for leisure, pleasure and recreation such as swimming, running, reading and so on. Had a component of their visit been for the purpose of learning about the sand dune ecosystem, then they would be considered as ecotourists.

- Nature tourism encourages productive use of lands which are marginal for agriculture, enabling large tracts to remain covered in natural vegetation.
- Cultural tourism enhances local community esteem and provides the opportunity for greater understanding and communication among peoples of diverse backgrounds.
- Environmentally sustainable tourism demonstrates the importance of natural and cultural resources to a community's economic and social well-being and can help to preserve them.
- Ecotourism monitors, assesses and manages the impacts of tourism, develops reliable methods of environmental accountability, and counters any negative effect.

Source of Ecotourism travel essentials: Adapted from Globe '90 Conference, Tourism Stream, Action Strategy adopted at Vancouver, BC, Canada

2

If ecotourism is not just an activity but a philosophy, which philosophy?

This chapter places ecotourism within its broadly historical context, in order to chart the major philosophic and social currents that have contributed to its development. We approach this chapter's question by looking closely at the human/nature relationship and the interaction between them for, as we have seen in Chapter 1, ecotourism by definition relies on the natural environment as its basic resource. This, however, tells us little, for the logging, mining, pastoral and fishing industries all rely on the environment in fundamental ways. However, differentiating specific activities is crucial in determining the relationship between human activity and the environment, especially in understanding the specific values that such activities embody and this will help us to understand the shift in value of nature that ecotourism embodies.

Human nature

Throughout human history it has been nature that has provided both the raw material and inspiration for human existence. Nature sustains our very existence, from the most basic of needs – water, food, air – to the materials from which

we fashion our distinct ways of life – our symbols, meanings and behaviours which constitute the diversity of our cultures; even our very conception of self is mediated by and through nature. Poets and artists, from our earliest beginnings – from the cave paintings at Lasaux in France, from traditional and contemporary indigenous art, to the Romantic poets, have turned to nature in expressing all that is human. However it was the Scottish empiricist philosopher John Locke (1632–1704) who expresses most succinctly our modern inheritance of the natural world in claiming that everything in nature is waste until people transform it into usable things of value (*cf. An essay concerning human understanding*, 1976). It is an ethos that Western societies have embraced with unrestrained enthusiasm. All over the world vital ecosystems are being replaced with infrastructure – houses, towns, industry, roads – all for the exclusive benefit and utility for the human species alone.

The environmental devastation that has resulted from this impetus to 'develop' and use nature for our own material ends is now becoming increasingly hard to ignore as we near the new millennium. It is indeed a grim harvest to reap and is a product of our own making, a result of our historical and contemporary human relations for our social customs, institutions and economy are the embodiment of specific systems of value, many of which have a long historical lineage: what we do about ecology depends on our ideas of the human–nature relationship (White, 1967). Indeed, many have argued that the remedy for our environmental predicament lies precisely here, in a change of values. However, it is of little real import to identify a certain set of values and to claim that we need simply to change them. Only by understanding the complexity of relations and the historical ideas that have contributed to our current position can we begin to make sense of the 'ethic' or behaviours that these values underpin.

Facts, figures and scientific data in themselves do not seem to have been enough to challenge the global trends of environmental decline: 'The spread of detailed knowledge about how man degrades and threatens his own planet has not produced of itself the likelihood of serious or permanent remedial action' (Pepper, 1984: 36). In December 1987, the Nobel Prize for Economics was awarded to Robert Solow of the United States for his theory of economic growth, not surprising in itself, but of particular interest was Solow's overt premise: the dispensability of nature. In his own words: '[t]he world can, in effect, get along without natural resources, so exhaustion is just an event, not a catastrophe' (Shiva, 1989: 219). Equally noteworthy was the former United States President Bush's address in 1992 before departure to the UN Earth summit in Brazil. He made his position and that of the United States clear in refusing to sign any treaty or document involving environmental controls that would inhibit US economic growth. As has been noted by a range of commentators, the motto for the industrialized North at the UN Earth Summit seemed to be 'What is yours is mine; what is mine is mine.'

This is the heart of the problem faced by not only ecotourism but all forms of activities that involve resource use: the question of *how* we use resources: 'If northern politicians are afraid to advise their public to buy fewer cars and use less oil, can a southern government really be expected to tell its people to tighten their belts further and make room for two structural adjustments: one forced on us by external debt, the other by new ecological imperatives? The legacy and inequality of anthropocentric policies followed by the industrial North is now being inflicted on the South' (Peng, 1992: 25).

Exchanging value(s)

Questions of value are central to considerations of the (often competing) conceptions of, and practices towards, the natural world. Godfrey-Smith (1980) identifies two primary ways in which value is assessed in Western society. If the value that something is said to hold is a means to a valued end then it is designated as being of 'instrumental' value. 'Intrinsic value' on the other hand is value that exists in its own right, for its own sake.

What is central here is the ethic that such ideas and values underpin.

● An ethic of 'use' – this is the normative or dominant mode of how human beings relate to nature: where nature is viewed predominantly as a set of resources which humanity is free to employ for its own distinct ends. It is an instrumental and anthropocentric view.
● An ethic 'of' nature – holds that non-human entities are of equal value with the human species. It is broadly intrinsic and ecocentric.

An ethic of use begins from a human locus and it is this univocal perspective that is often described as anthropocentrism. The ultimate grounding of value in the Western world is instrumental, as human beings are placed as the source of all value and, by extension, the measure of all things. Such a view allows nature no intrinsic value in itself and for itself as its value lies only in satisfying human needs and desires. However, it is unfair to make Locke the villain of this piece for anthropocentrism has a very long and deeply entrenched history. It has, to all intents and purposes, been the single deepest and most persistent assumption of (at least) all the dominant Western philosophical, social and political traditions since the time of the classical Greeks (Fox, 1990).

For the ancient Greeks it was the mind that set humanity apart from nature. As the exclusive repositories of mind we humans became the exclusive locus of meaning. Similarly the Judaeo-Christian tradition set the soul apart from, and above, a merely physical natural world and in doing so devalued nature and transformed it into an object. Matter, all that is not soul or mind, became the inert and dead and raw material which is possessed only by the value that we choose to project upon it (Mathews, 1987: 38).

The 'anthropocentric morality' and its ethic of use are difficult for us to argue against. The notion that a wilderness or natural area might have intrinsic value in itself is often dismissed as a transparent example of wishful thinking (Messer and Mosley, 1980), for in the great majority of cases it is an instrumental justification that is used to argue for the preservation and conservation of nature. Godfrey-Smith (1980: 56–71) places such justifications in four main categories:

- the aesthetic/spiritual (the 'cathedral' argument) – where nature is valued for providing spiritual revival and aesthetic delight;
- the biological/biodiversity (the 'silo' argument) – where nature is valued for its stockpile of genetic diversity;
- the scientific (the 'laboratory' argument) – where nature is valued for scientific inquiry;
- and the athletic (the 'gymnasium' argument) – where nature is valued for tourism and recreation.

Within the last few decades, however, an ecocentric philosophy has (re)emerged,[1] one which fundamentally challenges intrinsic and anthropocentric value systems. It is a broad philosophy that encompasses many elements and often includes:

- a belief in humanity's harmony with nature;
- attempts to alleviate (or eliminate) negative human impacts on the environment – atmospheric pollution, land degradation etc.;
- the argument for all life having its own specific intrinsic value;
- arguments against economic growth and consumerism;
- embracing of alternative technology – such as solar power, passive energy systems, recycling;
- the devolution of political and institutional structures;
- the promotion of minority, oppressed and marginalized groups into the political process.

It is a broad philosophical position which attempts to give validity to intrinsic value and which is holistic, strongly grounded in the biology and ecology of nature and rejects the view that the world is divided into mutually exclusive parts. Therefore it affirms the intrinsic interconnectedness of all things, both living and inert. It is a belief that the world is a shared web of life. A view:

shared by most indigenous peoples and environmentalists . . . that nature is the fabric of all life – a vast interconnected web that sustains life on earth, that humans are but one species among the millions and have no intrinsic right to dominion over all other life forms. Nor do humans have the exclusive right to decide whether other life forms have the right to survive. In this philosophy nature has the right to exist and thrive regardless of whether it delivers commodities or dollar benefits or in any way meets human needs and demands. (Nash, 1989: 149)

---

[1] Re-emerged in the sense that such a view is not particularly new, its origins can be traced back to at least the pre-Socratics – Pythagoras, for example – or many indigenous and non-Western cultures throughout the world.

Towards ecocentrism: modern roots

In *the Roots of Modern Environmentalism*, David Pepper (1984) cites four eras in recent history where deep-felt concerns of the public for the quality of the environment have been voiced – the 1890s, 1920s, late 1950s and the early 1970s. To these dates we could also add Chernobyl (1985), the Exxon Valdez disaster (1989), global warming and the systematic land clearing practices that reached their apotheosis in the late 1980s and 1990s and which continue unabated.

The serious questioning of anthropocentricism, however, was not taken up significantly until the early 1960s and 1970s, provoked in large part by the influence of Rachel Carson's (1962) *Silent Spring* and Lynn White's (1967) *The Historical Roots of our Ecologic Crisis*.

This shift, once begun, posed a fundamental challenge to the priority of a human-centred value system in a reorientation towards an identification with a more impartial, ecosphere-centred view of the world and of advocating behaviours appropriate to such a view (*cf.* Fox, 1990).

The type of behaviours, or ethic, appropriate to such a view, as we shall see below, can be interpreted in varied ways. However, those who dismiss that nature has an intrinsic value in itself argue that such a position is essentially not rational, or logically founded (often rhetorically characterized as overly 'emotional'), with no biological or economic justification (scientific basis), and would therefore define an ethic 'of' nature, or ecocentrism, on more pragmatic and rational grounds. Such a perspective is often referred to as technocentrism, or 'technological environmentalism' (Pepper, 1984).

For the technocentric, it is the function of economic growth and technological advancement to provide material well-being for humanity. Conservation, when advocated, is seen as the domain of efficient environmental management – the utilization of scientific and technological knowledge to provide responses to the environmental effects of industrial processes. Technol-ogy then is deployed to make the world a better place for all its peoples by converting a hostile nature into a benign productivity. Such a philosophy satisfies most people who are concerned about a global environmental issue as it lends comfort to the uneasiness felt in the face of the all-too evident damage of humanity's impact on the earth by providing a justification for not relinquishing any of the privileges and comforts currently enjoyed.

Beneath its rational facade however (for the technocentric the universe is indeed, above all, rational) is 'a raw and sometimes irrational faith – a faith in the idea of progress' (Pepper, 1984). For technocentrism's underlying principles are:

● an overt belief in the ability and efficiency of management;
● that problems can (indeed should) be solved by the use of objective analysis and recourse to the laws of physical science (and technology);
● that the 'natural' authority of the above is legitimated with recourse to economic 'laws' (Pepper, 1984).

An ecocentrist perspective on the other hand would argue that reform is fundamentally necessary at all levels – a re-evaluation of our social, economic and educational institutions, indeed a complete reorientation of society as we currently know it. A major element of this shift in values would be the recognition of nature's right to exist in its own right, apart from the benefits humankind can derive from it. In these terms maintaining biodiversity or the 'web of life' on earth is clearly in the interest of not only the human species but all species. Charles Birch speaks of the importance of a biocentric ethic:

Our way of life is tied to an anthropocentric ethic that sees the non-human world as simply the stage on which the drama of life is performed. All other creatures have no more than instrumental value to us. What is now urgently called for is a biocentric ethic that sees in all life some intrinsic value as well as instrumental value. Sentience, the capacity for feeling, gives life intrinsic value. A great achievement of our time could be to extend the concepts of compassion, rights and justice to all living creatures, not only in theory but in the practice of a biocentric ethic. (Birch, 1991: 82)

James Lovelock's (1988) GAIA hypothesis can be seen as the ultimate expression of this ecocentric view. For Lovelock, the earth is a living organism where its species and their environment are coupled together evolving as a single system, the largest living organism. As humans we are simply a part of this interdependent organism, but have a disproportionate effect on its life cycle. This organism, through its planetary feedback mechanisms, will optimize the necessary conditions needed to maintain life but not necessarily for human life.

This line of thought moves us into the ideas surrounding 'deep ecology,'[2] which is one of the most widely discussed ecocentric streams of thinking. Deep ecology is a comprehensive philosophical world-view that believes in a holistic view of nature in which the human being, through the self, is intrinsically connected to all life. No absolute boundaries exist between humanity and nature (a single ontology), therefore there is no point at which 'I', the individual or self, ends and other life-forms begin. The self encompasses the entire earth around us, and nature becomes an extension of ourselves (cf. Mathews, 1993). Thus it becomes incumbent on us to respect and serve cross-species common interests. A recognition of our interrelatedness with life and the intrinsic value of other things, deep ecologists argue, necessitate that we reduce our impact on the earth, taking only what satisfies our vital needs. Actions which follow from this philosophical position include not only 'treading lightly on the earth' but also actions

that respectfully attempt to alter the views and behaviour of those who persist in the delusion that self-realization lies in dominating nature and transforming it to satisfy our own needs (Young, 1990).

A platform for deep ecology

1 The value of non-human life is independent of the usefulness of the non-human world as resources.
2 The diversity of life forms has a value in itself and humans may reduce this variety only to satisfy vital needs.
3 The flourishing of non-human life requires a diminution of the size of the human population.
4 The increasing manipulation of the non-human world must be reversed by the adoption of different economic, technological and ideological structures.
5 The aim of such changes would be a greater experience of the connectedness of all things and an enhancement of the quality of life rather than an attachment to material standards of living.
6 Those who agree with this have an obligation to join in the attempt to bring about the necessary changes.

Source: Adapted from A. Naess, 'Deep ecology and ultimate premises', *The Ecologist*, 18 (4/5), 1988, 128–31

Aldo Leopold (1886–1948) can be considered as one of the first modern deep ecologists. Deep ecology's concern with addressing a 'transpersonal sense of ecological self' that embraces other beings (human and non-human) and ecological processes, would, in Leopold's terms, be an 'ecological conscience', which reaches its fullest expression in a 'land ethic'. For Leopold, our relation to the land, or earth, should not be

---

[2] Deep ecology begins primarily with the Norwegian philosopher Arne Naess (1912–) who was strongly influenced by ecology and the philosophy of Benedict Spinoza (1632–77).

governed solely by economics: 'our basic weakness in a conservation system based wholly on economic motives is that most members of the land community have no economic value' (1966: 20). In Antarctica, for example, some treaty countries are weighing up the economic value of oil and mineral exploration against the preservation of the existing unique ecosystem. But can the ecosystem be valued solely (or adequately) in economic terms? It is inextricably bound to existing (and future) relationships of species dependency, relationships between species and communities that are often intangible to our human dimension. As Leopold stated: 'these creatures are members of the biotic community, and its stability depends on its integrity, they are entitled to continuance' (1966: 21). The stability of an ecosystem depends on all of its members. Overharvesting the krill in Antarctica is having major impacts on the bird life, seals, whales and other members of the community, in fact the whole Antarctica marine ecosystem.

A land ethic, for Leopold, is based on the principle that each individual organism is a member of a complex community of interrelated parts. This community exhibits values such as diversity, connectivity and stability/change and, for Leopold, processes that preserve the integrity, stability and beauty of the biotic community are ethically the ones to pursue. Leopold argued that contemporary land economics does not achieve this, for economics places a 'value' on land that rests on 'ownership' and property rights.

Leopold advocated a drastic revision of society, a profound change in intellectual emphasis, human loyalties, affections and convictions. This change is based on an ethical relation to the land which requires care, respect and admiration for land and a high regard for its intrinsic value (*cf.* Leopold, 1966; Lovelock, 1988; Mathews, 1993; Young, 1991). Our relation to land, or the 'earth', or 'environment' should be determined by ethics in the social world, an ethic which 'reflects the existence of an ecological conscience and this in turn reflects a conviction of individual responsibility for the health of the land' (Leopold, 1966: 20).

Perhaps the most serious obstacle impeding the evolution of a land ethic, or ethic 'of' nature, is that Western societies are headed away from an intimate connection to land – a 'stewardship' of nature – through the dominance of a predominantly individualistic and economic value system. The pre-eminence of technology (backed up by enormous advances in scientific understanding) allied with a growing secularization of social institutions has led to an alienation of humans from the land and hence to the demise of an 'environmental ethos' or ethic 'of' nature (White, 1967). And this loss of a sense of stewardship has become institutionalized through the growth of private property and all of its associations of legal exclusivity, ownership and profit maxims (*cf.* Eckersley, 1992).

Most significant here is that Leopold's ideas reflect a concern for conservation based solely in economic terms. He maintains the basic weakness in a conservation system based wholly on economic motives is that most members of the land community (i.e. animals, plants etc.) have no economic values. 'Ecosystems' cannot be valued in economic terms for they are communities of inextricably linked elements. Removing one member or link, by valuing only one dimension, will damage the whole community.

However, resource conservation, resource preservation and alternative approaches to development do not necessarily challenge anthropocentricity or economic value as they are usually advocated on the grounds of nature's instrumental value to society (as we have seen above), be it for the cathedral, laboratory, silo, or gymnasium value.

Whose sustainability?

The concept of sustainability has become a mediating term in bridging the ideological and political differences between the environmental and development lobbies, a bridge between the fundamentally opposed paradigms of eco- and anthropocentrism.

'Perhaps it arises from the federal government's boundless ability to be gulfed by some greenies, in this case by sticking the adjectives 'ecological' on the front of the Brundtland term sustainable development. A sleight of hand unique in the world I believe. The choice of adjective has severely distorted the whole process and made any economic perspective a defensive one' (Hore-Lacy, 1991: 375). However, 'this sleight of hand' is not a particularly unique one to 'greenies'. Often the interests aligned with conventional development (growth in the production of commodities for profitable sale) have recourse to sustainability in justifying the present conditions of production against the environmental advocates who use it to promote alternatives. This is advanced through the magical transmutation of the term 'ecological sustainable development' into 'economically sustainable development' through the substitution of the letter E in the acronym 'ESD'. It is an indication of the latitude with which the concept of sustainability can be interpreted. Thus the concept of sustainability is both contested and deployed, often, for profoundly different reasons.

For the technocentrist the concept of what heritage we leave our children is not phrased in terms of clean air, water and biodiversity but in terms of 'intergenerational equity'; that is their inheritance should include an accumulation of community wealth generated by environmentally acceptable economic growth (Hore-Lacy, 1991). Apparently we are all entitled to a thriving economy.

Sustainability is inherently linked to conservation as it relies on the ability of the environment to renew itself without impairing or damaging its ability to do so. Definitions of conservation are numerous but most often include ideas such as: 'to keep from harm, decay or loss especially for future use'; 'protection, preservation and careful management of natural resources and of the environment'. Certain environmental groups, for example, believe that natural areas should be conserved by non-intervention, which means little or no human involvement (thus impacts) whatsoever. This is the 'hard' deep ecology orientation.

But is the 'preservation' or non-intervention position excessively utopian? As Eckersley (1992) suggests, it is self-defeating to focus solely on setting up small areas of pristine wilderness while ignoring the growing global population and pollution, since these problems sooner or later impact upon those remaining areas of 'wild' nature. Therefore deep ecology and non-intervention approaches must at least consider the influence of human beings. 'Soft technologists' exhibit one such approach in embracing the ideals of deep or transpersonal ecology in the conservation of nature but suggest that the human species play a necessarily evaluative role, one that recognizes the diversity of interrelationships between humanity and nature but not solely premised on an economic value. Such approaches realize the importance of the biotic community and are opposed to the technological optimism of the technocentrics. The 'soft technologist' approach[3] would also consider the welfare of humans as equally as significant as the biotic community because of their essential interdependence. This position advocates a 'stewardship' ethic that is premised on the belief that we must protect and nurture the biological systems on which we rely to exist. Human beings' role as stewards of nature is a necessary one in order for both the human and non-human species to survive. The continued study of nature in order to monitor human impacts on nature is central to such a position and underpins most approaches to resource management.

Resource conservation is thus a form of 'restrained development' in that, at a minimum, development must be sustainable in not endangering the natural systems that support life on earth – the atmosphere, the waters, the soils and all living beings. An early advocate of resource conservation was the first head of the United States Forest Service, Gifford Pinchot. In his book

---

[3] This approach is related to 'human welfare ecology' which also realizes that humans are necessary parts of the natural process.

The Fight for Conservation (1910), Pinchot's three principles of conservation were: development, prevention of waste, and development for the benefit of the many and not merely the profit of the few. Such an approach is evident today in many public resource management bodies. It considers natural resources as factors of production and as such, the term 'resource development' would be more appropriate.

However, the use of the terms conservation and development may seem incompatible. It could be argued that resource conservation and alternative approaches to development, such as resource development or restrained development, while acknowledging the need for a change from the practices of unrestrained exploitation and economic growth, merely change the temporal framework of exploitation by forestalling it. A technocentric frame is built into such a view in the belief that any impediments to the system – resource depletion and pollution for example – can be remedied by a technical solution. However, a technical solution may be defined as 'one that requires a change only in the technique of the natural sciences, demanding little or nothing in the way of change in human values or ideas of morality' (Hardin, 1968: 124). Moreover, it in no way guarantees its own success. For if humans continue to search for technical solutions to the world's economic, social and ecological problems, they will fall far short of producing an adequate solution.

According to Hardin's (1968) article that introduces the 'Tragedy of the commons', all resources owned in common – air, oceans, fish, bushland etc. – are or eventually will be overexploited. The rational individual has the incentive to take as much as possible before someone else does. No one is motivated to take responsibility for the resource. Because it belongs to everyone, no one protects it. Applying these ideas to tourism suggests that each tour company would seek to maximize its own gain, and becomes locked into a system that compels each to 'increase his herd' (maximize its profit by increasing the number of tourists) without limit, in a resource system which is finite. Hardin

(1968) proposes that to control this kind of undisciplined exploitation, an attitude of temperance rather than prohibition is required, through mediation of administrative law and 'coercion' (via taxes, incentives and other biased options). These are fundamental implications for policy and management regimes and will be discussed in detail in Chapter 3.

The commons argument has significant implications for ecotourism. The commons or destination area can only be justifiably used under low population (visitor) densities. As visitor numbers increase, the destination area has to be controlled or even abandoned. The only way to preserve and nurture other more precious freedoms (such as host populations) is by relinquishing the freedom to visit or the number of visitors. Freedom in these terms is the recognition of necessity, the necessity of relinquishing the personal or individual (human) freedom in placing restrictions on visitor numbers and experiences.

Hardin's answer to the ruin of commons is mutual coercion. This is not prohibiting certain acts, but having in place carefully biased options which makes these acts uneconomic for example. These options would coerce companies to not act in certain ways and the options would be mutually agreed upon by the majority. The end result would be less freedom for individual companies but more long-term sustainability, which could be seen as freedom in other ways. As Hardin suggests individuals locked into the logic of the commons are free only to bring on universal ruin; once they see the necessity of mutual coercion, they become free to pursue other goals.

'Freedom' in these terms is the freedom that comes with the necessity of mutual coercion, in other words, individuals are only free to pursue their own goals when abiding by laws mutually agreed upon by the majority of the people affected. Those who oppose any restrictions on their 'rights' – the rights to do as they please – will only bring on universal ruin.

These issues are at the heart of ecotourism and environmental management – the rights of individuals and their duty to others, to how far any person can understand the effects of their individual actions on the well-being of the ecosystem and the enjoyment of others, what the cumulative consequences are when many abuse an area (each in small ways), and how society should regulate individual use so that freedom of access is not unfairly restricted which maintains environmental quality.

Any form of government intervention requires that the exercise of Hardin's (1968) dictum of 'mutual coercion' is mutually agreed upon, because without public acceptance of authority regulation cannot be enforced. If tourists are made more aware of the consequences of their acts, will they become more morally concerned about the effects of these consequences on others and on future generations, and will they accept and respect the fact that some kind of governmentally imposed regulation of use is necessary in the public interest?

Ecocentrically informed resource management recognizes that modern science and technology cannot prevent environmental degradation if current economic growth and resource use trends continue. What is required is a change in philosophy, politics and economics to ensure that a sustainable human population can exist in balance with its environment. This 'preservationist' position (which we shall discuss in more detail in Chapter 4) emphasizes the need for prior macroenvironmental constraints, such as government legislation, scientific monitoring and use restrictions.[4]

Therefore conservation involves the management or control of human use of resources (biotic and abiotic) in an attempt to restore, enhance, protect and sustain the quality and quantity of a desired mix of species, ecosystem conditions and processes for present and future generations (Dunster and Dunster, 1996: 69).

It is becoming increasingly apparent that, at least for the immediate future, natural areas can only be defended for their instrumental value. But we shouldn't dismiss efforts to create new modes of ecological understanding simply as 'wishful thinking'. Even within the fields of economics, mathematics and analytic philosophy much work has been done on equating the value of non-measurable and non-comparable value dimensions.[5]

Ethics and (of) resource management

It can be argued that management itself is an anthropocentric concept, for if we accept that natural areas have intrinsic worth then why do they have to be managed? Further, if a localized ecosystem is protected as a wilderness area, 'management' itself can be seen to be an intrusion into the system. Similarly, in enclosing nature within certain boundaries, who is it we are trying to protect? Where do we draw the boundary line – are resource managers deciding what is natural? More pragmatically still, management requires expenditure – whose responsibility is it to finance the management of protected areas?

> ## Case study   The Himalayas: a protected ecosystem?
>
> In May of 1992 some thirteen expeditions totalling 250 climbers scaled Mount Everest in Nepal. At one stage thirty-two people were on the summit at the same time. If those 250 climbers had been asked why they chose to climb Mount Everest, somewhere in their answer would have been sentiments

---

[4] Deep ecology can be viewed as an extreme preservation position as it argues for the recognition of an intuitive acceptance of the notion of intrinsic (as opposed to instrumental) value in nature and thus the recognition of 'rights' for non-human species.

[5] Cf. Peterson *et al.*, 1988 in specific relation to natural resources.

expressing 'a desire to experience one of the wildest places on earth' (Edward, 1992). Technological innovations in mountaineering and clothing equipment, a growing class of people who are able to purchase such equipment and have the mobility and leisure time to join such expeditions, will ever increase the numbers of people attempting to fulfill that desire to experience wildness/wilderness.

The base camp at Anapurna has been described as the highest slum in the world – littered with bottles, noodle packets, sardine cans, film containers and wrappings and the ever-present toilet paper.

Deforestation and erosion, the increasing demands of the tourist industry, overgrazing and the changing land ethics of the Nepalese, as contact with the West increases through tourism, are resulting in major shifts within the Himalayan ecosystem. The present Nepalese government will continue to encourage tourism, as it is the country's highest income earner. International groups – such as the Mountain Protection Commission – advocate a drastic reduction in expedition numbers and call for the complete banning, for one year, of climbing on all peaks over 8000 m high. Many within this group would like to see all accommodation shacks at Anapurna removed 'to provide more of a wilderness experience' (Edward, 1992). This then is the looming tragedy of the Himalayas. It is a salutary lesson for any management body in trying to mediate a compromise between the conflicting needs of access, availability and presentability of an environmental or ecological product – wilderness – with those of the local population and the regenerative capacity of the ecosystem.

For environmental ethics to be of significance they must be able to be acted upon, that is, made operationally relevant:

The imposition of regulation reduces freedom, and by definition, reduces the need for individuals to exercise moral judgement . . . [e]thical behaviour willingly takes the rights, the needs and welfare of others into account. It is not behaviour that simply responds to the pressure of the law, regulation or code (Mackay, 1992: 3).

However, sustainable tourism development can only be achieved through international cooperation and agreed regimes for surveillance, development and management in the common interest (cf. World Commission on Environment and Development, 1987). But at stake is not just the sustainable development of shared ecosystems, our 'commons', but of all nations whose tourism development depends to a greater or lesser extent on their rational management. Without equitable rules future generations will be impoverished by the loss of these places to visit, and the people who suffer the most will be those who live in developing countries that are least capable of imposing regulation in the market global economy that tourism operates in.

Ecocentric management, in the case of tourism, would recognize that modern science and technology cannot prevent environmental degradation if the current economic growth and resource use trends continue, and that a change in human philosophy, politics and economics are needed to ensure that a sustainable tourism population (guest) can exist in balance with its social and physical environment (host). Further to this, ecocentrism can be viewed as 'communalist' – a preservationist position, which re-emphasizes the need for prior macro-environmental constraints on economic growth and favours a decentralized socio-economic system – or 'deep ecology' underpinned by the notion of intrinsic (as opposed to instrumental) value in nature for non-human species (cf. Pepper, 1984).

Mistakenly, ecocentrism is often criticized as a 'hands-off', 'only in theory', 'wishful thinking', 'put it on the agenda for future discussion' approach which is ideal yet impractical to implement on any real level. However it is important here to express ecocentricism's centrality for ecotourism clearly and purposefully in relation to the management question. Ecocentrism as an approach to management would argue that protected areas are not being conserved or preserved or protected for anyone but can exist because they have a value in and for themselves. This approach is a challenge to a more dominant world view that has been basically adopted by resource economists and which supports the idea that the non-human world is valuable only in as far as it is valuable to humans.

These are the extreme views of a continuum of perceptions, yet they deal with the same biosphere. What place and role does the market have in a finite natural world? Conversely, what is the place of the natural environment in an economically rationalist world? How do we begin, and is it possible, to reconcile or move from an economically based mass tourism system to a more eco-orientated system?

Conclusion

An economist sees tourism as a part of a 13 trillion dollar economy looking to expand five to ten times over the next few decades. To do this our tourism systems will raid the ecosystems of the biosphere for resources as raw materials for this growth. In order to achieve and justify such growth natural systems must be viewed through economic rather than ecological eyes. These natural systems will be valued for their resource utility rather than their ecological value.

As demonstrated through this discussion, numerous philosophical and political ideologies have contributed to the present form of ecological thought and the formation of the nature travel known today as ecotourism. Various other forms of tourism including 'nature tourism', 'low impact tourism' and 'sustainable tourism' have formed the basis of the definitions debate surrounding the ecotourism phenomenon. Common themes are evident in the numerous descriptions of ecotourism and can be linked to a number of underlying philosophical approaches which help to define it as an activity.

As ecotourism has the potential to impact on such a variety of sectors, debate by various bodies including governments, the tourism industry, the community and conservation groups is widespread and quite intense. These agencies play a major role in promoting, planning and implementing sustainable ecotourism practices as a means of satisfying the tourist, the economy and the environment. The next chapter will examine this exchange in an attempt to investigate how regulation might work for ecotourism.

3

Tourism development: government, industry, policy and planning

Tourism has become a central platform in many countries' development strategies. It is particularly attractive for governments in its potential for providing an alternative to other forms of economic development: through employment generation, for its ability to generate foreign exchange, and its ability to generate regional growth (Goldfarb, 1989: 131).

However, in many cases tourism has not lived up to these high expectations. Although tourism is highly regarded in its ability to generate significant levels of revenue in the form of Gross Domestic Product (GDP) – in many cases tourism's potential in generating foreign exchange has surpassed that of traditional commodity exports thus allowing for flow-on benefits in the form of local infrastructure such as roads and electricity – these benefits are often circumscribed by the significant impacts tourism engenders upon local communities, such as increased pollution and rising local prices and the export of profits from tourism out of the community itself. Even without considering the physical impacts, the flow of revenues out of the country or local region significantly challenges tourism's status as a foreign exchange generator. Many local communities and economies where tourism development takes place lack the infrastructure and necessary skills required in establishing

tourism operations – chief of which is capital – along with the range of goods and services desired by tourists. As a result leakages are usually high. Leakages are the flows of money out of a country or specific area as a result of the necessity to import certain skills, infrastructure, technologies and commodities along with the flow of revenue in the form of profits taken out of a locale by operators. This is significant for tourism development, for in many cases the necessary infrastructure required for tourism is provided by foreign owned corporations, particularly airlines, hotels, car rental agencies and package tours. In many cases[1] leakages have been estimated at up to 80%–90% in developing countries that do not have a significant share of the necessary tourism services such as airlines, hotels and transportation companies (Mathieson and Wall, 1982).

Tourism expenditure is considered to have significant flow-on effects throughout all levels and sectors of a local economy. This is the 'multiplier' effect whereby initial expenditure of tourist dollars is calculated to initiate

---

[1] Lindberg (1991: 24) estimates that only 10% of tourism spending remains in Zimbabwe: similarly Church (1994) estimated that only 10–20% of tourism spending is retained in Jamaica.

expenditure on local goods and services. That is, for every dollar spent an additional amount of dollars is further spent throughout the economy. Despite the multiplier effect, however, in many cases the negative economic, environmental and social effects of tourism build over time and are often not felt directly and are only experienced after the initial positive economic impacts. These problems are further exacerbated through the political imperatives to realize the short-term gains of tourism which often offset government intervention in planning or managing tourism. The result is that the immediate economic benefits are valued highly and accrue to national accounts while the often significant social and environmental costs have to be borne by local communities.

Similarly, tourism is often promoted by government or industry without an overall strategy, without adequate attention to legislative frameworks – such as determining if the planning and nature protection laws are adequate – without consultation or inclusion of local communities and without effective protected area management plans. This raises significant policy questions for government.

Against these effects we shall discuss ecotourism's potential to generate significant benefits to local communities as an alternative form of development, through employment, increased revenues for infrastructure and for community projects. Importantly is the potential for these benefits to be realized without compromising conservation or sustainability objectives. Indeed, ecotourism is a significant alternative development strategy due to its ability to link local income generation directly through conservation initiatives.

During the 1970s and 1980s, integrated rural development projects were used to raise rural living standards in developing countries, and focused primarily on irrigation, roads and social services. However, the World Bank (1992: 86) found that the results were often disappointing, with low success rates because of overemphasis in appraisals on outcomes, a tendency to select large and complex projects, and overly opti-mistic projections of project outcomes. The development of ecotourism and its infrastructure in providing for tourism experiences in the 1990s may suffer the same fate.

In order to ensure that tourism does not exceed its sustainable base, an understanding of the mechanisms that lead to the provision of infrastructure for development and the policy and institutional prerequisites for planning and managing ecotourism is fundamental. Through an examination of the principles of sustainable development, the nature of ecotourism and its potential environmental effects we will discuss the role of government and industry policy in facilitating ecotourism. We will discuss a range of sustainable approaches, from the role of government- and industry-led policy and planning initiatives along with the relative strengths and weaknesses of self-regulation. While there are many advocates for effective control measures developed through integrated programmes that incorporate federal, state and local legislation and policy (cf. McKercher, 1991a: 69), others present a case for industry-based 'best practice' (cf. Richardson, 1995). Regardless, the development of strategic plans and control mechanisms are only as effective as the will to implement them.

Case study   'Carrying capacity': Galapagos Islands, Ecuador

The Galapagos Islands are located 1000 km from the South American coast and form a unique ecotourism attraction based on native species endemic to the region. Conservationists involved in sustaining the resources of the islands have increasingly attempted to control the expanding tourism industry. In 1986, the island's second airport opened, with arrivals escalating to 41 000 per annum – almost four times the recommended carrying capacity of 12 000 visitors. A third airport on Isabella Island is expected to raise tourist numbers to over 50 000 per annum.

Despite the fact that the Galapagos Islands has had excellent controls on environmental damage per tourist, it has had few controls on the total number of tourists. Strict government regulatory policies include the control of zoning, the stipulation that tourists be accommodated on boats, the registration of naturalist guides and strict regulations for onshore visits. However, the focus on controlling damage per tourist often neglects the fact that most impacts are due to the volume of tourist arrivals.

A steady growth in migration to the Galapagos Islands has been attributed to the opportunity for profit derived from the booming tourism industry, and resulted in a proliferation of on-shore accommodation establishments (in breach of the regulations against such development). Local response also denotes a shift in income derivation, as traditional fishers convert their fishing boats to small tour vessels.

Notably, very little of the revenue is returned to the local community. Largely foreign owned cruise ships transport wealthy foreign tourists to the Galapagos, facilitating high leakage rates. More importantly, incentives for locals to maintain tight controls and regulations are non-existent and they compete to expand their own accommodation and boat tour operations.

The islands' ecology is the victim of this poor management. Agriculture is expanding and its effects are proving more disastrous than those of tourism. Depriving locals of their share of tourist revenue leaves them no choice but to expand the agricultural sector. The extinction of twelve native plant species is directly attributable to this expansion.

Placing locals in control of their tourism industry, or at least returning some of the financial benefits from visitation to local operators may reverse the current trends by providing direct incentives to operate within the regulatory frameworks. This may produce a shift in planning from a short-term reactive response to a long-term proactive one for the benefit of social and physical environments.

Source: P. Steele, 'Ecotourism, an economic analysis', Journal of Sustainable Tourism, 3 (1), 1995, 29–44

Sustainable tourism development

As we have seen in Chapter 1, ecotourism is an alternative to mass tourism due to its small scale infrastructure and the minimization of the environmental impacts that follow from it. This suggests that it can be regulated and controlled at a sustainable level. Sustainable tourism is tourism that produces economic advantages, in addition to maintaining environmental diversity and quality, thus 'combining conservation with economic development' (Wild, 1994: 12). A primary means of maintaining sustainability is by limiting tourist numbers and therefore the possibility for environmental degradation (Inskeep, 1991). In this way ecotourism is a supply-led approach (see Chapter 8) which involves determining visitor numbers based on the environment's capacity (its ability to support) rather than by the demand for it. However, what often sounds fine in theory is often not always the case in practice. According to the WWF (1992), although ecotourism is booming, much of its growth has been unsustainable (Steele, 1995). Sustainable development in relation to ecotourism is difficult to achieve because of the extraordinary expansion of ecotourism and the pressures of demand for access to natural areas. The question here is how should this demand (if it should at all) be controlled?

Unsustainable ecotourism is the result of inappropriate developments taking place in sensitive locations. The environmental effects caused by overcrowding, overdevelopment, unregulated recreation, pollution, wildlife disturbances and vehicle use are more serious for ecotourism than mass tourism (McNeely cited in Hvenegaard, 1994). This is due to the fact that ecotourism is more dependent on intact natural environments and is concentrated in ecologically sensitive areas. Without appropriate regulations, problems of overexploitation, and in particular ecological degradation, may be intensified with the development of ecotourism (Mieczkowski, 1995). This indicates that in practice the principles of sustainability are difficult to implement on a broad scale without a progressive planning and policy framework.

The negative effects of ecotourism are in large part due to the fact that visitation often precedes effective management and planning. Thus there is a need for suitable planning strategies to be formulated and implemented to ensure that the future expansion of ecotourism takes place in accordance with the principles of sustainable development. There is a need then for an overall policy framework to facilitate sustainable ecotourism development. Those responsible for ecotourism need to understand its philosophies and their associated requirements and consequences.

Planning and policy frameworks: who is involved and how?

Effective planning greatly enhances the sustainable development credentials of ecotourism: 'central to the goals of environmental conservation and resource sustainability is the protection and maintenance of environmental quality. To achieve this primary goal requires planning which is grounded in environmental protection and enhancement yet fosters the realization of tourism potential' (Dowling, 1991: 128). Planning involves anticipating and regulating change to encourage appropriate development so as to increase the social, economic and environmental benefits of the actual process (Murphy, 1985). Planning development means not only matching

its goals and objectives with the resource capabilities but also with conservation requirements. Sustainability of ecotourism practices is therefore possible if planning balances the demands of development with the supply of the environment in an attempt to manage potential benefits now and in the future (Mieczkowski, 1995: 98). However, as yet there are no clearly defined roles as to whose responsibility this is.

Government-led planning and policy initiatives

It is widely recognized that governments have the greatest potential to shape tourism in dictating how it is promoted, planned, managed, and regulated. They are the only body that can provide long-term planning and management as legislative and juridical protection of nature reserves for the benefit of future generations. Additionally, the importance of government planning and policy is credited to its power to provide an overall harmony, consistency and enforceable standards for the industry as a whole as the independent regulation of small areas is not enough to ensure environmental sustainability (*cf.* Mieczkowski, 1995: 467; Tolhurst, 1994).

Government policy, through its ability to enforce necessary environmental regulations, sets broad industry standards and therefore can assist in minimizing negative impacts, and hence has a major role to play in facilitating sustainable ecotourism practices. The significance of government policy and planning in accommodating sustainable ecotourism lies in its ability to effectively administer appropriate guidelines and consistent standards, taking into account possible effects.

Governments at all levels are becoming more involved in ecotourism as it is increasingly valued as an important source of revenue. This is evident especially in the Asia–Pacific region. Countries such as the Philippines are in the process of formulating an Ecotourism Act to safeguard the fragile ecosystem of tourism areas (Gabor, 1997). Similarly, Tonga in 1997 developed a Sustainable Tourism Strategy with a view to planning and implementing for long-term sustainable development of the tourism industry (Calkin, 1997). However, it has taken additional international funding and consultants to implement the strategy, highlighting the fact that governments alone are not always capable of delivering what they have planned.

The significance of government planning in regards to sustainability is highlighted by the various National Strategies for Ecologically Sustainable Development implemented throughout the 1990s in many countries around the world.[2] Such strategies recognized that through the use of government planning the tourism industry can be developed and managed in a way that conserves its natural resources and minimizes negative environmental impacts (*cf*. Evans-Smith, 1994). The main tools of government policy aimed at tourism-related environmental problems are:

- legislation
- regulation – including revenue collection and redistribution
- control
- the coordination of policies and programmes
- infrastructure and incentives
- planning and promotion between national and local level ecotourism ventures.

The primary means of minimizing impacts is to control tourist numbers, and as such much government policy is formulated around this intention. Such controls include quantity controls, for example zoning or limits to tour group sizes, as well as price controls, such as fees or taxes on local operators.

However, the practice of limiting visitor numbers is often a blunt and simplistic solution. Sustainability is about process, bringing stakeholders in to address the earliest stage of the planning process.[3] Governments also have changing interests and priorities which can lead to policies being inconsistent and unfulfilled. Countries with unstable political systems often cannot provide long-term vision and stability in policy and planning for tourism and ecotourism. Even in countries where the political and democratic processes are well established and secure, the frameworks and priorities for ecotourism change frequently.

Case study Bhutan

Bhutan limits tourism by requiring that visitors spend $200 per day along with limiting tourists numbers each year (Wells, 1993: 171). There are additional restrictions on development to regulate the scale and intensity of development.

Case study Australian government policy

The extent of tourism industry regulation, as an important aspect of government policy, has become a major issue in Australia. Since the late 1980s there has been a move by the Commonwealth to deregulate the tourism industry in an attempt to improve service provision. Despite this trend, the significance of conservation issues has meant increased demands for environmental protection regulation and legislation (Hall, 1991). Likewise, it can be argued that ecotourism's survival is reliant on regulation concerned with environmental protection. As such there is a need for increased

---

[2] *Cf*. Sachs, 1995: 16.

[3] For a comprehensive range of international case studies demonstrating alternatives to regulation see Hall and McArthur (1998).

regulation in regards to minimizing environmental consequences and promoting natural resource conservation. The implication is that while the future of the tourism industry will generally be characterized by decreased regulation, ecotourism's future development may well involve increased regulation, based on its environmental dependence.

The Federal Government of Australia established a National Ecotourism Strategy in 1994 with the intention of formulating an overall policy framework for the planning, development and management of ecotourism, to contribute to the achievement of sustainable tourism in natural areas (Evans-Smith, 1994: 4). Such a strategy highlights the importance of the government's role in establishing the necessary guidelines for which ecotourism can be developed in accordance with the principles of sustainability. Through the formulation of a broad framework promoting sustainable ecotourism the federal government potentially had a great amount of influence in determining the future direction of this type of tourism and thus its sustainability. However, since the change of government in Australia following the federal election of 1996, the National Ecotourism Strategy has not been promoted or recognized as a valid strategy by the newly elected government. In this instance, the government support in implementing this strategy has been withdrawn and leaves the impetus of any further actions with the industry and state governments. Some states in Australia have developed their own ecotourism or nature based tourism strategies.

Integrated policy and planning

The tourism industry is represented at the ministerial level in the form of specialist portfolios which indicate a government's recognition of tourism's importance. A government's priority for tourism can be derived from the position of the tourism portfolio within larger departments or if it is represented by a department designated solely for it.

Generally, where ecotourism planning occurs, it follows the development of an overall National Development Plan and a Tourism Plan. A Tourism Plan should revolve around the natural and socioeconomic environment of a country, taking into consideration domestic and international tourist market groups as well as residents' use of tourist attractions and facilities. Fundamental elements include:

- tourist attractions and activities;
- accommodation;
- transportation and other tourist facilities/ services;
- other infrastructure; and
- institutional elements (Inskeep, 1991).

The aim of planning for ecotourism is often to identify major issues that are likely to affect the development and management of ecotourism, as well as to develop policies and programmes to assist in making the industry more viable and sustainable. The actual content of an ecotourism plan should include the vision and aims of having such a strategy and a rationale for having it in the first place. The strategy also needs to identify and consult with the many stakeholder groups and representatives of the ecotourism sector before a definition of ecotourism or sustainable tourism is developed. A description of ecotourism impacts in relation to environmental, economic, social and cultural dimensions should raise issues that need to be covered through objectives and actions. Some of those issues can include ecological sustainability, regulation, infrastructure, impact monitoring, industry standards and accreditation, education and marketing. The most important part of any ecotourism plan is the implementation strategy, which needs to coordinate the actions identified into groupings and responsible stakeholders need to be assigned. Ideally, a resourcing or funding plan should accompany the implementation plan.

An ecotourism plan should ideally encompass the following steps:

- study preparation;
- determination of objectives;
- survey;
- analysis and synthesis;
- policy and plan formulation;
- recommendations;
- implementation and monitoring.

Effective control measures can only occur through integrated programmes that incorporate federal, state and local legislation and policy (McKercher, 1991b: 69). Clearly defined government roles and coordination of government policies are necessary to ensure effective planning for a sustainable tourism product (Hall, 1991). With a consistent and combined effort that seeks community support, governments have the potential to establish effective regulation which incorporates the principles of sustainability: 'its successful implementation requires integrated policy, planning and social learning processes: its political viability depends on the full support of the people it affects through their governments, their social institutions and their private activities' (Gunn, 1994: 244). Integrated regional planning, as outlined by Australia's National Ecotourism Strategy, has already proved successful in allowing for sustainable ecotourism practices in the Murray-Darling Basin and Cape York Peninsula for example, where community participation and support has provided a strong foundation for government policy development (Evans-Smith, 1994). Governments also need to examine regional planning across borders.

The coordination of government planning with private sector and non-government organizations is also fundamental, as is the establishment of links with tourism operators and local communities to facilitate sustainable practices (Wild, 1994). For sustainability to be achieved all levels of government, operators and developers, as well as tourists and local communities, must

Case study   Masai Mara

Following the closure of the Kenya–Tanzania border in 1977 the land of the Masai Mara became the terminus of a tourism circuit that had previously continued south through Serengeti, to the Ngorongoro Crater. As a result of this political action, the visitor load in Masai Mara increased rapidly, triggering ill-considered development. (Ceballos-Lascurain, 1996: 97)

each be involved in collaborative partnerships. Although government has the power to legislate regulative controls through policy and thus contribute to sustainable ecotourism practices, a cooperative approach between all involved parties under government guidance would enhance its ongoing success.

The government role in planning for sustainable tourism

Useful guidelines for the role of government in the planning and implementation of sustainable tourism were developed at the Globe '90 conference held in Vancouver in March 1990:

- Ensure that all government departments involved in tourism are briefed on the concept of sustainable development. The respective ministers (e.g. environment and natural resources) should collaborate to achieve sustainable tourism development.
- Ensure that national and local tourism development agreements stress a policy of sustainable tourism development.
- Include tourism in land-use planning.
- Undertake area and sector-specific research into the environmental, cultural and economic effects of tourism.

- Support the development of economic models for tourism to help define appropriate levels and types of tourism for natural and urban areas.
- Assist and support lower levels of governments in developing tourism strategies and conservation strategies and in integrating the two.
- Develop standards and regulations for environmental and cultural impact assessments and monitoring of existing and proposed tourism developments, and ensure that carrying capacities defined for tourism destinations reflect sustainable levels of development and are monitored and adjusted appropriately.
- Apply sectoral and/or regional environmental accounting systems to the tourism industry.
- Create tourism advisory boards that involve all stakeholders (e.g. the public, indigenous populations, industry, NGOs), and design and implement public consultation techniques and processes to involve all stakeholders in tourism-related decisions.
- Ensure that tourism interests are represented at major caucus planning meetings that affect the environment and the economy.
- Design and implement educational and awareness programmes to sensitize people to sustainable tourism development issues.
- Develop design and construction standards to ensure that tourism development projects do not disrupt local culture and natural environments.
- Enforce regulations relating to illegal trade in historic objects and crafts; unofficial archaeological research and desecration of sacred sites.
- Regulate and control tourism in environmentally and culturally sensitive areas (Ceballos-Lascurain, 1996).

Industry-led planning and policy

Planning and policy initiatives in the tourism industry are often seen as preventative methods in striking a balance between self-regulation and imposed regulation. This issue is of particular importance in managing the relationship between tourism and the environment, due to the fact that a proactive stance by industry on environmental issues will always be a preferred industry solution rather than reacting to legislative regulations. However, self-regulation of environmental impacts by industry has not always been successful in other sectors, such as mining and agriculture. It remains to be seen whether self-regulation can be effective in the tourism industry (Birtles and Sofield, 1996) as the very nature of the tourism industry, as a conglomerate of diverse segments, makes it increasingly difficult to regulate such diversity effectively.

Industry planning and policy initiatives for sustainable tourism have traditionally focused on improving professionalism, standards, training and quality of customer service, some with a business and marketing emphasis and others with an environmental emphasis. Manidis Roberts (1994) developed an 'Industry Quality Continuum' as a guide to the self-regulation measures for the tourism industry. Table 3.1 shows an adapted version of the continuum including an explanation and examples for each type of measure to improve industry standards. The continuum can also give an indication of the maturity of the tourism industry in a country or region, assuming that a Code of Practice is usually the first step in encouraging recognition of the need for environmental standards (Manidis Roberts, 1994).

We will now focus on the three most important measures – codes of practice, compliance and accreditation.

Codes of practice

The development of a code of practice for tourists and tour operators is typically one of the first industry initiatives on the path of

Table 3.1 *Industry Quality Continuum*

Codes of practice	Compliance	Accreditation	Quality system	Certification
Explanation				
• Industry general guide to behaviour	• Informal	• Formal	• Formal	• Formal
• No requirements for participation by individual or organization	• Complying with codes	• Voluntary	• Voluntary	• Compulsory
• No enforcement	• Voluntary participation	• Administered by industry or other body	• Externally driven	• Externally approved standard
• Little promotion	• Can possibly require the signing of an agreement	• Involves standards of skill, experience or activity	• Conformity with external standard or best practice	• May be regulatory
	• Rarely any enforcement	• May involve audit of individual or organization	• Involves audit and benchmarking	• Involves audit
			• The entire organization participates	• Withdrawal for noncompliance
				• Involves penalties
Examples				
• Ecotourism Association of Australia	• PATA Green Leaf	• Savannah Guides	• AS3902 (Quality in Service)	• Builders' licence
• Pacific Asia Travel Association (PATA)	• Green Globe	• National Ecotourism Accreditation Program	• ISO 9000	• May include Natural Resource Manager permits
• New Zealand Tourism Industry Association		• Tourism Vanuatu Accreditation	• ISO 14000	
• The Ecotourism Society			• BS7750	
• Tourism Council Australia				

Source: adapted from Manidis Roberts, 1994

sustainable development: 'one of the most promising features of the ecotourism industry is its willingness to both educate its operators and provide guidelines for their activities' (Duff, 1993: 18) in the form of codes of practice and guidelines. These codes of practice and guidelines seek to establish standards of environmental performance and minimize the environmental impacts of tourism. Numerous codes of practice for ecotourism operators, tourists and developers have emerged in the early 1990s (*cf.* Dowling, 1992; Duff, 1993). Examples include the Ecotourism Association of Australia's code of practice for ecotour operators (Duff, 1993), New Zealand Tourism Industry Federation code of practice (NZTIF, 1991), Pacific Asia Travel Association code of practice (PATA, 1992), the Tasmanian Professional Trout Fishing Guides Association code of ethics (Department of Tourism, Sport and Recreation, 1994) and the Tourism Council Australia *Code of Sustainable Practice* (TCA, 1998).

Case study   Kingfisher Bay Resort and Village, Queensland, Australia

Environmental codes of conduct for developers were written into all contracts ensuring environmental protection in the development stages was not neglected (Hackett, 1992). The most important aspect to note in this example is that the guidelines were legally enforceable and as such there were penalties involved for non-compliance.

The above example is unfortunately a relatively isolated case. Most guidelines or codes of practice are ineffective as they lack any enforcement policy, statements of objectives, targets or evaluation procedures (Blangy and Nielsen, 1993). Further, such codes of practice and principles have also been criticized as they are usually adopted as narrow checklists, thus creating strict frames of reference that do not encourage actions or thoughts beyond those detailed on the lists (Gertsakis, 1995). As such, although codes of practice and guidelines are an attempt by the industry to minimize its impacts they lack enforcement and as such are limited in effectiveness and value.

Conversely, there are many advocates for the development of codes of conduct for tourists (*cf.* Weiler and Johnson, 1991: 125). This would encompass appropriate social, cultural and environmentally responsible behaviour. Examples of codes of conduct developed specifically for visitors include the Himalayan Environmental Trust 'Code of Conduct' and the American Society of Travel Agents Code of Conduct, which was one of the earliest proponents of responsible tourism. While many sensitive regions have regulations governing visitor and operator behaviour, such as the regulations governing visits to New Zealand's Sub-Antarctic Islands being some of the most rigorous, none of the codes of practice is in any way binding on the industry or the individual. Distribution and enforcement are major issues that underline its usefulness (*cf.* Hall *et al.*, 1991).

There have also been attempts to introduce affirmation programmes, requiring operators to display codes of practice and become signatories. However, their main role has been to create a sense of awareness within industry and visitors of environmental responsible practice (Manidis Roberts, 1994).

Case study   Codes of conduct – the Arctic

The use of codes of conduct in the Arctic has attracted debate as to the effectiveness of their use, particularly in relation to the often inadequate implementation of such codes. A draft visitor code for the Artic is presented below as an indication of the content which has fuelled debate on the effectiveness of such documents:

Conserve resources:

● Please leave wildlife habitats alone; where this is not possible, keep disturbance to a minimum.
● Please do not take plants, animals and other samples from nature – these must be left where found.
● Please limit damage by vehicles such as snowscooters.
● Hunting and fishing are under the strict control of national and regional authorities. Permits can be obtained from . . .
● Accessibility to nature reserves and National Parks is strictly restricted through the use of permits. These can be obtained from . . .

Stop pollution:

● Please do not leave behind any equipment or litter – this will decay only slowly, may injure wildlife, and could cost you a fine.
● All materials that have been brought in and not consumed during your visit should be taken out.

Respect indigenous cultures:

● Almost all indigenous cultures in the Arctic have developed in harmony with nature, without overexploiting resources or creating unnecessary waste. Pay respect to these cultures.

Be a guest:

● Please do not expect to come to a wilderness and find all home comforts supplied.
● Be a true guest – one who is welcome in the landscape and amongst the local people.

Enjoy yourself and remember:
Take nothing but photographs,
Kill nothing but time,
Leave nothing but footprints.

Source: P. Mason, 'Tourism codes of conduct in the Arctic and sub-Arctic region', *Journal of Sustainable Development*, 5 (2), 151–164

Mason and Mowforth (1996) identify four main areas of concern in relation to codes of conduct, namely:

● Monitoring take-up and effectiveness.
● The use of codes as a marketing tool.
● The need for coordination.
● The question of whether self-regulation or external regulation should be utilized.

The critical component to any code of conduct is the need to evaluate the effectiveness of the code through an assessment of effects and record the results. The validity of such issues is well illustrated by the Arctic Case Study, with behaviour reliant on the interpretation and honesty of the tourist.

Compliance

Compliance schemes are an attempt to develop environmental constraints for the industry and improve the type and nature of the experiences for visitors. They are similar to codes of practice for, unless binding agreements are made between individual operators and an industry body who is responsible for the enforcement of the principles, the rigour and effectiveness of any such scheme is questionable. However, compliance schemes are distinguished from a code of practice in that they may require operators to become signatories to a set of principles and intentions.

An example of a compliance scheme in the tourism industry is the Green Globe Programme (GGP) which was developed by the World Travel and Tourism Council (WTTC) in 1994. The WTTC brings together the chief executives of over seventy of the world's largest travel and tourism companies drawn from the accommodation, catering, recreation transportation and travel-related services sector. The GGP was designed to help tourism businesses take targeted environmental action to enhance both business and environmental performance (Hawkins, 1995). It is a world-wide environmental management and awareness programme for the travel and tourism industry, open to any companies of any size, type and location (WTTC, 1994). Research shows that operational changes to minimize or negate adverse effects on the environment which have a cost to the individual operator, will not necessarily induce the operator to introduce the required changes (Birtles and Sofield, 1996). The GGP, however, is based on the assumption that tourism operators will be motivated to introduce operational changes for cost savings, increased turnover and profit, moral pressure, or a competitive advantage.

The promised services to members of the programme include a telephone hotline information service, training, education and information guides, a global network of environmental advisers, annual survey, member's directory and extended support services. To become a member of the programme, an organization is required to complete an annual survey on the state of environmental practice and targets for the coming year, as well as make a formal commitment to improvement in environmental practice and accept the Green Globe goals.

While there are many positive elements that the GGP achieves in the greening of the tourism industry, there are also some questionable aspects. While the WTTC has the potential to have a global influence due to its high profile amongst the international industry, government and policy makers, it is difficult to provide one set of guidelines and training materials for the diverse range of tourism destinations and operations in the world. Its objectives are also constrained by the lack of rigorous controls to ensure that standards are met. Often however any environmental conservation program is better than no program at all. The WTTC advocates a self-regulation approach for the industry with the rationale that if the industry acts now it may through self-regulation be able to prevent constrictive governmental regulation (*cf.* Birtles and Sofield, 1996).

A recent study conducted by Sirakaya and Uysal (1997) investigated the compliance behaviour of 127 tour operators with ecotourism guidelines in the USA, Canada and Ecuador. The study tested major factors that promote the adherence to codes of conduct and compliance schemes. Those factors included rewards, sanctions and enforcement, education and communication of policies as potential predictors of compliance. The study results showed that within a voluntary system of compliance, sanctions and deterrent measures did not play an important role in achieving conformance behaviour to the guidelines. Instead the positive reinforcers, such as education of tour operators with respect to the benefits of compliance, were identified to be far more effective in achieving adherence to the guidelines. Accreditation programmes involve a far greater degree of rewards and education than codes of practice or compliance schemes and therefore have the potential to be a more effective instrument in managing sustainable tourism.

Accreditation

Choice, risk, involvement and interaction with the natural environment are vital parts of the ecotourism experience. The ecotour operator (provider) needs to instil trust in the ecotourist (client) in order to attract and encourage them and this can be achieved through professionalism and accreditation. However, while these provide the ecotourist with security, they can, in turn, reduce the excitement and interaction found in the natural environments visited.

Accreditation has been proposed as one solution to the provision of security and a quality of experience. It offers the opportunity to improve industry standards generally and the opportunity to provide a degree of quality assurance in a highly competitive market. It may also improve the protection of the natural environment on which ecotourism depends and ensure appropriate practices and more informed decision making by ecotourists.

Accreditation involves the formal acknowledgement of adherence to agreed standards (Allcock *et al.*, 1994: 39). Benefits often associated with accreditation include quality assurance to both operators and tourists and the creation of a competitive edge in marketing. In accreditation systems, the primary responsibility for the integration and adoption of changes is with the tourism operator, through the identification and evaluation of a number of the environmental best practice initiatives within the ecotourism industry. However, a number of issues limit the effectiveness of 'environmental best practice' initiatives of the ecotourism industry, one of which was highlighted by PATA (1992) in that the industry does not control or own any major part of its assets. As such this leads to the industry developing a 'selling mentality to the resource as distinct from a sense of ownership and stewardship' (PATA, 1992: 9). Although this is the case, the diversity of not only the bodies involved in ecotourism but also destinations makes it extremely difficult to create and implement a national accreditation scheme, as indicated by both Allcock *et al.* (1994) and the Department of Tourism, Recreation and Sport (1994). The high level of fragmentation of the tourism industry further reinforces such anticipated difficulties (Forestry Tasmania, 1994; Gilbert, 1984).

Nevertheless, the world's first National Ecotourism Accreditation scheme was developed and launched by the Ecotourism Association of Australia (EAA) and the Australian Tourism Operators Network in 1996. The programme is based on ecologically sustainable development principles and gives operators the opportunity to be innovative and continually improve their practices. The application process involves the completion of self-assessment in relation to minimum standards, compiled in a comprehensive application document and the nomination of three referees. An appropriately qualified and appointed Ecotourism Accreditation Assessor evaluates the self-assessment and forwards the application to the Ecotourism Accreditation Committee for approval or rejection. Apart from the referee checks, there are other forms of verification used to determine whether the application is bona fide, such as feedback from clients and random audits on a certain percentage of accredited operators. Should it be revealed that an accredited business is not fulfilling their

nominated criteria, their accreditation status may be suspended or revoked. The aim over time is to increase the minimum standards on a regular basis and to ensure best practice can be realized on an ongoing basis (EAA, 1996).

While initiatives such as the National Ecotourism Accreditation Program are more accountable and enforceable than any code of practice or compliance scheme, there are still concerns over the credibility of its self-assessment component. However, this concern will most likely decrease with the increasing amount of accredited ecotourism operators who have the capacity to act as 'watchdogs' amongst themselves, and the continual review and raising of the minimum standards: 'if we have switched the emphasis from defining ecotourism to improving its performance, then we have come a long way in a short time. The challenge now is to go beyond rewarding bona fide ecotourism operators to establish measures that help other operators change their practices and become bona fide themselves' (McArthur, 1997b).

Case study   Great Barrier Reef Marine Park, Queensland, Australia

The issuing of licensing and permits is one method used to control both the numbers and types of users of a particular area. An example of their use is in the Great Barrier Reef Marine Park where commercial tourist operators require a permit to operate. All permit applications are assessed for possible impacts upon the conservation of the park's natural resources in order to reduce or prevent potential adverse impacts (Shurcliff and Williams, 1992). In this way access is restricted to a select number who have met certain conditions or criteria which are seen as being compatible with the area's values and desired uses. The main strength of the use of licences and permits is that they are legally enforceable. An associated problem with regard to industry-led best practice is that it is dependent upon the resource manager and not the user (such as the ecotour operator) to establish and instigate the conditions or criteria for the granting of the licences and permits. As such, all the operator has to do is fulfil the required conditions of the use situation.

Cooperative government and industry initiatives: community involvement and cooperative approaches

Depending on the political and economic system of a country, the ideal solution to the debate over self-regulation versus regulation is a cooperative approach to tourism planning and policy. Sustainable tourism relies heavily on stakeholder involvement, and 'efforts must be made to improve the links between nature conservation, local community development, and the tourism industry' (Ceballos-Lascurain, 1996).

One of the most critical aspects of the development for models to monitor and manage tourism activity has been the establishment of stakeholder endorsement and support (Prosser, 1986). Stakeholders from the local tourism sector and community are critical in implementing these models. The stakeholders can provide valuable input into desired conditions and acceptable standards, and are usually essential in providing the economic and political support necessary to maintain monitoring programmes and implement management decisions.

However there has been a consistent failure to establish sufficient stakeholder support for sustainable management models – such as the Visitor Impact Management Model (VIMM) and the Limits of Acceptable Change (LAC) which we discuss further in the following chapter – largely due to the fact that management organizations responsible for these models simply aren't attuned to attracting wider stakeholder involvement. There are three primary impediments to achieving this outcome:

- the use of the terms 'impact' and 'limits', which the tourism industry has interpreted as being discouraging to growth and thus business;
- the conventional narrow focus on the condition of the physical environment and to some extent, the nature of the visitor experience; and
- the lack of cooperative involvement of the tourism sector in identifying indicators and standards that are acceptable to the industry.

Without the involvement of all stakeholders, the monitoring of results becomes conflictual and prone to conjecture, particularly if they reveal surprising or controversial implications (McArthur, 1997a).

Case study   TOMM

The recent implementation of a tourism planning and monitoring model on Kangaroo Island in South Australia has attracted world attention due to its strong focus on involving all relevant stakeholders from local and state government to tourism operators, the island's community at large and natural area managers (Manidis Roberts, 1997). Its success was largely due to the Tourism Optimization Management Model (TOMM), which builds on the Limits of Acceptable Change (LAC) system developed by Stankey et al. (1985). (See Chapter 4 for a full discussion of the LAC system and other sustainable management models.)

TOMM was designed to serve a multitude of stakeholders with a multitude of interests, and can operate at a regional level over a range of public and private land tenures. Specifically, TOMM has been designed to:

● monitor and quantify the key economic, marketing, environmental, sociocultural and experiential benefits and impacts of tourism activity; and
● assist in the assessment of emerging issues and alternative future management options for the sustainable development and management of tourism activity (Manidis Roberts, 1997).

TOMM is being used to help change the culture of the tourism industry and its stakeholders by generating tangible evidence that the viability of the industry is dependent upon the quality of the visitor experiences it generates, and the condition of the natural, cultural and social resources it relies on.

Using policy to achieve best practice

Tourism has the potential to be an 'environmentally friendly' industry. Yet there are well-documented examples of tourist destinations becoming polluted, degraded and congested by mass market travel (PATA, 1992: 7). One way of attempting to deal with such problems of increasing environmental degradation of the natural environment is through the incorporation of 'environmental best practice'. This concept not only plays a role in the ecotourism industry but also the 'mainstream' tourism industry. We will now turn our attention to 'environmental best practice' in ecotourism as a practical and effective approach to generating solutions to environmental management and its

potential to give direction to the rest of the tourism industry with regard to the environmental issues the industry is facing as a whole.

Best practice involves 'striving for excellence, keeping in touch with innovations, avoiding waste and focusing on outcomes which are in the community interest' (Edwards and Prineas, 1995). It involves managing change and continual improvement and in this way it encompasses all levels of an organization. Examples of best practice include aiming to increase customer service, improvements in productivity or in the management of people. Best practice is not limited to particular types of organizations or bodies, nor is it to particular aspects or issues within those organizations or bodies. Rather it is an extremely diverse practice, which can be implemented in an array of different situations to serve different purposes. However, its central concern is related to change within an organization.

Following from this, it seems fairly straightforward that best practice can be associated with tourism or ecotourism, especially in regard to the increasing levels of environmental concern and awareness world-wide. The form of best practice in this case can be referred to as environmental best practice, which is defined by the Ecologically Sustainable Development Steering Committee (ESDSC) (1992) as business/industry culture and practices which align operational competitiveness to improved environmental performance. In this way it links environmental management and operational management in a positive way, leaving the primary responsibility for both with the organization itself. Numerous forms of environmental best practice are currently employed by ecotourism operators, ranging from the issuing of licences and permits for access to the development of codes of practice for tourists, operators and developers. A number of these forms will be discussed below, with emphasis placed on their relative strengths and weaknesses.

Tourism is no different from any other industry in its imperative for profitability. This profitability imperative is somewhat limited in ecotourism ventures as they must realize and incorporate limits to growth and volume. (The following chapter will elaborate on operational techniques to achieve these objectives.) There is an inverse relationship between how environmentally friendly a local nature tourism operation is and how economically successful it can ever hope to be (Cohen and Richardson, 1995). In this sense the environmental best practice initiatives of ecotourism are often not adopted within the greater tourism industry as they can be seen to place limits on profitability. This issue is further compounded by the tourism industry's overt pursuit of ever increasing volumes and the measurement of performance being exclusively linked to this increase (PATA, 1992).

It would be a grave mistake, however, for the tourism industry to disregard the environmental best practice initiatives of ecotourism. As we have seen, the most effective forms of regulation are those instigated by the industry itself and ecotourism is a leader in recognizing its environmental responsibilities by attempting to address these responsibilities through the establishment of codes of practice, guidelines and suggested accreditation schemes. Even though such initiatives are not yet supported by penalties for non-compliance, they provide a starting point or springboard with which to further foster and encourage environmentally sound practices in the tourism industry into the future. However, the major drawback with ecotourism-led environmental best practice is that actions are only adopted if they are seen as desirable within the organization. If they are not legally enforceable their use and effect is limited to those organizations already oriented towards environmental philosophies or which have the aspiration to incorporate such values.

In understanding the mechanisms for policy and planning we may be able to achieve a certain flexibility in approaching future ecotourism development by adopting a broad range of approaches which may assist in:

- achieving lower infrastructure cost;
- reducing the number of inbound visitors – which could conserve natural and cultural sites;
- an increase in the quality of visitor experience through understanding group and community interactions;
- a means to increase long-term benefits for local communities.

The extent to which ecotourism adheres to the principles of sustainability appears to be greater with cooperative approaches between government and stakeholder planning and policy. The principal role of such planning and policy, which mainly occurs through legislation and regulation, is therefore to ensure that ecotourism does not negatively impact on the environment, but rather creates environmental, economic and sociocultural benefits.

Case study Rwanda: diversification of ecotourism product

Many lesser developed nations are shifting to ecotourism as a primary source of income in preference to traditional agricultural pursuits. In such cases, management of this shift may be strengthened by diversification of the ecotourism products promoted.

In Rwanda, data available suggests that 75% of the country's tourism income is derived from gorilla visitation. The revenues in 1991, estimated at $1 million through direct expenditure and $9 million via indirect expenditure, are derived through international visitation, as high tourism costs in the country deter domestic visitors to gorilla populations.

Most visitors to Rwanda are attracted to the Parc National des Volcans which houses the gorilla population; however, the country has been attempting to promote its other protected areas. The Parc National d'Akagera, created in 1954 and covering an area of 2500 square miles, and the Nyungwe Forest Reserve in Southern Rwanda, one of the largest untouched montane forests, with 250 species of birds, are two such areas. With Rwanda still reeling from the recent civil war, genocide and mass population exodus, advertising of new ecotourism destinations has understandably been given lesser priority. The effects of economic and political upheaval in less developed nations illustrate the influence external factors may have on already limited government expenditure on tourism, and such volatility threatens successful ecotourism ventures which operate in areas of significant natural beauty. Where governments cannot afford to promote the region/attraction, operators are left to bridge a large gap with finite resources.

Source: M. Shackley, 'The future of gorilla tourism in Rwanda', *Journal of Sustainable Development*, 3 (2), 1995, 61–72

Land use zoning is associated with the use of carrying capacity. Generally carrying capacity attempts to establish the level of use possible within the given environment without environmental deterioration. Hall (1994) takes the issue of carrying capacities a step further, highlighting that they must include social and cultural aspects as well as the above mentioned environmental issues. An example of the effective use of an environmental carrying capacity is at the Point Nepean National Park in Victoria, where once the assigned quota of daily visitors is reached the gates to the park are simply closed (Wescott, 1993). Once again though, the identification and implementation of the carrying capacity is the duty of the resource manager not the user. There are also inherent difficulties involved in quantifying the associated environmental, social and cultural impacts (Dowling, 1992; Norris, 1994).

Zoning

Land use zoning divides sections of land into areas based on their sensitivity and conservation values (Buckley and Pannell, 1990). By doing so areas are designated for different purposes in an attempt not only to protect the valued areas but also to balance this with appropriate use. It has the ability to facilitate sustainable tourism through the regulation of development and the implementation of design standards for tourist facilities to ensure they do not impact to the detriment of the environment in which they are developed (McIntyre *et al.*, 1993). The main advantage of zoning is that it is one way in which conflicting activities can be separated, enabling the identification of the suitability of particular areas/sites for particular uses, and the protection and conservation of selected sites or areas (Simmons and Harris, 1995: 14). Zoning is an effective means to limit the extent of tourism activities within the sustainable boundaries of the region.

Ecotourism travel essentials: planning guidelines for ecotourism

● To encourage community, environmental, and tourism constituencies to work together toward a common goal.
● The success of ecotourism depends on the conservation of nature. Many parks are threatened, and it is critical for everyone involved with ecotourism to realize that intact natural resources are the foundation.
● Ecotourism sites need revenue for protection and maintenance, much of which can be generated directly from entry fees and sale of products. Many protected areas charge nominal or no entrance fees and provide few if any auxiliary services. Ecotourists also desire gift shops, food services and lodging facilities and expect to pay for them.

- Ecotourists are a valuable audience for environmental education. In many parks, opportunities are missed to provide environmental education. Whether 'hard-core' nature tourists or 'new' visitors with little background in natural history, all tourists can enhance their appreciation of the area through information brochures, exhibits and guides.
- Ecotourism will contribute to rural development when local residents are brought into the planning process. For ecotourism to be a tool for conservation and rural development, a concerted effort must be made to incorporate local populations into development of the tourism industry. In some cases, tourism to protected areas is not benefiting the surrounding population because they are not involved.
- Opportunities are emerging for new relationships between conservationists and tour operators. Traditionally, these groups have not worked together; often they have been in direct opposition. However, as more tourists come to parks and reserves, tour operators have the opportunity to become more actively involved with the conservation of these areas through education for their clientele and donations to park management (Boo, 1990).

4

Ecotourism and protected areas: visitor management for sustainability

Conservation issues are now at the forefront of public opinion. The decline of natural rainforests, loss of endangered species, global warming and increasing land degradation have galvanised public support for conservation. It is no accident that the interest and growth of ecotourism and nature-oriented tourism has coincided with this world-wide concern.

Ecotourism and nature-oriented tourism often take place in protected and remote regions, areas of exceptional beauty, ecological interest and cultural importance. Today these areas are established to conserve biodiversity and to halt the large scale loss of natural ecosystems. Globally there are approximately 8500 protected areas which cover about 5.17% of the earth's land surface[1] and the growth in the designation of protected areas has increased remarkably over the past twenty years[2].

However, protected areas are increasingly coming under pressure a range of fronts:

● the demands for 'multiple use' parks allowing extractive industries;

● the demands of lobby groups seeking access for a range of recreational activities – four-wheel driving, horse riding, hunting, fishing;

● and the aspirations of indigenous groups for title and management of parks.

These demands raise distinct challenges for protected areas. Indeed, in the face of these increasing challenges can (indeed, should) these areas remain as protected refuges?

The traditional conception of protected areas is the uninhabited, minimal interference park, and as we have seen in Chapter 2, this is an overtly 'preservationist' position. However, in much of the world population pressures are dictating that excluding human presence from protected areas is no longer feasible.

The preservationist position is also under attack from the opposite end of the spectrum, by those that believe nature has one primary value or function – for human use. 'Use' adherents range from industry representatives seeking access to park resources, such as the logging, grazing and mining industries, to the many diverse special interest groups who are generally hostile to nature-centred management, such as hunters and off-road enthusiasts.

Historically protected area policy has moved significantly in the direction of human use. In the Caracas Action Plan, the major strategy

---

[1] Over 773 million ha.

[2] Currently, 80% of the world's protected areas were established after 1962 (World Conservation Monitoring Centre, 1992). Protected areas in Costa Rica for example from 30 in 1970 to more than 230 by 1990 (Cornelius, 1991).

document to come out of the IVth World Congress on National Parks and Protected Areas in Venezuela in 1992, the shift away from an overt preservationist position towards a human-needs orientation is unambiguous: 'Protected areas must be managed so that local communities, the nations involved, and the world community all benefit (IUCN, 1992).

We can see here, in both the use and preservationist positions, the centrality of the anthropocentric premise. Nature conservation's most acceptable and prevalent form[3] is a utilitarian one in that such areas are deemed necessary to preserve or protect for their potential human benefits, be it for 'aesthetic', 'gymnasium', 'cathedral' or 'laboratory' potential (see Chapter 2). Thus the use and preservationist positions are constrained by two orientations: at one extreme lies the emphasis on human needs being met in parks, while the other leads to overt opposition to the preservation and protection of natural areas as valueless 'locking up' of land. This conflict intensifies with the pressures of an exponentially increasing global population and the concomitant consumption of resources this entails.

As we have seen in Chapter 2, ecocentrically oriented philosophies have raised significant challenges to the anthropocentric focus on nature's value lying in its relation to human needs. However, an extreme ecocentrist approach would actually challenge the fundamental rationale of protected areas themselves as a 'Noah's Ark solution', for protected areas are in effect isolated islands of biodiversity. An ecocentric perspective would argue that we would not need protected areas if we did not have such an exploitative relationship with nature (see Chapter 2) and this is the heart of the protected area debate, particularly in relation to ecotourism, for in essence 'humanity depends upon that which it threatens'.

Tourism and protected areas

Nowhere are the conflicting views over intrinsic and utilitarian value more evident than the current debate over the function and purpose of protected areas. It is a conflict over two primary orientations, 'preservation' versus 'use', and tourism in protected areas embodies precisely this dilemma. For tourism is in essence a recreational activity in which the value for nature aligns with both the 'cathedral' and 'gymnasium' dimensions we have discussed in Chapter 2. Protected areas seemingly are incompatible with such activities for their primary function lies in the preservation of natural ecosystems. Such an opposition is illustrated and reinforced through accepted institutional arrangements in which tourism and conservation goals are pursued by independent organizations. The current focus of the debate on tourism in parks is the extension of a long controversy, a controversy that has existed since the conception of protected areas and equivalent reserves.

The originating conception of national parks placed recreation rather than conservation at the centre of park functions. Yellowstone National Park in the United States of America for example was originally conceptualized as 'pleasuring grounds for the benefit and enjoyment of the people . . . for gaining great profit from tourists and pleasure seekers' and as 'a national domain for rest and recreation' (Strom, 1980: 3). Similarly, the Royal National Park, established in Australia in 1879, was originally established as a recreational park. Historically then parks were established for utilitarian reasons but since the early conception of parks there has been a significant reorientation away from a predominant recreational/tourism focus towards conservation objectives. In the past recreation and tourism were only a minor threat to parks because of distance and difficulty in access and the low levels of visitation. However, this has changed significantly in the past 15–20 years as protected areas are becoming of increasing significance through increases in mobility, leisure and environmental awareness (Sheppard, 1987; 25), both

---

[3] This is often the only grounds accepted for its argument.

in terms of visitor numbers – and hence impacts – and their centrality for conservation.

To accept increased levels of visitation as the price of support significantly compromises the natural qualities upon which parks are founded. Every day we witness increasing pressure on natural resources and a need for escalating protection of resources, particularly those found in protected areas and equivalent reserves. The major problem is in deciding what directions and actions should be taken to ensure the future of such areas.

Although protected areas are not conceived identically across the world, the International Union of the Conservation of Nature (IUCN) identifies their common characteristics:

1 The area contains one or more ecosystems not materially altered by human activity and it contains fauna, flora, geomorphological sites, and habitats of scientific, educational and recreational interest.
2 The highest competent authority of the country has taken steps to prevent or eliminate as soon as possible exploitation or occupation in the area and to enforce protection of its ecological, geomorphological, and aesthetic features that led to its establishment.
3 Visitors are allowed to enter, under special conditions, for inspirational, educational, cultural, and recreational purposes (IUCN, 1985: 7).

This definition clearly identifies conservation values as a major purpose. This includes the protection of genetic and biological diversity, and the provision of settings for base-line measurements of biological conditions for the comparison of effects associated with development. However, it also recognizes the legitimate right of public entry 'under special conditions' – recreational purposes for example.

Protected areas and capitalist realism

Across the industrialized West the role of government is shrinking, with many former govern-ment controlled sectors – insurance, health, education, energy, water, transport, banking – being increasingly removed from public owner-ship and control in a shift towards a business rather than public interest model. The impact of this change has seen no sphere of government as quarantined from the market-based rationale. In this way protected area agencies have also found themselves under intense pressure to be more 'commercial', 'customer focused' and to produce more of their revenue from the services provided by parks.

Case Study   Funding United States national parks

With the drive to meet budget targets and increased discussions on corporate sponsor-ship the National Parks Service has been forced to pursue alternative funding options whilst still maintaining their stewardship role. In 1997, in budget submissions to the Department of Interior, the Park Service requested ($US) 1.5 billion. Congress allot-ted ($US) 1.42 billion. For the 1998 fiscal year, the agency is seeking ($US) 1.6 billion, including ($US) 100 million for an ambitious upgrading of the Everglades National Park. Although funding has steadily increased from ($US) 900 million in 1984 to the 1997 figure of ($US) 1.4 billion, if this figure is measured in constant 1983 dollars, the appropriations have decreased 14%

Increased land management responsibili-ties have increased the strain on resource managers – consider these statistics along-side the decline in real funding:

- Visits have steadily risen from 210 million in 1984 to over 260 million in 1996.
- The number of parks has increased from 335 in 1984 to 374 today.
- In the past five years, staff numbers have been reduced by 10%.

In addition, there are estimated costs of ($US) 6–8 billion required to rectify a backlog of repairs and improvements. A debate rages over appropriations, budgeting and priorities, but the essence of the argument is that parks need more money. One critical concern is that the Park Service maintain its stewardship role in the face of the funding crisis. Congress approved a three-year pilot programme to introduce entrance fees at 100 parks Nearly all of the money collected goes back into parks, providing in 1998 an estimated ($US) 48 million for repairs and maintenance. Congress is considering:

- Concession reform legislation. This could generate $50 million annually from private businesses operating within the park.
- A revenue bond programme, allowing private non-profit groups to finance capital parks projects by issuing bonds.
- A bill to let taxpayers check off part of their return to go towards funding parks.

However, the primary fear for the parks service is that the reduction in appropriations due to such an offset would in effect defeat the purpose of such fund raising.

Source: W. Mitman Clarke, 'Insufficient funds', *National Parks*, July/August, 1997, pp. 26–29

Contemporary questions about whether to utilize or conserve are really questions about who controls the resources (Stretton, 1976). They are therefore like any other question of distributive justice and are inherently political. In our current economically dominant world-view, protected areas are considered as no different from competing land use claims and most argue for their survival on these terms.

The imperative for conservation advocates becomes *how* to conserve rather than *whether* or not to conserve. However urgent it may be to wake people up to physical and ecological changes, environmental reformers also need political philosophies (Stretton, 1976) and for quite practical purposes. In this way ecotourism, as a sustainable development strategy, is increasingly being turned to as part of a political philosophy for protected area managers and conservation agencies as a means of providing practical outcomes in the struggle to provide a basis for continued protection for these areas. These outcomes include:

- a source of finance for parks and conservation and therefore providing a justification (economic) for park protection;
- an alternative form of economic development;
- the broadening of conservation issues within the general public;
- the facilitation of a private conservation ethic.

To operationalize conservation goals in a context which involves decisions on the allocation of scare resources dictates that arguments for protected areas will almost inevitably involve economic rationalist and utilitarian premises. Being realistic (some would say pessimistic) it also seems unlikely that the potential value of protected areas to future generations will be a sufficiently strong argument to cause current generations to set aside scare resources for their future offspring.

However, to argue that protected areas are a resource that can be enjoyed for recreation and tourism poses a serious dilemma. This dilemma is one of current protection based on utilitarian objectives and of future conservation based on intrinsic value. Are these approaches compatible or, more importantly, can either contribute towards conservation?

With such a variety of pressures on natural resources, the need for more and more intensive protection of those resources which are currently found in protected areas and equivalent reserves is all too evident. The manpower and financial resources which are needed for the protection of the 2% of the Earth's terrestrial surface that are currently in protected areas are far from adequate. Can we rest with any confidence that the 98% of the globe which is not covered by the UN list of protected areas and Equivalent Reserves is adequately managed?

[P]rotected areas are but one mechanism for attaining conservation objectives. They are an important mechanism but in themselves they are inadequate. (Eidsvik, 1980: 187)

Many authors[4] suggest that the use versus preservation question is an 'appropriate use' dilemma. This dilemma of 'appropriate use' is a conflict of values which will always arise in any anthropocentric approach to conservation and management of ecosystems:

Wilderness, however defined, belongs to all Americans, yet to enjoy the wilderness is to destroy it – particularly if the enjoyment is seen in terms of mass recreation. (Coppock and Rogers, 1975: 510)

Although protected areas are considered as primarily conservation based (*cf.* Runte, 1997; Strom, 1980), there will always be conflicts between use and conservation.

Protected areas have been, are, and will continue to be used by people, irrespective of what park management agencies say and do. (Sheppard, 1987: 23)

Section 72(4)(e) of the New South Wales, Australia National Parks and Wildlife Act, 1974 requires:

The encouragement and regulation of the appropriate use, understanding and enjoyment of each national park, historic site and state recreation area by the public.

Tourism as a key

Society expects optimal use of natural resources as an integral part of the process of continual economic development. In this circumstance the economic justification of ecotourism in protected areas offers a means of providing outcomes that can demonstrate to society the benefits of protected areas. Increasingly, tourism is often used to provide an economic rationale to preserve natural areas rather than developing them for alternative uses such as agriculture or forestry. In current analyses of natural or protected areas it is this element that has become central, pushing debate onto the question of maintaining an area in its natural state as opposed to exploiting the resources it contains.

This economic valuation is increasingly being used to justify the existence of protected areas through the demonstrable 'value' of both the wildlife and ecosystem features. Tourism is becoming increasingly central to these strategies given that tourists are willing to pay to experience these natural areas.

Many studies are now being used to show that protected areas make an economic contribution of some significance.[5] These studies have variously used econometric modelling, input–output analysis and multiplier analysis to estimate the impact of natural resource-based recreation and tourism on local and regional economies.

Case study   Amboseli National Park

Mount Kilimanjaro is the majestic backdrop for this park which features five different wildlife habitats: the seasonal lake bed of Lake Amboseli, sulphur springs surrounded by swamps and marshes, open plains,

---

[4] (*cf.* Nash, 1989; Runte, 1997; Turner, 1988)

[5] *cf.* For a review of these, see IUCN (1996) *Economics of Protected Areas.*

woodlands, and lava rock thornbush country. These habitats support elephant herds, black rhino, lion and cheetah as well as Masai giraffe, eland, Coke's hartebeest waterbuck, impala and gazelle.

Amboseli National Park is estimated to be worth 18 times the annual income of a fully developed commercial beef industry. The value of a single lion as a tourist attraction is estimated at $US27 000 a year, while an elephant herd may be worth as much as $US610 000 per year – thus they are 'worth' more alive than dead (MacKinnon *et al.*, 1986). The total net return for a park such as Amboseli in utilizing tourism, is estimated to be 50 times more per hectare a year than the most optimistic agricultural returns.[6]

Tourism in protected areas can lead to increased economic benefits through both the direct expenditures of tourists and the associated employment opportunities it generates, both within and adjacent to the park. This can be capitalized upon in promotional strategies – a poster in Tanzania reads: 'Our protected areas bring good money into Tanzania – Protect them' (Nash, 1989: 344). This economic rationale in support of parks (*cf.* Machlis and Tichnell, 1985; MacKinnon *et al.*, 1986) is especially important where competing resource uses, such as agriculture or forestry, are involved.

The economic benefits of tourism have the potential to provide additional support for park protection and for giving parks a role in supporting rural development. However, there are questions about the distribution of the economic benefits of tourism. Large-scale developments

involving millions of dollars may be appearing to contribute to local or regional economies but, in fact, such benefits may only be illusory. Rates of leakage of tourist expenditures can be very high; in the Caribbean for example, first-round leakage rates range from 30 to 45% and second-round leakages from 15–20%.

The question of who gets the benefits and who pays the costs is complex. Although visitors expect some tourism money to directly benefit the local population surrounding the area, in some cases little of that money actually is distributed to the local communities. Moreover, much of the economic impact literature focuses only on benefits. Limited attention has been given to the economic costs imposed by the infrastructure developed to attract, accommodate and facilitate tourism or to the costs of maintaining and/or restoring park resources adversely affected by tourists. This raises the concern of whether the perceived economic returns of tourism in or associated with protected areas will lead to inappropriate developments and/or use levels that threaten the conservation objectives upon which the park is founded.

Arguments for tourism's ability to generate employment are also problematic, as often employment goes to persons residing outside of the area which directly experiences the impacts of tourism. Wages also are typically low and tourism is highly seasonal in many areas. Economic benefits are also subject to external changes, such as shifts in exchange rates that can rapidly change the 'attractiveness' of a location as the cost of holidaying is one of the most important factors in determining the desirability of a region.

This illustrates several key limitations in the economic justification of protected areas. Current economic analyses are capable of extending only to those more tangible economic measurements, such as willingness to pay, travel costs and expenditure rates. These methods have been effective to an extent in evaluating some human behaviour associated with national parks and protected areas, but they have not been widely

---

[6] Similar studies abound in the literature: one study in Costa Rica showed that the value of a tropical rain forest reserve in its natural state was at least equal to or twice as high than the economic 'price' of the land itself; a macaw in Peru is estimated as generating between $750 and $4700 annually in tourist revenues (Munn, 1991: 471).

accepted as adequate methods for estimating accurately the value of national parks and protected areas.

Economics is by definition a zero sum equation and must therefore take account of all costs that are associated with a particular project in order for the economic equation to balance fully. In terms of natural areas, a large proportion of the costs in changing the use of an area are social costs which, in many cases, are intangible and difficult, if not impossible to measure.

Economic concepts do not readily adapt to measurement of the intangible values of protected areas. The valuation of natural areas has its basis in the framework for land use planning in developed countries which centres around the idea of 'highest and best use'. For an economic cost, the highest and best use of land invariably refers to the most economically viable purpose. Inherent in this judgement are the limitations of economic indicators to value all relevant factors with a consistent degree of accuracy. Clearly it is easier to quantify the value of raw materials, land (as private real estate) or development opportunities in accurate monetary terms, than it is to identify the more intangible social impacts of utilizing a resource.

When an economic valuation of a natural area is proposed, it is usually done so in order to compare alternative uses of the resource. This comparison is almost always for the purposes of decision making, and this decision-making process is inherently political. While the concept of economic cost seeks to provide a figure that provides a platform upon which a political argument is built, almost inevitably this argument moves to analysis of non-economic matters or the concept of 'social cost,' or, in economic terms, externalities.

In basic economic terms a quality environment is a 'good' producing 'satisfaction' and therefore must be accounted for in some way. Environmental impact assessment has been developed as a mechanism to begin accounting for these less tangible values. However, the consideration of social costs presents significant problems for economic analyses. Economic analysis has, in the past decade, expanded its theoretical parameters to include non-financial benefits. However, there is an inherent bias for measurable economic returns.

The solution to the problem should not be based on the development of better economic and social indexes: 'Indexes can't alter the fact that what one citizen sees as goods another sees as costs or waste. What one wants to consume another wants to leave in the ground. Indexes of net welfare have to be constructed by controversial judgements of good and bad. They are still worth having (though every person may want their own). Better accounting can serve all sorts of good purposes, and reconcile some mistaken conflicts of opinion, but it can't reconcile real conflicts of interest outside' (Stretton, 1976: 314).

Ecocentrically informed management recognizes that modern science and technology cannot prevent environmental degradation if the current economic growth and resource use trends continue, and that a change in philosophy, politics and economics are needed to ensure that a sustainable human population can exist in balance with its environment. This is a preservationist position which re-emphasizes the need for prior macroenvironmental constraints, such as government legislation.

Therefore, conservation involves the management or control of human use of resources (bionic and abiotic) and activities on the planet, in an attempt to restore, enhance, protect and sustain the quality and quantity of a desired mix of species, ecosystem conditions and processes for present and future generations (Dunster and Dunster, 1996: 69).

Resource conservation is thus a form of 'restrained development' in that, at a minimum, development must be sustainable in not endangering the natural systems that support life on earth – the atmosphere, the waters, the soils, and all living beings.

An ecocentric systems approach to protected areas management allows a shift from the utilitarian/instrumental justification toward the intrinsic values of the protected areas. However, without this change in values the long-term future of protected areas could be placed in jeopardy.

Sustainable management techniques

While more conventional forms of tourism modify the surrounding environment to suit the specific needs of their clients, ecotourists do not expect or even desire substantial modifications of the natural environment. Rather than measuring the quality of the tour by conventional standards such as predicability and uniformity of experience, 'ecotourism's success is based on the unexpected' (Williams, 1990: 84). Ecotourism provides the tourist with opportunities to discover and actively participate and interact with the surrounding environment, encouraging the tourist to assume a proactive role in creating their own tourism experience.

Despite increasing interest from larger tour operators, ecotourism remains largely an activity of small operators (O'Neill, 1991). Thus it occurs at a different scale to traditional mass tourism as small operators are restricted in the numbers of clients that they are able to handle at any one time (cf. Choegyal, 1991: 94; Williams, 1990: 85). Due to the small scale of operations, political support, market stability, business costs and employment are not as reliable as conventional tourism. However, limited group size provides a higher quality experience for the tourist.

There is concern, however, that ecotourism will act much in the same manner as mass tourism only destroying the resource at a slower rate (Butler, 1992). In the short term ecotourism is viewed as 'less conducive to causing change in destination areas than mass tourism, in part because of its dimensions and in part because of the need for fewer and smaller facilities' (Butler, 1990). However, it is thought that, over time, the cumulative effects of this activity may penetrate deeper into the environment and the surrounding communities, paving the way for mass tourism development. For every traveller prepared to meet the wilderness on its own terms, there exist hundreds of others who demand that it be modified for their use – surfaced roads, cafeterias, toilets, parking, picnic facilities and a range of other amenities.

This is a fundamental issue for ecotourism and protected areas. Ecotourists prefer to experience natural areas in an unspoilt state and therefore there is a significant crossover of interest for conservation objectives. However, although ecotourism to natural areas may have positive outcomes, it is important for management to be aware of possible adverse effects so that they might be addressed through careful planning and effective management strategies (McNeely and Thorsell, 1989). Protected area agencies may be significantly attracted to the economic benefits of tourism which may compromise conservation objectives. Managers must be clear of the park's objectives along with the significant differences between forms of tourism and their impacts. Common issues associated with tourism in natural areas that need to be considered by managers include visitor crowding, conflict between different user types, littering, user fees and information distribution (Lucas, 1984).

Thus, an important consideration for management involved in ecotourism activities in natural areas is the way in which a balance may be provided in order to maximize visitor enjoyment, while at the same time minimizing the negative impacts of tourism development (cf. Ceballos-Lascurain, 1990; McNeely and Thorsell, 1989).

It is essential here to note that even when ecotourism is deployed in order to supply protected areas with economic benefits, the park itself must be strictly managed, monitored and controlled through protective measures to prevent degradation of the site by tourists. Most protected areas with the highest biodiversity are fragile and even the smallest human impacts have significant environmental effects. Protected areas are themselves areas that are in much demand for nature-based tourism because of the very features that they are designed to protect – their biodiversity, remoteness, pristine ecosystems. However many of these areas lack infrastructure and park managers therefore have few resources to cope with increasing tourist levels.

The defence of protected areas for their intrinsic value alone has proven to be difficult. In capitalist societies such as ours, expensive and often expansive claims on scarce land resources must be based on broad grounds and integrated within a robust management framework; ecotourism has presented an opportunity to achieve this.

As we have seen in previous chapters, one critical element of ecotourism is sustainability. Ecotourism's goal then is sustainability which attempts to provide a resource base for the future, and seeks to ensure the productivity of the resource base, maintain biodiversity and avoid irreversible environmental changes while ensuring equity both within and between generations.

Ecotourism seeks to capitalize on the increase in tourism to protected areas renowned for their outstanding beauty and extraordinary ecological interest and return the benefits of this to the host community. Ecotourism is premised on the idea that it can only be sustainable if the natural and cultural assets it is reliant upon survive and prosper. This involves reducing social and biophysical impacts caused by visitors, reducing the leakage of potential benefits away from developing countries, increasing environmental awareness and action among tourists and opportunities for the people who would otherwise depend on the extraction of local resources.

Management guidelines for natural attractions are frequently expected by nature-oriented tourists. Management control serves to protect and conserve the area, ensuring that the expectations of visitors are met, thus ensuring that patronage continues along with the natural resource bases. Factors which should be under management control and which may affect natural attractions as well as tourist expectations include tourist infrastructure and development, visitor levels, guides, vandalism, souvenir collection, access to areas, driving off-road at night, feeding animals and others.

Ecotourism groups ideally should be small in scale in order to provide a higher quality experience to the customer as this aids in the ability to keep environmental stress and impact levels to a minimum, as well as allowing the tourist's intrinsic goals to be realized. Ecotourism is able to foster an appreciation of natural areas and traditional cultures by enabling the tourist to experience an area first hand. It is this first hand experience with the natural environment, combined with the quest for education and other intrinsic enjoyment, that constitutes a true ecotourism experience (Butler, 1992).

Carrying Capacity, Recreation Opportunity Spectrum, Limits of Acceptable Change, Visitor Impact Management and Visitor Activity Management Process are sustainability decision-making frameworks used in protected area management. When implemented they help to protect a country's natural and cultural heritage, enhance public appreciation of the resource, and manage the conflict between resource and user (Graham *et al.*, 1987: 292). To gain an appreciation of these strategies and their relationship to managing ecotourism operations, protected areas will be used to elaborate the specific issues relating to sustainability practices; their historical development within the context of an increasing environmental awareness and the ability to consider broad social factors will be examined.

A short history of protected areas and sustainable management strategies

The balancing of the tension between the resource and the user during the late nineteenth century and into the late 1960s was largely achieved by focusing research, planning and management efforts on the resource base in determining infrastructure and facilities in the park. Social and economic factors were not an integral component of park planning and management and little was known about the dimensions and nature of human use (Graham *et al.*, 1987). In this respect, management did not have an understanding of the interdependent relationship between social and biophysical systems. There was no overall approach to the selection and management of visitor opportunities, and the effectiveness of services could not be measured, with incorrect decisions often being made about the size and location of facilities with little public involvement in the development of park plans, and often confusing information was given to visitors (Graham, 1990: 276).

Increasing recreational and tourism use of protected areas is generally accompanied by negative environmental and social impacts. These impacts have to be managed to conserve ecological and recreational values. Numerous planning and management frameworks have been developed to assist managers in preventing, combating or minimizing the effects of recreational use on natural environments.

The concepts of Carrying Capacity, the Recreation Opportunity Spectrum (ROS), Limits of Acceptable Change (LAC), Visitor Impact Management (VIM), Visitor Activity Management Process (VAMP) and the Tourism Optimization Management Model (TOMM) are examples of visitor planning and management frameworks. Each is intended to complement existing management and decision-making processes.

Carrying capacity is fundamental to environmental protection and sustainable development. It refers to the maximum use of any site without causing negative effects on the resources, reducing visitor satisfaction, or exerting adverse impact upon the society, economy and culture of the area. Carrying capacity limits can sometimes be difficult to quantify, but they are essential to environmental planning for tourism and recreation.

Carrying capacity

The carrying capacity concept originated in the 1970s. Its central idea 'is that environmental factors set limits on the population that an area can sustain. When these limits are exceeded, the quality of the environment suffers and ultimately, its ability to support that population' (Stankey, 1991: 12). It was believed that objective, biological studies could determine the capacity of an area's natural resources, establishing how much use the environment could cope with and regulating access to the resource. According to Stankey (1991: 11), this 'scientific' basis explains the wide appeal of carrying capacity as a recreation and tourism management concept.

There are three main elements of tourism carrying capacity:

- Biophysical (ecological) – which relates to the natural environment.
- Socio-cultural – which relates primarily to the impact on the host population and its culture.
- Facility – which relates to the visitor experience.

Carrying capacity varies according to season and, over time, factors such as tourists' behavioural patterns, facility design and management, the dynamic character of the environment, and the changing attitudes of the host community will all vary in differing ways, thus affecting its determination.

However, carrying capacity has not been as useful as anticipated. Perhaps it was expected to reveal precisely 'how many is too many?' Instead, depending on assumptions and values, the result has been 'widely varying capacity estimates' of types and levels of use (Stankey, 1991: 12). There are a wide range of differing values and perceptions of what an 'unacceptable impact' is. There are no absolute measurements of the resource's condition that can be defined as constituting 'crowding' or 'resource damage' (Stankey, 1991: 13).

As social issues, management, as well as natural resources, affect the calculation of carrying capacity, it is not possible to come up with a number beyond which unacceptable impacts occur: 'To prevent most impact it would be necessary to limit use to very low levels' (Stankey, 1991: 13). People continue to use an area for recreational activities even when it is obviously having an impact on the resource. This stems from the absence of an adequate framework that links the relationship between visitor expectations, use and impact and management decisions (Stankey and McCool, 1985).

Carrying capacity analysis then has been virtually ignored because of the complexity of the parameters, and although tourism operators can be conscious that too many visitors will degrade the environment and diminish the experience of their clients in both recreation and tourism, there are very few examples of it being used by agencies to successfully limit tourism (*cf.* Stankey *et al.*, 1990).

Solutions to the problems of overuse and crowding differ depending on the policies of agencies managing wilderness (Watson, 1989: 394). A study conducted in 1987, for example, found that only 6 out of 38 wilderness managers had estimated recreational carrying capacity, even though most were concerned about overuse of parks (Watson, 1989).

Canada recognized the concept's deficiencies, such as ignoring the social aspects, and went on to develop more broad-based concepts. Recreation Opportunity Spectrum (ROS) is based on assumptions and tenets borrowed from other lines of research (Driver *et al.*, 1987: 210).

The Recreation Opportunity Spectrum

ROS is a framework for prescribing carrying capacities and managing recreational impacts. The process is largely a judgemental one, but establishes explicit standards regarding appropriate conditions for each opportunity class. Determining carrying capacities for recreational areas establishes conditions of use which are considered appropriate for each opportunity type, and provides a means of assessing the relative numbers of persons as a result of changing opportunity types (*cf.* Stankey, 1991).

The ROS approach shifted attention from the type and amount of use an area receives to the biophysical, social and managerial attributes of the park setting (Prosser, 1986: 7). ROS was further developed to provide a logical series of interrelated steps for natural area planning. This new framework is known as the Limits of Acceptable Change (LAC) system (Prosser, 1986: 6).

The ROS focuses on the setting in which recreation occurs. A recreation opportunity spectrum is the combination of physical, biological, social and managerial conditions that give value to a place (Clark and Stankey, 1979). ROS has been described as a framework for presenting carrying capacities and managing recreational impacts. The ROS provides a systematic framework for looking at the actual distribution of opportunities and a procedure for assessing possible management actions.

Clark and Stankey (1979) initially proposed a series of four levels of development, or management classes under the ROS, i.e.:

- semi-modern
- modern
- semi-primitive
- primitive.

Factors used to describe management classes were:

- access
- other non-recreational resource uses
- on-site management
- social interaction
- acceptability of visitor impacts
- acceptable level of regimentation.

Limitations of the ROS are related to its basis in recreational carrying capacity, which is seen as the product of technical assessments, as opposed to value judgements that weigh resource and social impacts, along with human needs and values (McCool, 1990).

Limits of Acceptable Change

The Limits of Acceptable Change methodology is an extension of the ROS concept and recognizes both the social and environmental dimensions of recreational impacts. It involves both resource managers and stakeholders in:

- identifying accptable and achievable social and resource standards;
- documenting gaps between desirable and existing circumstances;
- identifying management actions to close these gaps; and
- monitoring and evaluating management effectiveness (Payne and Graham, 1993).

The LAC planning system consists of nine steps.

- Identifying concerns and issues.
- Defining and describing opportunity classes.
- Selecting indicators of resource and social conditions.
- Carrying out an inventory of resource and social conditions.
- Specifying standards for the resource and social indicators.
- Identifying alternative opportunity class allocations.
- Identifying management actions for each alternative.
- Evaluating and selecting an alternative.
- Implementing actions and monitoring condition (Stankey et al., 1985).

Relative to the ROS, the LAC framework offers more opportunity for public participation which results in a consensus planning approach to natural area management. However, few LAC systems have been implemented with any great success and this is thought to be due to a lack of political and economic support from stakeholders (McArthur, 1997c). LAC systems also require considerable resources to establish inventories of resource and social conditions.

The LAC system is a technical planning system. It provides a 'systematic decision-making framework which helps determine what resource and social conditions are acceptable and prescribes appropriate management actions'

(Stankey, 1991: 14). The LAC framework mitigates the conflict between recreation, tourism and conservation. It defines the impacts associated with different levels of environmental protection. It also helps set the basis for allowing environmental change consistent with, and appropriate and acceptable to, different types of recreational opportunities (Stankey, 1991: 13). By establishing specific indicators and standards related to conservation values, coupled with monitoring, it is possible to define what impact levels can be permitted before management intervention becomes necessary (Stankey, 1991: 12).

Significantly, the LAC system does more than develop and extend the ROS framework. It also represents an important reformulation of key elements of the carrying capacity concept (Prosser, 1986: 8). By directing attention away from the question 'how much recreation use is too much?' towards desired conditions, the LAC approach skirts around the use/impact conundrum. Because the resource and social conditions of an area are most important, the LAC emphasis is on management of the impacts of use (Lucas and Stankey, 1988).

Visitor Impact Management

The Visitor Impact Management process involves a combination of legislation/policy review, scientific problem identification (both social and natural) and analysis and professional judgement (Payne and Graham, 1993). The principles of VIM are as follows.

- Identifying unacceptable changes occurring as a result of visitor use and developing management strategies to keep visitor impacts within acceptable levels.
- Integrating visitor impact management into existing agency planning, design and management processes.
- Basing visitor impact management on the best scientific understanding and situational information available.

- Determining management objectives that identify the resource condition to be achieved and the type of recreation experience to be provided.
- Identifying visitor impact problems by comparing standards for acceptable conditions with key indicators of impact at designated times and locations.
- Basing management decisions, to reduce impacts or maintain acceptable conditions, on knowledge of the probable sources of, and interrelationships between unacceptable impacts.
- Addressing visitor impacts using a wide range of alternative management techniques.
- Formulating visitor management objectives, which incorporate a range of acceptable impact levels, to accommodate the diversity of environments and experience opportunities present within any natural setting (Graefe *et al.*, 1990).

Both LAC and VIM frameworks rely on indicators and standards as a means of defining impacts deemed unacceptable and place carrying capacities into a broader managerial context. However, VIM makes reference to planning and policy and includes identifying the probable causes of impacts, whereas LAC places more emphasis on defining opportunity classes (Graefe *et al.*, 1990; Payne and Graham, 1993).

Visitor Activity Management Process

Whereas Recreation Opportunity Spectrum and Limits of Acceptable Change relied on management of the resource, the emphasis with Visitor Activity Management Process (VAMP) shifted back to the user of the resource. VAMP built on the previously developed Visitor Impact management (VIM). It has received relatively little attention in recreation management journals, whereas VAMP has been written about extensively in the USA and Canada.

The Visitor Activity Management Process relates to interpretation and visitor services. This framework involves the development of activity profiles which connect activities with:

- the social and demographic characteristics of the participants;
- the activity setting requirements; and
- trends affecting the activity.

The VAMP framework is designed to operate in parallel with the natural resource management process.

VAMP is a proactive, flexible, decision building framework which can contribute to a more integrated approach to management of protected areas. It has the potential to develop better information about customary users, stakeholders, visitors and non-visitors (Graham, 1990: 280). Information on both natural and social sciences is used to 'build' decisions about access and use of protected areas. It also incorporates a format for evaluating the effectiveness in meeting public needs (Graham, 1990: 281).

VAMP is not a process to justify random development at a site; rather, it is an aid to understanding visitor behaviour and, where necessary, to modifying it. The questions that guide the process include needs and expectations, what interpretive services and educational opportunities should be offered at a site, level of service for current and projected use, and visitor satisfaction (Graham, 1990: 283).

VAMP provides a framework to ensure that visitor understanding, appreciation and enjoyment of the resources is just as carefully and systematically considered as protection of natural resources. VAMP does not stand alone, but operates within a strong planning and management context as it represents how social science data are integrated within a park's management planning process.

The application of the basic VAMP concept to management of visitor programmes follows the traditional approach to planning used by most resource management agencies. However, a major emphasis throughout each stage is on understanding park visitors (Taylor, 1990). The task is to determine the current situation when comparing the park's expectations to the visitor's, and then to assess the actual activity on offer in terms of services, their use and visitor satisfaction (Taylor, 1990). VAMP's proactive approach to profiling visitor activity groups, suggesting target messages and evaluation before the development of interpretive programmes, may lead to more effective interpretation and environmental education programmes (Graham, 1990: 291).

Tourism Optimization Management Model

The Tourism Optimization Management Model was developed by Manidis Roberts Consultants. It builds on the LAC system to incorporate a stronger political dimension and seeks to monitor and manage tourism in a way that seeks optimum sustainable performance, rather than maximum levels or carrying capacities. TOMM involves the following.

- Identifying strategic imperatives (such as policies and emerging issues).
- Identifying community values, product characteristics, growth patterns, market trends and opportunities, positioning and branding, and alternative scenarios for tourism in a region.
- Identifying optimum conditions, indicators, acceptable ranges, monitoring techniques, benchmarks, annual performance and predicted performance.
- Identifying poor performance, exploring cause/effect relationships, identifying results requiring a tourism response or other sector response, and developing management options to address poor performance (McArthur, 1997a).

Managing visitor use

The frameworks we have discussed above are effective means to assess and project the sustainable and desired limits of human impact on natural ecosystems. Once identified, these limits must be strictly monitored in order to ensure that baseline sustainability limits are maintained. Protected area authorities must then implement strategies to ensure that these limits are maintained.

Use limitation

One fairly common and direct regulatory type of visitor management is that of use limitation. For instance, in Grand Canyon National Park, private and commercial rafting parties have been limited to approximately 2000 per year (Todd, 1989). Also, Skomer Island, Wales, is a bird sanctuary with access controlled by a daily ferry, limiting the quota of visitors to 100 per day (Valentine, 1991a). While the small size of ecotour operators serves to limit tourist numbers somewhat, there may also be a need for managers to implement built-in limits to control the size and number of tour operations acting within natural areas (Bunting, 1991). Private operators may be restricted by permit or other such regulations to guard against excessive or destructive impacts (Ceballos-Lascurain, 1990). As well as controlling the negative impacts on the natural environment, this would also serve to increase the quality of the visitors' experience, as most ecotourists perceive crowding to be a problem. Research indicates that by reducing crowding, particularly in camping areas, the quality of visitor experience tends to increase, although fewer people are able to experience the benefits of this.

Therefore, intensity of use (how many people are engaged in particular activities?) is an important consideration for managers of natural areas. Regulations can be used to control the numbers of visitors entering a particular area in any given time period, their access points and the types of activities they may undertake. As well as implementing these controls, managers may find it necessary to employ some form of deterrent to the breaching of regulations. These deterrents are usually in the form of fines and other penalties which may be difficult to enforce due to limitations in surveillance.

In order to limit the number of visitors to an area, management must first establish a visitor carrying capacity – an estimate of the capacity of an area to absorb visitors so that such use is sustainable (McNeely and Thorsell, 1989). Environmental, social and managerial resources must be evaluated as all of these factors represent constraints on the carrying capacity of a given area. One problem associated with the establishment of carrying capacities is that it is subjective issue, each interest tolerating various levels of environmental degradation. Thus management must determine the level of visitor use that an area can accommodate, 'maintaining high levels of visitor satisfaction and few negative impacts on the environment' (McNeely and Thorsell, 1989: 33).

Use redistribution as a visitor management technique may be either direct or indirect in nature. Such techniques are most commonly used by managers to reduce the concentration of use in general, by shifting some visitors from heavily to lightly used ares (Lucas, 1984). It is believed that tourists tend to confine themselves to small segments of wilderness in accordance with the ease of access and viewing attractions (Todd, 1989). Although this may not be desired by the ecotourist, they are often restricted in their experiences by the operators or guides of such tours who, whilst seeking to provide their client with the best view of wildlife, produce a highly commercial activity. An example of this includes operators in the Serengeti National Park in Tanzania, where tour bus drivers 'concentrate on the "Big 5" – lion, leopard, elephant, buffalo and rhino' (Todd, 1989: 78).

Use redistribution has been implemented in East Africa's Amboseli Game Park where, in the late 1970s, it was estimated that 80% of visitors used only 10% of the total area of the park. This technique was used to disperse visitor movement throughout the park, allowing carrying capacity to rise from 80 000 to 250 000 visitors annually, for the same level of impact (Todd, 1989: 78). However, this may not be conducive to

the ecotourism experience as impact levels spread, making it more difficult to experience a truly unspoilt wilderness tract.

Managers may wish to shift use in site-specific ways, to reduce use in particularly fragile or overused areas and shift some of it to specific places better able to sustain it. This can be achieved through zoning measures and the restriction of access points to control the movements of ecotourists and other visitors within wilderness ares.

Zoning

Zoning may also be used to control different uses in different parts of the region. It is a multi-dimensional technique that is driven by ecological data to balance the demands of protection and use in determining the most appropriate levels of use for specific areas within the park. One of the most important outcomes is to ensure that 'activities in one zone do not impinge on the planned functions of another' (Buckley and Pannell, 1990: 29). Where tourism is concerned, zoning should include areas that are not open for visitation in order to minimize the impact of infrastructure on wildlife. For example, 'tourism and recreation in the upstream part of a catchment may adversely affect water quality in the downstream region; so if the latter has been zoned purely for conservation, it may suffer water quality deterioration even though there are no recreational activities in the conservation zone itself' (Buckley and Pannell, 1990: 29).

As ecotourism involves low impact travel requiring few facilities and minimal disturbance to the environment and other wilderness users, it is not so prevalent to zone ecotouristic activity from other users as it is to zone more commercial activities from them. For example, it is necessary for managers to limit or prohibit areas in which mechanized recreation, horse riding and other such activities are not permissible in order to minimize the negative impact on the wilderness area, as well as to protect other visitor experiences. Visitor facilities act as a powerful management tool. They allow managing authorities to attract tourists to areas of significance/interest, control activities within these areas and divert visitors from more sensitive areas. Thus more traditional forms of tourism may be restricted from areas important to ecotourism by simply a lack of facilities that adequately satisfy their needs. This indirect management technique of restraint in providing facilities in natural areas seems to be 'consistent with what is known about wilderness visitor preferences; visitors are not clamouring for facilities that managers refuse to provide' (Lucas 1984: 135).

Trail system design

Trail system design is also an indirect management action that may not only be effective in the redistribution of use, but also for improving the quality of visitor experiences, by setting the level of challenge, the scenic quality and the opportunities to observe and learn about natural communities and processes (Lucas, 1984). The design of trail systems may be an important factor in improving the quality of the ecotourist's experience as they rely on trails to provide an experience in themselves, rather than just a route to attractions. Much of the negative impact that occurs in natural areas can be specifically related to visitor behaviour and actions, rather than to sheer numbers of users. It is the minority 'few unskilled, uninformed, careless groups rather than the many typical parties' that cause most of the damage (Lucas, 1984: 133). Perceptions of natural areas may be altered through various means of providing visitors with information. This indirect management technique can act to increase the visitors' enjoyment of the area and also to stimulate 'modes of behaviour which enhance the environmental quality of the site' (McNeely and Thorsell, 1989: 37). It is recognized by Buckley and Pannell (1990) that education as a management option may be the most effective of all management techniques, particularly in natural areas where it may well be the only option. Lucas (1984: 133) notes that wilderness visitors 'tend to be highly educated, most with university educations and often with graduate

study, as well as strongly committed to wilderness'. Ecotourists possess these same characteristics and it is thought that these allow education programmes to be successful in informing tourists of how to minimize the negative impacts of their visit on the surrounding environment. It is important, however, that the information provided to visitors be interpretative in nature, explaining possible interactions between visitors and the environment as well as methods to reduce any impacts that might occur from these interactions. This information may be provided in such forms as brochures, maps and pamphlets and is preferred by visitors to be distributed prior to entering the resource area. The majority of information aimed at changing visitor behaviour deals with the reduction of environmental impacts through minimal impact camping and hiking information. These education programmes commonly address issues such as littering, campfire use and vegetation impacts (Lucas, 1984).

Education

No natural resource can be effectively managed without the support and backing of its users. It follows that no system of natural area reserves can adequately fulfil its roles without the guidance of appropriate management objectives. Failure to fulfil such roles and provide appropriate information is likely to alienate some recreational users and decrease the level of public support for the reserve system as a whole. This would be a very serious situation, for without public support it is unlikely that we would have such a diverse and extensive range of environments protected. The fate of reserve systems is determined largely by social and political pressures (Hall and McArthur, 1996). Even the best planned management procedures will fail without public support. A strong base of public support for the aims and objectives of protected areas is one of the first prerequisites for their management. From this comes the political will, financial support and staffing necessary to achieve the aims and objectives of management. For this reason it is essential that natural area management provides information that seeks to change behaviour, not just awareness (Forestell, 1990). As we shall see in the following chapter, interpretation and education are key components of ecotourism and protected areas provide one of the essential ingredients for successful interpretation. They provide the opportunity for natural processes to be observed, for the inter-relationship of natural ecological systems to be appreciated and for the consequences of human change and ultimate degradation to be understood (Kenchington, 1990). Outdoor recreation has been the major function of all parks and reserve areas, even though conservation may be the more vital and immediately necessary role of these areas (Cameron-Smith, 1977). Recreation in this context is generally limited to those activities that are 'consistent with preserving the natural state' of these areas, although this definition in itself can cause problems. Activities such as bush walking, picnicking, camping and nature photography for example, are generally considered acceptable within national park and reserve areas; however, even such restricted recreational use can cause problems, including physical damage to ecological and cultural resources. User/user or user/manager conflicts in the perception of what constitutes acceptable recreational behaviour at any given site can and do still arise (Beckmann, 1991).

Priorities in outdoor recreation management should therefore include a balancing of supply and demand, 'a matching of resource adequacy with human recreational needs and desires' (Kenchington, 1990). Management strategies which reconcile recreation with other priorities such as conservation have become essential with increasing visitor demand. Visitor, rather than resource management, is now regarded as the most important component of recreation management (Wearing and Gardiner, 1994).

Ecotour operators in wilderness and other protected areas must also assume responsibility for minimizing the impacts of their operations in the destination region. Examples of education techniques that may be applied by tour operators include 'slide shows, lectures and discussions to further familiarize guests with the wildlife, history and culture of the remote area in which they find themselves' (Choegyal, 1991: 95). However, with tour operations it is also necessary to educate and inform tour leaders of the most appropriate behaviours for environmentally sensitive regions. The Tiger Mountain group of companies operating in Nepal believes 'in educating trek clients before leaving Kathmandu with detailed briefings of ecological issues and how to behave. Our sherpa guide groups which seldom exceed a dozen people, leave campsites as they find them and carry out all non-biodegradable rubbish' (Cheogyal, 1991: 101).

A more direct benefit of interpretation is as a visitor management tool to manage visitors and reduce visitor impacts. One of the chief criticisms of ecotourism is that it threatens to destroy the environment which it is trying to protect. Interpretation is an effective way management can encourage appropriate behaviour, thus alleviating any potentially damaging behaviours of ecotourists. For example, the ecotourist trekking through the Himalayas in Nepal in search of an understanding of subalpine environments can leave trails strewn with toilet paper, empty cans and bottles, and ashes from fires used for cooking. However, they can be educated through interpretive means so that they are aware of the devastation that their impact is causing.

While other strategies for reducing environmental impacts from visitor pressure have been developed and implemented in protected areas and national parks, interpretation is a key approach due to its long-term effects (Cameron-Smith, 1977). For example, interpretation can help visitors to understand and appreciate the differences in permitted activities, management practices and conservation values among national parks, state forests, reserves and privately owned bushland, as such interpretation is an important part of any strategic management plan.

Although interpretation is believed by many to be the most powerful tool for visitor management it has rarely been incorporated fully into major planning mechanisms (Roggenbuck, 1987). None the less, the relationship between interpretation and management is now recognized as a fundamental one and the two are often linked directly in management policies (Wearing and Gardiner, 1994). For example, interpretation significantly influences the carrying capacity of an area. By limiting the number of unwanted encounters or experiences in a recreational environment and restricting unsuitable behaviour in the area and reducing conflicts between users, the current acceptable field carrying capacity limits can be increased.

User fees and charges

User fees and charges have been gaining increased consideration as natural areas have become more popular for recreational use. There are a range of each and they are methods of capturing revenue from visitation that is essential to channel back into conservation objectives:

- *User fees*: charges on 'users' of an area or facility such as park admission, trekking fees etc.
- *Concession*: groups or individuals that provide certain services to visitors are often levied a fee for the permission to operate within a location – food, accommodation and retail stores for example.
- *Sales and royalties*: fees levied on a percentage of earnings that have been derived from activities or products at a site – photographs or postcards for example.
- *Taxation*: an extra cost imposed upon goods and services that are used by ecotourists– airport taxes for example.

- *Donations*: are often sought from tourists which may be used to contribute to maintaining a facility (*cf.* Hedstram, 1992; Marriott, 1993).

Fees can provide an important source of revenue for managers, particularly in developing countries where protected areas are traditionally underfunded (Swanson, 1992). The rationale supporting user fees is that most foreign visitors travel to remote protected areas to experience their very isolation and unspoilt natural features. The visitors should be willing to contribute to the costs of maintaining such conditions (Bunting, 1991). Ecotourists travelling in tour groups pay a fee which is usually incorporated into the price of the tour.

This chapter has presented the issues relating to ecotourism and protected area management (national parks). It has reflected upon the compromise between current views on management of our natural resources, and allows for evolution towards future management based on ecocentric management using ecotourism as a catalyst. Given the dominance of economic rationalism and increasing competition for scarce resources, protected areas are going to come under more and more use pressure. Park supporters need to join the political debate and look at ecotourism as a means of achieving the economic justification that will ensure the short-term survival of protected areas while developing a political constituency enabling a longer-term perspective. Conservation and preservation of natural resources and cultural heritage are global as well as local concerns. For tourism to be sustainable, the type and extent of tourism activity must be balanced against the capacity of the natural and man-made resources available.

5

The role of interpretation in achieving a sustainable future

It has been suggested that there is limited value in science (which provides the data upon which conservation is based) and management (which provides the tools) without communication to share their respective insights and directions (McCurdy, 1985). Past experience has shown us that many of the answers to today's environmental problems are far from clear, based as they are on scientific prediction only after the accumulation of evidence and therefore after significant impacts have already occurred. This is compounded by scientists being notoriously poor at imparting information that is readily understandable to the lay person, and as such the message is often lost to the community at large. As science increasingly informs ecology it is essential for it not only to communicate the facts and current theories, but to promote understanding of resource management as a dynamic process with a continuing need for monitoring, assessment and research.

As we have seen in Chapter 1 it is this recognition of interpretation and education's centrality to ecotourism that helps to differentiate ecotourism from other forms of nature-based tourism. A focus on the dimensions of visitor experience reveals that the visitor is concerned not with simply looking at a setting or object, but

with feeling and realizing some of its *value*. In this way, interpretation is oriented towards a visitor's cognitive and emotional state in order to raise awareness, enhance understanding and, hopefully, clarify or enlarge each participant's perspective and attitude. In this way, interpretation is essential to conservation goals.

Regulations and restrictions do not necessarily change people's activities or attitude towards our environment (Cameron-Smith, 1977). Few people are satisfied in the knowledge that small pockets of natural wilderness exist if they cannot gain access to the areas. We can focus on regulation, but as we have seen in previous chapters, there could never be enough resources – rangers, firearms or patrol vehicles – to protect parks from visitors who do not care about them (Cameron-Smith, 1977; McCurdy, 1985). Visitors to sensitive protected area sites who lack awareness of the value of the place can become bored, and then directly or indirectly cause impacts which could have been avoided if they had been offered a more enriching experience pitched at their interests.

Interpretation is effective because rather than regulating and enforcing behaviours and practices, it works with, rather than against the visitor.

Defining interpretation

Before exploring some of the interpretive techniques utilized by ecotourism, we need to clearly define what interpretation is and understand how attitudinal and behavioural outcomes are generated by interpretation.

Many definitions of interpretation limit it to a kind of 'dressing-up' exercise for facts and figures, usually the translation of the technical language associated with natural science into terms and concepts that people can easily understand and enjoy (Ham, 1992). While this may be a part of what interpretation is, it is not limited to this aspect alone. Indeed, Freeman Tilden (1977), in providing one of interpretation's most recognized definitions, states that it is 'an educational activity which aims to reveal meaning and relationships through the use of original objectives, by first-hand experience, and by illustrative media, rather than simply to communicate factual information' (Tilden, 1977: 8).

Tilden stressed that interpretation was not simply 'jazzed up information'; it had a larger purpose – that of revelation. Although an environmental interpreter may use factual information to illustrate points and clarify meanings, it is concepts and ideals that they are first trying to communicate, not simply facts. This is what distinguishes interpretation from conventional education and instruction and it is in these terms that effective interpretation can be used as a basis for developing a conservation ethic within the community.

The Queensland National Parks and Wildlife Service (Carter, 1984) defined interpretation as: 'a special process of stimulating and encouraging an appreciation of the natural and cultural heritage of a region, as well as a means of communicating nature conservation ideals and practices.' This definition suggests that the service uses interpretation to get visitors to appreciate the heritage it is responsible for managing. This single perspective or value base is commonly known as a *unicentric* approach (Machlis and Field, 1992). From the visitor's perspective, interpretation is a means of value-adding to their experience because most sights become that little bit more interesting when you know a little more about them. Ecotourism operators have recognized this value-adding and incorporated it into their product. For the operator interpretation and education are important because they provide an opportunity to offer something extra that may lead to market advantage.

However, interpretation and education need not necessarily focus on natural and cultural heritage and the raising of appreciation. Ecotourists are, after all, on holiday, and are therefore resistant to the imposition of 'too much information' and particularly of having it 'shoved down their throats', meaning that they are sensitive to the continual presentation of one perspective and position. As a result, interpreters and educators have widened their definition and use of interpretation to present a range of values, perspectives and positions. This approach, known as a *multicentric* approach, places the responsibility back with the visitor to arrive at their own understanding based on their collective experiences.

The definition provided by the Interpretation Australia Association is worth noting because it was generated after extensive consultation with its 400 or more members from various interpretation professions. The definition endorsed by the association was that interpretation 'is a means of communicating ideas and feelings which helps people enrich their understanding and appreciation of their world, and their role within it' (Interpretation Australia Association, 1995). This definition builds on the multicentric view and Tilden's stress on revelation, then adds the concept of empowerment, so that the end benefit rests with the audience of the interpretation – the visitor, or the ecotourist.

It is worth contrasting interpretation from education, particularly since in the field of ecotourism the two are so often used interchangeably. Education is a more formalized version of interpretation. Whereas interpretation tries to capture the attention of visitors, education typically has a 'captive audience' and can therefore develop facilities and programmes specifically designated for education. Environmental education mirrors the basic philosophy and characteristics of interpretation in that it also takes place in the natural environment and its subject matter concerns the environment.

Case study   New Zealand

Customized educational resources for tour operators and their customers have been designed for a series of themed heritage trails in New Zealand which aim to enhance the tourist experience. The production of something tangible or physical, through the provision of interpretive materials and certificates as a result of participation on the trails, has been clearly identified as value-adding and building on the natural competitive advantage of New Zealand's ecotourism industry (Hall *et al.*, 1991).

Changing understanding, attitudes and behaviour

In order to understand how interpretation works, it is important to understand how interpretation relates to attitudinal and behavioural change in contributing to environmental awareness. This in turn requires an understanding of what attitudes are and what kinds of cognitive processes are involved in their change. If we argue for greater use of interpretation as a means of generating attitudes and behavioural choice that will assist in conserving our environment, we must have some idea of how the process of gaining an environmental consciousness occurs.

In order for natural areas to stimulate environmental awareness, people presently uncommitted to conservation must be encouraged to visit both national parks and reserves. In order to achieve a change in attitude, they must be provided with much more than simple informa-

tion and propaganda when they do visit. Recent research by Beaumont (1997) suggests that interpretation can induce a change in understanding and a positive shift in attitude amongst individuals who already have some form of conservation ethic. However, the same research suggests that visitors with a limited understanding and narrow attitude are less likely to be influenced by interpretation provided by an ecotourism operator. Thus, interpretation may not necessarily lead to a conservation ethic and flow-on behaviour, nor even retention of a positive attitude (Carter, 1979). However, this may be due to the standard of interpretation being delivered not reaching a level that induces visitors to shift their position. Fundamentally, they require an experience that will change their fundamental thinking about the environment and its preservation (Forestell, 1990).

Clearly, the ability of interpretation to enact attitudinal change is in large part dependent upon the availability and effectiveness of resources to provide material that can be understood by the general public and is able to maintain their interest both on-site and post experience. Given the relative lack of research on interpretation finding its way back to interpreters, this situation seems to be intractable for the short to medium term. The effects of limited research and subsequent poor planning in the past were largely responsible for a culture of interpreters that was overtly focused on technique delivery, at the expense of a sound rationale (McArthur, 1996). It therefore seems pertinent briefly to examine some of these techniques that interpreters typically concentrate on providing.

Interpretation techniques

There are more ways to interpret than one could hope to cover, because each technique is like a piece of artwork, crafted from the creativity of the interpreter. In this sense, some of the most creative interpretation is barely recognized as such.

For example, within the lobby of an ecolodge or museum the materials used in construction, the pattern of pavers on the floor, and the choice of music, all suggest ideas and feelings of which the visitor may or may not consciously be aware. Another example is the presence of staff within a site and the way in which they present themselves to visitors (McIntyre *et al.*, 1993; WTO, 1990). As staff move about their normal duties they can casually engage visitors in conversation, provide relevant information and obtain some feedback. In order for the contact to be effective, however, the staff must be knowledgeable, which may require training in visitor communication and hospitality. The most widely recognized interpretive techniques therefore tend to be the more tangible ones, such as visitor centres, publications, guided tours and educational activities, displays and exhibits and signs.

Visitor centres

Visitor centres are special buildings or rooms in which exhibits and displays can be presented in relative comfort and controlled surroundings. Exhibits may include photographs arranged in wall or panel displays, map models, mounted specimens, or diagrams. Visitor centres are very useful for showing 'the big picture' – such as processes, histories and other features that cannot be easily depicted on-site. Visitor centres often house permanent and continuous audiovisual presentations in an auditorium. The visitor experience within a visitor centre typically finishes with a gift shop selling extension material such as detailed guidebooks and maps. Where necessary, visitor centres can be enlarged or combined with education centres. The most effective visitor centres are designed from the inside out, meaning that their interpretive theme and purpose drives the design and construction of the building, rather than vice versa.

Education centres

Education centres are designated buildings, or separate spaces within a visitor centre, designed to deliver educational activities and house facilities and supporting material. Education centres usually feature low key classrooms to hold activities and discussion sessions, though the surrounding environment outside the environment centre is critical to delivering many of the activities. The most effective education centres are those containing one or more full-time education officers who have developed their programmes to dovetail with school curricula.

Displays and exhibits

Displays and exhibits are typically developed as permanent features within a museum or visitor/education centre, or as a mobile 'mini-centre', or mobile display. They typically feature objects and specimens, dioramas, scale models, live exhibits, panels of text, diagrams and photographs. Displays and exhibits are useful because they are relatively cost effective, and are portable enough to be located indoors or outdoors. The most effective exhibits are designed with a specific audience in mind, and the most effective mobile displays are those that are staffed to add a more personal touch to the interpretation.

Case study   'The Environment Express': Trinidad and Tobago

'The Environment Express', is a mobile interpretation centre which continuously travels through Trinidad and Tobago. The interpretation centre is a converted passenger bus and was introduced as part of an integrated environmental awareness programme on the two Caribbean Islands. The audience was clearly identified as the local community and the most obvious advantage of the programme was the dedicated staff who adapted the design of the bus and the programmes to better serve the users (Meganck, 1992).

Publications

Publications are a cost-effective way of reaching a lot of people. Publications can come in the form of brochures, leaflets, note-sheets, maps, books, posters, postcards, calenders and stickers. Publications tend to be based around information rather than interpretation. For example, the standard brochure promoting a region or site tends to be more information-oriented. None the less, there have been some highly interpretive posters that use layered presentations of images and ideas to progressively reveal underlying ideas. Some of the disadvantages of publications are that they have limited capacity to respond to different visitor needs, they are expensive to distribute and manage, and they can quickly date and need upgrading.

Case study   The *National Geographic Traveller*

The *National Geographic Traveller* is an American-based magazine publication, whose mission is to 'increase and diffuse' geographic knowledge. The editor, Richard Busch, stated in his address to the 1994 World Congress on Adventure Travel and Ecotourism that publications such as the *National Geographic Traveller* had two responsibilities – one to their readers and the other to the environment. The readers need to be provided information on worthwhile places to visit, and simultaneously informed on the importance of protecting the environment.

The publication 'communicates with a conscience' by following several important steps. Firstly, the editor insists that writers discuss relevant ecological issues in the stories themselves. This is often supplemented by side stories and sidebars on the subject. Secondly, an 'Econotes' component of the trip-planning section details the environmentally friendly do's and don'ts, and often covers policy governing the subject area. Thirdly, the editor's notes have often addressed ecotourism-specific issues, particularly when they relate to articles.

Busch used an example article on the Amazon to illustrate the type of article produced. The piece centred around an Amazon ecotour that took the photographer from Belem, near the mouth of the river, westward to Iquitos, Peru, 2300 miles upriver. The article illustrated the forest flooding during the rainy season and the role of fish in seed dispersal as they swam among trees. The article also depicted tree-top lodges at the the Explornapo Camp, a low-impact ecolodge facility near Iquitos, and most importantly, the native guide who interprets the rainforest. Thus, there was a balance between environmental and cultural presentation.

Busch's presentation ended in a reiteration that the needs of the environment and reader are not mutually exclusive, and that if other publications took care to inform readers on the fragility of ecosystems, and ways to minimize impacts, such advertising could benefit both the environment and the consuming public.

Source: R Busch, 'Ecotourism: responsibilities of the media, World Congress on Adventure Travel and Ecotourism, Hobart, Tasmania, 7–10 November 1994

Self-guided trails

Self-guided trails involve a series of prescribed stops along a route that visitors travel. The route may be a road, a walking track, a river or a railway line. Each stop provides a feature that is interpreted via a brochure, a sign or an audio facility such as radio or cassette. Each stop is usually marked by a numbered post, label or sign. A self-guided trail allows the visitor freedom to move at their own pace, stopping for as long as they want. Self-guided tours have similar problems to publications but are similarly cost-effective per visitor contact. A study in Sweden of self-guided tours for campers found that it was much easier to attract the independent travellers to self-guided tours for exactly those reasons (Hultman, 1992).

Guided tours

Face-to-face interpretation is considered to be one of the most powerful and worthwhile interpretive techniques available because it can be continually tuned to the type of visitor(s) participating. In terms of commercially run ecotourism, guided tours are perhaps the most widely used technique. The method is especially useful with school children and formal tour groups, or as a means of controlling where visitors go and what they do. A trained guide accompanying a group discusses features along a predetermined route, adding additional detail or perspectives according to the interests and responses of the group. One of the strengths of guided tours is that the guide can adapt what is said to the particular interest of each group. Guides working for ecotourism operators must be knowledgeable about many aspects of the attractions and be fluent in the major languages of visitors. One of the limitations of guided tours is their high cost per visitor, and their continual reliance on the personality and commitment of the guide to deliver a high quality experience. In addition, large proportions of visitors may find guides an interference that impinges upon their desired sense of freedom.

Principles for successful interpretation

Successful interpretation typically reflects a number of key principles:

- People learn better when they are actively involved in the learning process.
- People learn better when they are using as many senses as appropriate. It is generally recognized that people retain approximately 10% of what they hear, 30% of what they read, 50% of what they see and 90% of what they do.
- Insights that people discover for themselves are the most memorable as they stimulate a sense of excitement and growth.
- Learning requires activity on the part of the learner.
- Being aware of the usefulness of the knowledge being acquired makes the learning process more effective.
- People learn best from first hand experience (Lewis, 1980).

With these factors in mind, it should be possible to develop an effective communication network that promotes ecotourism and subsequently a conservation ethic. Interpretation should leave the ecotourist with a sense of enjoyment and satisfaction, and a perception that environmental conservation and the principles of sustainability are worthwhile, thus satisfying conservation objectives (Forestell, 1990).

Protected areas provide one of the essential ingredients for successful interpretation. They provide the opportunity for natural processes to be observed, for the inter-relationship of natural ecological systems to be appreciated and for the consequences of human change and ultimate degradation to be understood (Kenchington, 1990). If these opportunities are realized, then people can look forward to a more informed society, capable of weighing up the implications of local, national and international decisions which may affect the environment, fostering a willingness to participate actively in the decision-making process (Ham, 1992).

The benefits of interpretation

Along with interpretation's role in value-adding to the visitor experience through enhancing and facilitating the setting being explored, there are four key areas of potential benefits:

- promotional benefits;
- recreational benefits;
- educational benefits;
- management/conservation benefits (Beckmann, 1991).

In practical terms these benefits may overlap significantly, but for clarity we will discuss them individually.

Promotional benefits

Because interpretation generally requires contact between the public and the agency staff, it often crosses into the public relations role of effective management. The interpretation services of the Canadian National Parks for example have been described as a 'propaganda service' due to promotion not only of the need to manage the natural resources, but of an understanding of the management agency itself (Sharpe, 1982).

The potential promotional benefits of interpretation are summarized in Table 5.1.

Effective interpretive services can be of use in promoting the 'image' or 'visual identity' of the agency. This is particularly beneficial for protected area and conservation agencies, as a favourable image and prominent visual identity is fundamental for conveying the objectives of an organization. Many people make a rapid appraisal of an organization based on the 'image' presented and since most conservation authorities communicate their message and ideas with the use of visual media, the relevance of an interesting and easily recognizable design or logo is central.

An easily recognizable graphic design will improve communication of the conservation message by allowing the public to identify the management agency and the management practices associated with that agency. It will also promote a favourable corporate image for the organization and thus promote support within the local community. Although a prominent visual identity as such is hardly a prime objective of a conservation agency, it necessarily plays a leading role in creating an independent, competent and forcefully competitive impact.

The political leverage which can be exerted by interpretation is a promotional benefit that should also be identified and utilized. Interpretation is often used to achieve political objectives and to control volatile conflicts between advocacy groups. For example, the United States National Park Service was able to promote valuable community support for its management policies by presenting interpretive seminars on local natural history and by placing qualified interpreters into uniform to capitalize on the well-accepted ranger image of the management authority (Beckmann, 1991).

Table 5.1 *The promotional benefits of interpretation*

Promotional benefits	Explanation of benefits
Diversity of subjects that can be promoted	Interpretation can promote values, sites, land tenures, management objectives and practices, and the corporate mission of the managing authority
A subtle and sophisticated form of promotion	Interpretation can weave promotion into a story without making it sound too promotional and self-centred
Added dimensions for follow-on promotion	Interpretation can provide on-going advisory services to reinforce and expand initial ideas

Recreational benefits

One expectation common to most people in an outdoor leisure setting is a relaxed atmosphere and activities which enhance the feeling of relaxation (Wearing and Gardiner, 1994). Many park visitors seek some level of recreational involvement with the landscape, flora, fauna and/or cultural sites, although social interaction with other visiting groups may be either actively sought or actively rejected. To be effective, therefore, any educational activity offered within such a setting must retain this informal, relaxed atmosphere (Ham, 1992) and cater for the level of friendly interaction required by the visitor. Compulsory activities will be rejected, while the diversity of visitors can be satisfied by an equally diverse range of educational experiences (Sharpe, 1982). Interpretation, by focusing on the visitor's desire to be involved in their surroundings, provides educational opportunities while at the same time enhancing recreational experiences (Lewis, 1980).

By helping visitors to match their recreational needs and expectations with the available resources, and by influencing visitor behaviour, interpretation may aid recreation management directly. Satisfied visitors may be encouraged to make return visits, with a more realistic idea of what to expect from the site and of the most appropriate behaviour for the area. This pro-vides benefits for managers through a reduction in depreciative behaviour and increased community support for the protection of the site. Pre-visit interpretation may be as important as on-site interpretation in maximizing visitor satisfaction, and establishing visitor expectations prior to visiting the area (Sharpe, 1982).

Outdoor recreation has been the major function of all parks and reserve areas, even though conservation may be the more vital and immediately necessary role of these areas (Cameron-Smith, 1977). Recreation in this context is generally limited to those activities that are 'consistent with preserving the natural state' of these areas, although this definition in itself can cause problems. Activities such as bush walking, picnicking, camping and nature photography for example, are generally considered acceptable within national park and reserve areas; however, even such restricted recreational use can cause problems, including physical damage to ecological and cultural resources. User/user or user/manager conflicts in the perception of what constitutes acceptable recreational behaviour at any given site can and do still arise (Beckmann, 1991).

Priorities in outdoor recreation management should therefore include a balancing of supply and demand, 'a matching of resource adequacy with human recreational needs and desires' (Kenchington, 1990). Management strategies

Table 5.2 *The recreational benefits of interpretation*

Recreational benefits	Explanation of benefits
Value added to the visitor experience	Interpretation is an added activity to those typically expected. For example, interpretation signs enhance a walking track just as interpretive guides are preferred over one that merely points out significant attractions as they come into view
Making the experience more enjoyable	Interpretation that is stimulating and connects with emotions tends to make the experience more enjoyable
Enhance a sense of meaning to recreational activity	Interpretation provides a greater sense of meaning to activities such as sightseeing

which reconcile recreation with other priorities such as conservation have become essential with increasing visitor demand. Visitor, rather than resource management, is now regarded as the most important component of recreation management (Wearing and Gardiner, 1994). Table 5.2 illustrates some of the recreational benefits of interpretation.

Educational benefits

Tilden's (1957) original definition of interpretation refers to an educational activity. However, educating simply to improve the satisfaction gained from recreational experiences has ceased to be the only or even the dominant role of interpretation in protected areas and equivalent reserves. Although these areas are recognized as important resources for environmental change, management agencies now recognize that it is not enough simply to interpret the site itself (Cameron-Smith, 1977). As the United States National Park Service emphasizes in all its interpretive programmes, interpretation should communicate an environmental consciousness both within and beyond the park (McCurdy, 1985). As a result, environmental interpretation is rapidly becoming an adjunct to formal environmental education programmes. Table 5.3 presents some of the educational benefits of interpretation.

Many environmental educators and interpreters alike identify that the knowledge base of the individual is the key to attitudes, and that with changing attitudes comes an instinctive change in behaviour (Lewis, 1980). However, it must be stated that knowledge is not sufficient alone to change attitudes. With knowledge must come understanding (Cockrell *et al.*, 1984). It is not enough for an individual to know that a plant is the main food source of a given species of bird. What must be taught is that without this plant being present in the area the bird life of the area will change. This gives the individual a reason to ensure that their activities do not affect the potential survival of the plant or bird species found in the area. This change in attitude also has some value for interpretive planners in the evaluation process. If attitude changes can be identified then interpretive programmes can be evaluated accordingly. Popular outdoor recreation sites obviously attract large numbers of visitors and on-site interpretation can expand latent interests in nature and scenery of an area into a more active concern for conservation (Carter, 1979).

The fundamental differences between interpretation and environmental education lie not in the basic philosophy but in the procedures and methodologies used to present the message.

Interpretation as a conservation management tool

A more direct benefit of interpretation is as a visitor management tool to manage visitors and reduce visitor impacts. One of the chief criticisms of ecotourism is that it threatens to destroy the

Table 5.3 *The educational benefits of interpretation*

Educational benefits	Explanation of benefits
Opportunity for learning	Interpretation generates learning experiences for visitors that increase their knowledge and understanding of the environment
Opportunity for self-discovery	Interpretation generates experiences for visitors to gain a clearer understanding of their role within their environment, and this aids in self-discovery and self-actualization

Table 5.4   *Conservation and protected area management benefits of interpretation*

Conservation benefits	Explanation of benefits
Stimulation of an environmental consciousness and broad-based conservation ethic	Interpretation stimulates thoughts of personal responsibility for using resources and contributes to improvements in quality of life
Raise awareness of regulations and codes designed to minimize impacts	Interpretation programmes such as minimal impact campaigns can subtly present requirements for changed visitor behaviour in a way that is non-confrontational
Stimulation of behavioural change to minimize personal impacts upon the environment	Interpretation presents ideas for people to adopt
Support for protected areas	Interpretation presents the value of protected areas from a range of perspectives
Support for protected area management organizations	Interpretation presents the challenges for management in a candid way that exposes the constraints facing protected area management agencies

environment which it is trying to protect. Interpretation is an effective way management can encourage appropriate behaviour, thus alleviating any potentially damaging behaviours of ecotourists.

Table 5.4 presents some of the conservation and protected area management benefits of interpretation.

While other strategies for reducing environmental impacts from visitor pressure have been developed and implemented in protected areas and national parks, interpretation is a key approach due to its long-term effects (Cameron-Smith, 1977). For example, interpretation can help visitors to understand and appreciate the differences in permitted activities, management practices and conservation values among national parks, state forests, reserves and privately owned bushland. As such, interpretation is an important part of any strategic management plan.

Although interpretation is believed by many to be the most powerful tool for visitor management, it has rarely been incorporated fully into major planning mechanisms (Roggenbuck, 1987). None the less, the relationship between

interpretation and management is now recognized as a fundamental one and the two are often linked directly in management policies (Wearing and Gardiner, 1994). For example, interpretation significantly influences the carrying capacity of an area. By limiting the number of unwanted encounters or experiences in a recreational environment and restricting unsuitable behaviour in the area and reducing conflicts between users, the current acceptable field carrying capacity limits can be increased.

Economic benefits

Tourism that utilizes interpretation as a key part of its product generates economic benefits. Whether the tourism is ecotourism, cultural tourism or some other form, the delivery of interpretation can give the product additional value that attracts higher yield markets.

Similarly, by encouraging conservation and modifying visitor behaviours that affect damage to natural resources, effective interpretation programmes can reduce the costs of managing recreational resources (Sharpe, 1982).

Table 5.5 *The economic benefits of interpretation*

Economic benefits	Explanation of benefits
Business activity	Tourism operations utilizing interpretation contribute significantly to wealth. For example, the turnover for Australia's ecotourism industry in 1995 was estimated to be $250 million (Econsult, 1995)
Direct employment	There are many people employed as interpreters. For example, the Interpretation Australia Association has a membership of 450 members, most of whom are interpreters for heritage managers (Interpretation Australia Association, 1995). In 1995 some 6500 people or 4500 full-time equivalent staff were employed in the Australian ecotourism industry (Econsult, 1995). The payroll from ecotourism employment in 1995 was estimated at $115 million (Econsult, 1995)
Indirect employment	The business activity generated by organizations employing interpreters itself generates additional indirect jobs and wealth. For example, interpreters need training providers, graphic artists, sign and display manufacturers and visitor centre builders
Investment	Investment in tourism businesses to deliver interpretation via facilities (e.g. visitor centres, signs, displays etc.) and services, e.g. guides and counter staff. Total expenditure in North Queensland by visitors to the Wet Tropics World Heritage Area (WHA) equated to $443 million in 1994. At the time this equated to 3.6% of Australia's total export earnings from tourism

While Table 5.5 illustrates that effective interpretation has important economic benefits, these benefits are not always easy, or indeed possible, to prove to management agencies (Hill, 1993). Economists have spent vast amounts of time in recent years attempting to place a dollar value to natural resources. Techniques such as measuring the actual costs incurred in attaining a recreational experience or in identifying people's willingness to pay for an interpretive experience have all been attempted but all, it seems, underestimate the value of our natural resources. However, measuring benefits in monetary terms is particularly important when cost–benefit analyses are required as management is interested in the cost-effectiveness of different interpretive methods in order to rationalize its continued use given budgetary constraints.

Problems limiting interpretation

Interpretation has suffered from the perception that it is simply 'the icing on the cake' instead of being an integral part of the ecotourism product base. Indeed, Australia's National Ecotourism Accreditation Program in its first year of operation found the quality and commitment to interpretation to be one of the weaker elements of the operators seeking accreditation (McArthur, 1997a).

No natural resource can be effectively managed without the support and backing of its users. It follows that no system of natural area reserves can adequately fulfil its roles without the guidance of appropriate management objectives. Failure to fulfill such roles and provide appropriate information is likely to alienate some recreational users and decrease the level of public support for the reserve system as a whole. This would be a very serious situation, for without public support it is unlikely that we would have such a diverse and extensive range of environments protected. The fate of reserve systems is determined largely by social and political pressures (Hall and McArthur, 1996). Even the best-planned management procedures will fail without public support. A strong base of public support for the aims and objectives of protected areas is one of the first prerequisites for their management. From this comes the political will, financial support and staffing necessary to achieve the aims and objectives of management. For this reason it is essential that the natural areas management provide information that seeks to change behaviour, not just raise awareness (Forestell, 1990).

Case Study   Savannah Guides, Australia: interpretation with a difference

The Gulf Savannah of Northern Australia, along the Gulf of Carpentaria, is a remote 200 000 square kilometre wilderness, which up until the early 1980s was virtually unassessed. The new breed of 'recreational explorers' which emerged about this time began to accelerate negative environmental impacts in the region. The local response was the development of a Wilderness Management Plan by GLADA (Gulf Local Authorities Development Association). GLADA is a grouping of four remote local authorities specifically responding to the emergence of tourism.

One major recommendation was the establishment of a ranger/guide organization that was professional, and moved beyond interpreting the environment to being empowered to protect it. A community/ranger guide system was subsequently

established across Northern Australia, and these were the founders of Savannah Guides.

The mission of Savannah Guides is:

'To be economically sound, community based, identifiable professional body maintaining high standards of:

Interpretation
Public education
Tourism and resource management
Leadership, and
Staffing

And through ecologically sustainable tourism principles to enhance and maintain the regional lifestyle and encourage the protection and conservation of the environment and cultural resources of the Gulf Savannah region.'

From its inception, founding members agreed to fund the setting up of the Savannah Guide system. This included an agreement collectively to fund a biannual five-day training school at a Guide Station, where professionals such as behavioural scientists, geologists and aboriginal elders etc. would lecture. Additionally, a grant of US $10 000 was secured from the PATA Foundation to produce educational material for use in interpretation, and the development of Guide Station signage.

All Savannah Guides are long-term residents, whose role covers both education and training of visitors and the community to protect natural and cultural assets. Each Guide Station is administered by one Savannah Guide. Any other employees are classified following their completion of on-site training and Joongai (local indigenous community) assessment as site interpreters. In the event that a guide leaves the service, it is from this pool of employees that a new guide would be selected.

The Savannah Guides use education as their tool for managing impacts and visitation. The guides are able to access stations and National Parks often closed to individual visitors. Each National Park or grazing lease has an associated management regime, with which the local guide is extremely familiar, eliminating conflicts that may arise with a tour party, and generating additional income for landholders, charged at a per head basis.

The key words which have been used to describe the interpretation skills of Savannah Guides are 'accurate' and 'authentic'. Each guide is encouraged to have a reference library, which is utilized in the event that they and the client do not know the answer to a query. Communication skills are considered a critical aspect to continued training within the ranks of Savannah Guides. Each guide utilizes these verbal communication skills in conjunction with a more traditional marketing effort to distribute information on other stations across the Savannah.

The concept of Savannah Guides has facilitated the development of positive benefits from tourism, introduced ecotourism to numerous cattle properties, and provided an opportunity for small businesses in creating environmentally sensitive tourism products. Currently this system is one of the few private organisations that mans a National Park. It demonstrates the potential success of a proactive and managed wilderness scheme.

Source: John Courtenay, Savannah Guides, Australia: British Airways Tourism for Tomorrow Awards 1996, Pacific Region

Although the premise underlying interpretation and interpretive services is that it is worthwhile and valuable, it would be naive to consider it as a field without flaws. The implementation of effective interpretation is not without its problems and it is for this reason that any interpretation should included monitoring and periodic evaluation.

Interpretive services have a role in developing visitor expectations for their recreational experience of an area and thus inappropriate interpretation may result in disappointment being experienced. Even something as simple as the photograph chosen for use in a promotional poster can convey an inappropriate message to visitors. Inaccurate promotion has proved to lead to unsatisfied visitors and inappropriate behavior (Jenkins and McArthur, 1996).

Inappropriate interpretive facilities and services can in fact diminish the natural resources of an area. No one who visits a wilderness area or marine reserve known for its natural beauty wishes to be confronted with a series of unattractive and overpowering concrete signs conveying information about the area. Similarly, a visitor centre that dominates the landscape and reduces the aesthetic appeal of an area is not an effective management tool. For this reason, many sound interpretation plans actually prescribe 'Interpretation Free Zones' for, in some cases, the most effective interpretation is no obvious interpretation at all, just the right setting for individual inspiration and imagination.

Case study   Dolphin Discovery Tours, Port Phillip Bay, Victoria, Australia: The importance of interpretation in ecotourism tour operation

Dolphin Discovery Tours operates a luxury charter yacht which ferries tourists to Port Phillip Bay, Victoria, to learn about and interact with the mammals. The tour was designed to educate and develop awareness about the environment in Port Phillip Bay and the need to protect the area and its wildlife populations. At present, 12% of revenue is redirected to support of the Dolphin Research Institute, and the yacht itself is made available to media and sponsorship special events.

The educative component of the tour is what sets it apart from other such ventures. The delivery of information to passengers is achieved through comprehensive commentary and access to guides, all of whom are actively involved in the Dolphin Research Institute or its research and education programmes. In addition, a booklet, *The Dolphins of Port Phillip Bay*, is made available for purchase at a significantly reduced price.

The tour itself commences with a familiarization and safety demonstration, during which participants are invited to ask questions during the course of the tour. On route to dolphin-prone waters, the vessel sails to Chinaman's Hat, the site of a colony of Australian fur seals. The passengers are provided with information on the biology and behaviours of the animals, and informed about the detrimental effects of sealing during the last century. Other unique islands and channels en route provide the commentator with a multitude of topics to which all passengers are encouraged to listen. Unique ecosystems and wildlife species such as gannet rookeries and defence forts bearing testimony to the development of early Australia provide a historical and biological context to the area.

Dolphin Discovery Tours operate with a definite community focus, with the aim to 'give participants a direct experience which is properly and thoughtfully interpreted'. Interpretation itself is channelled primarily through crew members and professional and volunteer guides. A comprehensive training programme educates guides to the standard required by management, and the inclusion of volunteer guides provides all passengers

with the opportunity to seek information in a relaxed and informal way without the necessity of approaching the principal commentator. Minimization of environmental impacts, interpretive quality and the management of visitor expectations are critical to the owner–operators of this product. The emphasis of commentary is on the diversity and value of Port Phillip Bay's ecosystems, the need to protect it, threats currently posed and, most critically, what individuals can do to help preserve the area.

The dolphins themselves are not interfered with in any way. Dolphin Discovery Tours is the only tourism experience in the Bay that operates within the whale-watching guidelines of not approaching the mammals within 100 metres.

The quality of interpretive strategy is summarized by Bill Fox, Tourism Manager for Parks Victoria:

'The high quality interpretation of the natural environment of Port Phillip Bay offered to tourists by this operator plays a significant role in enhancing awareness and understanding of the need to protect and sustain our natural asset. Dolphin Discovery Tours offers an excellent example of a partnership between conservation and tourism interests, and the value of an ecologically sustainable tourism industry.'

Source: Philip Tubb, Victoria: British Airways Tourism for Tomorrow Awards 1997, Pacific Region

Interpretation is not just the communication of information, regardless of how jazzed up and enjoyable it becomes. Interpretation seeks to reveal meaning and stimulate a cognitive and emotional response. This response should impel people into reconsidering their value base and behaviour. The way in which interpretation is delivered can be as varied as the individual imagination, and, generally speaking, the more imaginative the approach, the more successful the interpretation. Interpretation is a core part of any ecotourism experience. As such, interpretation adds real value for the operator, distinguishing the product from nature-based tourism. Interpretation is also critical to the protected area manager, as it offers a chance to present values and conservation ethics, and at a more practical level, provides the opportunity to minimize visitor impact. Within both these sectors, interpretation is yet to realize anything like its full potential. When it does, it will become quite an awe-inspiring player in the world of ecotourism, conservation, and personal commitment to a sustainable future.

6

Linking conservation and communities: community benefits and social costs

A significant contribution to ecotourism's global following has been its potential to deliver benefits to communities remote from centres of commerce, benefits that do not involve widespread social or environmental destruction. Too often in the past the only opportunities for many communities remote from urban centres, particularly in the developing world, were provided by extractive industries – mining, logging, or fishing – which had massive impacts on local communities and often left an unacceptable legacy of long-term environmental damage.

Tourism is often advocated as a way of solving some of the problems that have arisen in developing nations through inappropriate economic growth. Tourism is a diverse and decentralized industry, which affects other sectors of local economies; it is a 24-hours a day, 7-days a week industry, labour-intensive, creating employment opportunities across all sectors and skill levels. However, conventional tourism brings with it many of the problems we have found in the exploitation of developing nations in the past.[1] It is often driven, owned and controlled by developed nations with a high return to these nations – conventional package tours in many cases, for example, utilize local people through the use of their resources and labour at a minimum (or often zero) cost to the operator. Employment is often seasonal and lowly paid in contrast to the profits accruing to investors and operators. Such practices are defended on the pretext that if these operators did not initiate tourism then there would be no money injected into the community at all. However, tourism can no longer be justified on its supposedly low impact–high return.

It is this dominant economic focus that serves to obscure significant dimensions of tourism impact. Tourism produces a diverse range of both social and environmental impacts that are often complex and mutually related. Some indigenous communities often put it in simple terms: a frequently used phrase is 'Tourism is like fire. It can cook your food or burn down your house.' The tourism industry makes extensive use of natural assets – forests, reefs, beaches and parks – but what does it contribute to management of these assets? The provision of tourism infrastructure, and the costs of managing the impact of tourism on host communities, is often borne

---

[1] *cf.* Butler, 1991; Lea, 1993, 1995; Mieczkowski, 1995.

by the environment, the community itself and the government. A significant body of research has challenged the claims of industry and government agencies that the aggregate benefits of tourism far outweigh the costs: benefits are rarely uniform, accruing to those actively involved in the tourist industry, while costs are often borne by those who derive no compensatory benefits from tourism (cf. Butler, 1991).

Local communities are significantly vulnerable to the deleterious impacts of tourism development – particularly indigenous cultures – as they directly experience the sociocultural impacts of tourism. The subsequent impact of tourism's dynamic growth on communities has in some cases precipitated strong protests by community groups, which, being sensitive to the impacts of tourism, have actively opposed large-scale tourism developments for their locality. Other community groups have been more accepting of a gradual growth in tourism to their region over many years, only to become aware of the negative impacts at a later date when these impacts cannot easily be ignored.

Disruption to established activity patterns, anti-social behaviour, crime and over-crowding caused by tourism development can also have a negative impact on local lifestyles and the quality of life of both indigenous and non-indigenous communities.

In many cases indigenous cultures are used extensively to promote destinations to overseas markets yet opportunities for visitors to interact with and experience their cultures and lifestyles are limited, while the opportunities that are provided for tourists often trivialize or exploit those involved and the communities they represent. Many indigenous people rightly feel that the tourism industry has a poor track record, in disregarding their legitimate interests and rights, and profiting from their cultural knowledge and heritage.

The tourism potential of local areas is also compromised by the environmental impact of other industries. According to the Economist Intelligence Unit, the entire tourism industry is under attack from other business interests which are virtually stealing its assets (Jenner and Smith, 1991). In the late 1980s the development boom initiated the emergence of many so-called 'tourism developments' which were nothing more than land speculation, or a means of making otherwise conventional residential developments acceptable to planning authorities. It led to bankruptcies, inflated profits, overloaded infrastructure, residential sprawl and unwanted social and environmental impacts which led many local communities to be suspicious about the benefits of the tourism industry. The ecological and cultural impacts and social impacts of tourism often lead to diminished community and political support for the industry, particularly at local levels.

The interdependence of tourism and the social and physical environment is fundamental to the future of each, and seeking a way to accommodate the needs of all parties, without control being external to those who experience its effects most directly, is essential. Features of the natural and cultural environment and supportive host communities are the foundations of a successful industry. Neglect of conservation and quality of life issues threatens the very basis of local populations and a viable and sustainable tourism industry.

As we have discussed in Chapter 1, ecotourism involves travel to relatively undisturbed or protected natural areas, fostering understanding, appreciation and conservation of the flora, fauna, geology and ecosystems of an area as well as local community culture and its relationship to the land. The flora, fauna, geology and ecosystems of an area highlight the nature-base aspect. There is thus a significant overlap between conservation and sustainability between the natural and social environment. As we have seen in Chapter 2, sustainability is at the forefront of policy-oriented literature about conservation and development. Unfortunately, however, little or no discussion has yet taken place about the sustainability or otherwise of communities adjacent to, or surrounding, ecotourism ventures.

Ecotourism has the potential to create support for conservation objectives in both the host community and in the visitor alike, through establishing and sustaining links between the tourism industry, local communities, and protected areas. As social and environmental benefits are essentially interdependent, social benefits accruing to host communities as a result of ecotourism may have the result of increasing overall standards of living due to the localized economic stimulus provided for in increased visitation to the site. Similarly, environmental benefits accrue as host communities are persuaded to protect natural environments in order to sustain economically viable tourism (Ceballos-Lascurain, 1990).

Many tourists, and especially ecotourists, are sensitive to decreases in water quality and air quality, loss of vegetation, loss of wildlife, soil erosion and a change in the character and visual appeal of an area due to development. Degradation of the natural environment will severely reduce visitor demand in the long term because the natural attributes on which ecotourists depend will be perceived as less attractive, less legitimate and less able to provide satisfying ecologically based experiences.

Ecotourism and local communities: conflict, compromise or cooperation?

Local communities comprise groups with different, and potentially conflicting interests (see Figure 6.1). That is, not all groups want the same things.

The tourist industry seeks a healthy business environment with:

* financial security;
* a trained and responsible workforce;
* attractions of sufficient quality to ensure a steady flow of visitors – who stay longer and visit more often;
* a significant return on investment.

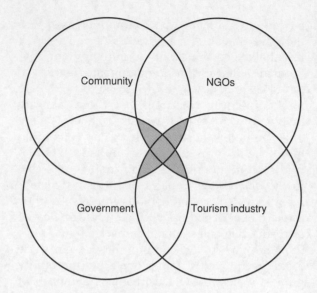

Figure 6.1   *Stakeholders and their needs*

Those interested in the natural environment and cultural heritage issues seek:

* protection of the environment through prevention, improvement, correction of damage, and restoration;
* to motivate people to be more aware – and therefore 'care for' rather than 'use up' resources.

Community members seek a healthy place in which to live with:

* food, adequate and clean water, health care, rewarding work for equitable pay, education and recreation;
* respect for cultural traditions;
* opportunities to make decisions about the future.

Some concerns that each may hold in common include:

* issues of access, such as when, where and how tourists visit and move from place to place;

- host and guest issues, such as cultural impact or common use of infrastructure;
- land use issues, such as hunting/wildlife habitat, agriculture/recreation, preservation/ development, etc.

Ecotourism and local communities

There are a number of reasons why local communities may consider ecotourism:

- a desire to be part of strong growth in tourism generally and see the potential of catering for special-interest tourism (niche markets);
- an awareness of the high value of natural attractions in the locale;
- empathy for conservation ideals and the need for sustainable tourism;
- a desire to responsibly rejuvenate the local tourist industry.

As we have seen in Chapter 1, one of the main principles or elements of ecotourism is its ability to maximize the benefits of tourism, not only as regards income to a region but also the preservation of social infrastructure and biosphere conservation. Specifically, these benefits include:

- increased demand for accommodation houses and food and beverage outlets, and therefore improved viability for new and established hotels, motels, guest houses, farm stays, etc.;
- additional revenue to local retail businesses and other services (e.g. medical, banking, car hire, cottage industries, souvenir shops, tourist attractions);
- increased market for local products (e.g. locally grown produce, artefacts, value-added goods), thereby sustaining traditional customs and practices;
- employment of local labour and expertise (e.g. ecotour guides, retail sales assistants, restaurant table waiting staff);

- source of funding for the protection and enhancement/maintenance of natural attractions and symbols of cultural heritage;
- funding and/or volunteers for field work associated with wildlife research and archaeological studies;
- heightened community awareness of the value of local/indigenous culture and the natural environment.

As these benefits suggest, ecotourism is about attracting visitors for the 'right' reasons, and not simply the promotion of tourism for the sake of the 'tourist dollar' at the expense of a community's natural and cultural attributes. However, local communities are not immune from ecotourism impacts.

The issues and problems

The conflictual issues expressed by representatives of host communities to tourism development generally fall into a number of interrelated categories:

- the lack of opportunities for involvement in decision-making relating to ecotourism;
- inadequate responses from governments when administrative or legislative mechanisms have been established to involve them in such decision-making;
- the lack of financial, social and vocational benefits flowing to these communities from projects that commercially exploit what they regard as their resources;
- the need to establish better tools for evaluating socio-cultural impacts and ensuring this is completed over the more emphasized environmental impacts on the natural environments which are usually of more interest to the outside investors and conservation groups;
- impacts on community cohesion and structure;

● the rapidity of tourism development that in many cases significantly accelerates social change.

These concerns embrace a wide range of issues relating to the management of natural resources adjacent to these communities. The central issue is the inadequate levels of participation perceived by these communities in the management of what they regard as their traditional domains. Control is exerted over local communities both economically and culturally. Tourism involves an interactive process between host (both human and environment) and guest and therefore 'the culture of the host society is as much at risk from various forms of tourism as physical environments' (Sofield, 1991: 56). In many cases tourists view indigenous cultures and local communities as 'products' of the tourism experience that exist to be 'consumed' along with all the other elements of their trip. As tourists are often paying to watch and photograph indigenous people, the tourists feel that it is their 'right' to treat them accordingly – as providing a service, and as a product being purchased as a component of their travel cost. Significantly, however, many local cultures may actively 'construct' what appears (to the tourist's camera) to be an 'authentic' cultural display but which in reality is a staged event specifically for tourists' consumption. This phenomenon, known as 'staged authenticity' (cf. MacCannell, 1976), in many cases serves a strategic purpose in satisfying the tourist's curiosity while allowing the maintenance of actual cultural rituals to escape the hungry tourist's lens. This is the positive side (from the indigenous culture's perspective) of the commodification of tourism, as in many cases it is the interest in local cultures that in many ways helps to sustain and even revive traditional cultural practices.

However, the commmodification of culture often has significant impacts on local communities. 'Staged authenticity' is often actively encouraged by operators whose chief concern is often with providing a 'cultural experience' for tourists that can be experienced in comfort and safety and which is aesthetically pleasing. These cultural performances often become detached from their actual cultural meaning and begin to be performed purely for the viewing public. Too often cultural attractions become overtly commercialized in nature, satisfying the visitors' needs but losing all meaning and significance for the indigenous population. Similarly, indigenous communities often have little or no say over whether they want tourism and they derive few real benefits from their 'performance'. Sustaining the well-being and the cultural traditions of the local community where ecotourism takes place becomes fundamental to definitions of ecotourism.

Case study
The commodification of culture: the Arctic

Over the past 20 years, much of the presentation of indigenous Sami culture has been by those who have lost their traditional Sami heritage or by non-Samis. This has led to the overt commercialization of Sami culture with an often manufactured culture being promoted with the economic benefits being diverted away from the traditional Sami groups to those involved in the provision of unauthentic services. 'The danger is that the people of the north will become human animals in a cultural zoo, mere objects of curiosity for adventurous southerners wealthy enough to enjoy the temptations of glossy travel magazines, luxury cruises through the icebergs, reindeer round-ups or photographic safaris amongst the walrus and polar bears' (Hall, 1987; 217).

Source: P. Mason, (1997) 'Tourism codes of conduct in the Arctic and Sub-Arctic region', *Journal of Sustainable Development*, 5 (2), 1997, 151–164

As we have seen in Chapter 3 ecotourism is in large part a sustainable development strategy: 'whereby natural resource amenities, the local community and the visitor benefit from tourism activity' (Pearce *et al.*, 1996).

The following definition of ecotourism incorporates the above points:

travel, often to developing countries, to relatively undisturbed protected natural areas for study, enjoyment or volunteer assistance that concerns itself with the flora, fauna, geology and ecosystems of an area – as well as the people (caretakers) who live nearby, their needs, their culture and their relationship with the land. (Wallace, 1992: 7)

Similarly, many organizations are now beginning to recognize the integral part that local indigenous people play in tourism by including cultural understanding and appreciation in their definitions of ecotourism. In this way ecologically sustainable tourism is increasingly becoming aligned to conservation, environmental and cultural understanding and appreciation (EAA, 1996).

Thus ecotourism aims to promote and foster a respect and an increase in awareness of other cultures, in fostering mutually beneficial relationships between hosts and tourists.

Case study The Anangu and Tiwi Island response

For the indigenous Australians of the Northern Territory, tourism was perceived as being able to 'offer some employment in remote parts of the Territory where alternative economic opportunities were few' (Burchett, 1992: 6). Guided walks, demonstrations of tracking skills and food processing techniques and other aspects of aboriginal life are carried out at Uluru. Performances of traditional dance are undertaken by three different groups who maintain control of their dance routines (Burchett, 1992). Similarly, specialized small group tours are undertaken by the Tiwi community of Melville Island who saw 'the development of an isolated, comfortable safari camp as being an ideal way for them to combine their needs for employment, cash flow and cultural underpinning' (Burchett, 1992: 7). Produce from traditional hunting and fishing activities undertaken by tourists is returned to the local community with only sufficient amounts for tasting for the tourists left at the safari camp (Burchett, 1992). Tourists experience the traditional and authentic activity and can taste the 'catch' but these vital resources, necessary food stocks for the aborigines, are not depleted just for the sake of the tourist.

While it is important for the traditional values of local and indigenous communities be maintained, indigenous people must not be asked to maintain their traditional practices simply for the sake of tourist entertainment. However, it must also be recognized that cultures undergo a constant process of change and it is this process of *genuine* culture change and exchange that is a fundamental component of ecotourism. 'Genuine' in this sense may be read as synonymous with *sovereignty*. Local communities must be in an empowered rather than a subordinate position from which they have autonomy over their culture, its artefacts and rituals, its very direction, while engaging in and with cultures that interact with them but do not exploit them.

In this way, both the visitors and the hosts benefit from the tourism experience while at the same time avoiding negative cultural impacts on the indigenous population. Participation of local communities in the activity of tourism, therefore, is an essential element to sustaining the well-being of local people.

Through the interactive process between the visitor and the host population both can benefit experientially from ecotourism. By developing an appreciation of local communities and their customs and traditions, 'a process of mutual respect and understanding between societies can be greatly enhanced' (Burchett, 1992: 10) and the achievement of successful interaction between hosts and guests will only benefit and sustain the well-being of local communities. Local communities can benefit from ecotourism economically if they play a greater participatory role in the tourism process. The greater the control over tourism in their region, the more culturally sustainable they will become.

Employment

One of the most obvious and immediate benefits of tourism associated with local communities is the increase in employment opportunities and income generation for the host region:

● direct employment (associated service industries such as hotels, restaurants, concessions);
● indirect employment (generated as a result of increasing industry inputs such as employment at a retail souvenir outlet);
● induced employment (generated as a result of increased spending capacity of local residents due to increased receipts from tourism; consumption of goods for example) (Healy, 1989: 21).

Unfortunately, however, employment opportunities for local communities are extremely restricted. Tourism is often extolled as a major employer in local communities due to the assumption that high levels of capital investment equate with a corresponding increase in employment. Conversely, tourism is often advocated as a major employment generator due to its labour-intensive nature. However, these assumptions are often misleading as tourism often does not essentially generate significant amounts of employment and is less labour-intensive than sometimes espoused by operators seeking community support.

The primary employment opportunities through ecotourism are in the areas of hotels, craft makers, shop owners, tour operators, government agency staff, park wardens/rangers and the like. Kusler (n.d: 2) sounds a particular warning to those who may hail ecotourism as invariably solving endemic unemployment as he notes that in some circumstances little (if any) employment benefits have accrued to local communities because infrastructure, such as accommodation establishments, have already been developed (and staffed) in the area.

Case study   Papua New Guinea

Papua New Guinea is the most rapidly westernizing nation on earth, and as a consequence there are growing social problems, unemployment and a rapidly diminishing culture (Bates, 1991: 4). The Ambua Lodge in the Highlands of Papua New Guinea is an example of an ecotourism establishment providing employment opportunities to local people which, in part, assists in halting the urban drift towards the crime ridden major cities, and thus providing the incentive not only to preserve the natural environment, but the unique features of the local culture. The construction and operation of Ambua Lodge provides a diverse range of long- and short-term employment to locals, in the positions of construction workers, art and crafts makers, performers, waiters, cooks, guides, gardeners, room cleaners, laundry operators, maintenance personnel, vegetable growers and the like (Bates, 1991: 4).

Currently, the general lack of skills and resources has meant that many ecotourism ventures are owned and operated by expatriates (Weiler and

Hall, 1992). Often it is unfeasible to expect the local population automatically to assume employment positions within ecotourism: 'The hard truth is that a local farmer, fisherman or plantation worker cannot always be changed overnight into a tourist guide or hotel manager' (Clark and Banford, 1991: 9). It is often common that the planning, staff and management of parks is done by developed country personnel or expatriates in developing countries and this can have negative effects on the affected local communities, often leading to 'homogenization' of cultures, and in many cases the trivialization of local and traditional methods of managing the natural resources, as well as hostility and bitterness.

Training and education should not solely be concerned with utilitarian skills that may enhance employment opportunities. Partnerships between the tourism industry, government agencies and the local population are needed in which local populations are able to articulate their initial concerns, wants and needs in relation to any development, and which allow them to evaluate in their own terms whether they wish to benefit from tourism (even before they gain employment).

However, participation by local communities in tourism must not be limited simply to employment opportunities. Local communities must be involved in the complete tourism development process, from the planning stage to the implementation and management of tourism projects, through avenues of consultation and partnership. In conjunction, tourism ventures need to be driven by the local communities themselves in all aspects, particularly through locally owned operations or vested interests in local operations which would see greater economic benefits accruing to local communities. Joy and Motzney (1992: 457) suggest locals should buy and manage small accommodation establishments. However, despite the lack of capital intensity of ecotourism, it may not be a viable economic possibility for many local populations to enter the market.

Case study   Belize, Central America

Belize is attempting to counter this problem by developing policies that provide feasible financial avenues and 'competitive advantages' for locals to invest in small to medium scale private tourism enterprises, such as food and beverage outlets, accommodation establishments, sport and activity operations and so on. Government enforcement of the policies is through the restriction of trade licences, concessions or duty exemptions, and vetting procedures (Maguire, 1991: 6).

Extensive training and education is needed before local communities can gain meaningful benefits from ecotourism, particularly language, environmental and natural history skills (Weiler and Hall, 1992: 117). While the skills for running private business enterprises may not be available within the local community, local expertise and knowledge can be a powerful tool for tourist guides and park wardens in protected areas:

proper management of protected areas requires employment of park rangers and guards, as well as workers to maintain park buildings, roads and trails. Ecotourism in protected areas creates demand for guide services . . . providing employment for . . . local people familiar with the flora and fauna of the area. (Bunting, 1991: 3)

According to Ceballos-Lascurain (1992: 5), local people not only possess the 'practical and ancestral knowledge of the natural features' of the area, they also have the incentive to become dedicated to ecotourism in positions such as park rangers since 'their subsistence would depend in a major degree on the sustained preservation of the natural qualities of their environment'. Similarly, instead of promoting a colonialist model of development which would seek to bring locals 'up to speed' through training in 'necessary' skills, a recognition of the particular range of skills *already* possessed by local communities matched with their own expectations and outcomes for tourism projects proposed for their locale would be more beneficial in any real sense. Local communities must be involved in the complete tourism development process, from planning, through to the implementation of tourism projects, through avenues of consultation. Consultation is 'a process which aims to reconcile economic development with the broader interests of local people and the potential impact of development on their natural, social and cultural environment' (World Wide Fund for Nature, 1992: 25).

Case study   Sakau Rainforest Lodge: an ecotourism model

Sakau Rainforest Lodge (SRL) was developed with an intention to blend with the sociocultural and physical environment of the region, and to create an alternative source of employment for the local population, particularly those being retrenched from the logging industry. The lodge is located 130 km from Sandakan, with a further 15 minute boat trip up the Kinabatangan River from Sakau itself. A 7-acre land site was purchased in the remote location on the Kinabatangan River bank, but in order to minimize disturbance of natural vegetation, the built-up area is limited to 10 000 square feet.

The management recruit local people as boatmen, gardeners, general workers and kitchen hands. All boats used to ferry passengers are built by local fishermen, with other jetty and furniture requirements subcontracted to local tradespeople. In the event that the lodge operates at maximum capacity, local boats are hired for use in ferrying and guiding guests.

Staff slide shows are the primary tool used to upgrade current local interpretive skills, understand the conservation policies of the company and government, and of course, the needs of the tourists.

The lodge is sited 100 feet from the river and separated by a buffer zone of trees to prevent soil erosion and minimize the effects of noise on proximal areas. SRL is built on stilts 5 feet above the ground with a 10-foot ceiling to optimize air circulation and cooling. To maximize the benefits of the location, solar lighting and a supplementary generator are used wherever possible. Rainwater and river water are collected for showering, toilet and household usage, with no waste discharged to the river.

In order to minimize the effects of lodge-controlled tours along the river, all boats are painted green and powered by the smallest possible engine size of 15 h.p. When the tour group stops to observe wildlife, power is derived from a solar-charged battery, connected to an electric engine.

Management of SRL set aside 1000 room nights in 1996 for volunteers to clear weeds in the nearby Kelenanap ox-bow lake. Wildlife, birdlife and local fishing have been affected as a result of weed infestation. Working in cooperation with the University of Malaysia and overseas students, the problems of weed infestation and waterway eutrification are being addressed.

Finally, SRL has begun to raise funds from overseas tour operators – the money being channelled to a local NGO, Sabah Environmental Protection Association and used for research purposes. In the near future, an area of the lower Kinabatangan River will be gazetted as a wildlife sanctuary. Management is using this sustainable lodge as a catalyst and incentive in preserving the natural and cultural environment, encouraging a move from illegal logging and bribery of local enforcement officers to sustainable ecotourism, where locals receive long-term benefits.

Source: Albert Teo, Managing Director, Sakau Rainforest Lodge, Malaysia: *British Airways Tourism for Tomorrow Awards 1996*, Pacific Region

Even small-scale development may have significant negative impacts. As a result of tourism to various areas, local people have lost access to land and resources they had previously enjoyed. According to Johnson (1993: 2) ecotourism often leads to a change in resource ownership and management, beneficial to the tourism industry but detrimental to the local people.

Similarly, 'flourishing employment, living standards and consumption levels for some, added to the unequal distribution of benefits to a portion of the population, can contribute to social tensions and hostility' (WWF, 1992: 19). This has significant import for protected area agencies for local resentment towards designated conservation areas often arises when the park is viewed as principally of benefit to tourists with no reciprocal benefit for the local population. This is often due to the fact that local people no longer have the right to use land they consider was theirs, but at the same time see it frequently visited by foreign people; the reaction to this is often negative.

Extreme cases can lead to the destruction of natural areas as 'malicious destruction may occur if landowners believe that their lands are being singled out for protection . . . and they are not receiving the benefits' (Kusler, n.d.: 2).

Local planning and development

The ideal for planning ecotourism development is cited by Clark and Banford (1991):

There is no reason why countries or communities should not decide what type of tourism they are willing to accept and set limits to the amount of change they are prepared to put up with. This applies to ecotourism. (1991: 7)

Such a process would involve goal setting at the national, regional and local level. Clark and Banford (1991: 7) suggest the development of a tourism masterplan to document the desirability and limits of acceptable tourism for the area. Ideally, communities could develop their own masterplan, but presently it is dependent on the priorities of those in positions of power to determine (such as the above-mentioned policies for ecotourism in Belize).

Several examples exist where local people have taken moves to ensure they both personally, and as a community, benefit directly from ecotourism. In many small communities such as that living on Easter Island accommodation becomes a key factor. On Easter Island over 300 beds within local houses are open to tourists, providing the major source of accommodation on the island. The additional income gained has been spent beautifying homes and providing for local infrastructure. In Papua New Guinea's highlands, villagers have a source of income from the accommodation huts they have built on their land (Bates, 1991: 4) which, with the cooperation of the local tour operators, provide accommodation to groups of tourists.

Similarly the Pax World Friendship Tours and Co-op America's Travel Link programmes are all designed specifically so that the local community can benefit from ecotourism to that area. The programmes involve local people opening their homes to tourists, who in turn use this time in the local community to work on 'community development projects' (Johnson, 1993: 3)

However, it is often the power struggle at national, state or local levels which is the determining factor of where tourism occurs, what is seen and done, and who, among the local community, receives the economic benefits. In practice, the planning system itself is often set up in a way that gives indigenous people little or no opportunities for input. According to Johnson (1993: 4), 'development projects are often

Case study South Pentecost, Vanuatu

The Pentecost Land Dive is a traditional ceremony of the villages in this area that occurs annually in April/May. In response to increasing negative cultural impacts as a result of tourism, the local chiefs of the villages established the 'South Pentecost Tourism Council' to manage the event, its 'primary responsibility [being] to safeguard the cultural integrity of the event' (Sofield, 1991: 59). This involves maintaining customs with tourist visits, preventing filming of the event and limiting numbers of tourists attending the performance. This not only provides the tourist with an 'authentic' cultural experience but also maintains the cultural significance of the ritual to the villagers themselves and allows them some degree of control over the activity of tourism.

Case study Costa Rica

Costa Rica's joint UNESCO–MAB and Costa Rica National Park project intentionally prefers residents to foreign involvement. The restoration of denigrated forest (known as the Guanacaste project) emphasizes Costa Rican residents, employing and training locals in the areas of park maintenance, management and habitat restoration. This programme has the long-term benefit of the gradual transfer of control over the research, management, and public education sectors from the currently dominant North Americans to Costa Rican industry (Johnson, 1993: 3).

designed and implemented in a political context in which indigenous people have minimal voice in policy and management'. In contrast, Nepal has developed a system (through a resource management plan) specifically benefiting local people by giving them increased power and a greater role in decision-making.

Increasing access to information for indigenous people provides them with greater scope for involvement in planning and decision making. Education plays a powerful role in increasing local involvement.

Programmes such as these will eventually lead to greater local control over protected areas and the tourism industry. Therefore, when local people are involved in studying, discussing and devising strategies to control or capture control over the development decision making process they are taking a critical step towards increasing their role in ecotourism and development decision making (Johnson, 1993: 4).

Consideration for local cultures can be incorporated into the planning and marketing of ecotourism destinations and products in many ways. Blangy and Epler Wood (1992: 4) recommend that government agencies, tourism boards, the tourism industry and local inhabitants could all play a role in the education of tourists about cultural issues by the implementation of social guidelines. They suggest government should be responsible for developing guidelines but recommend significant input from the local community. The local community can be incorporated into the development of these guidelines by using government funding (if available) to get assistance with the preparation and editing of brochures for distribution. Alternatively, the local community could collaborate with international and local non-governmental organizations and become involved with environmental education projects.

Social guidelines could incorporate desirable and acceptable behaviour in the following areas:

1 Local customs and traditions
2 Permission for photographs
3 Dress

4 Language
5 Invasion of privacy
6 Response to begging
7 Use and abuse of technological gadgetry
8 Bartering and bargaining
9 Indigenous rights
10 Local officials
11 Off-limits areas (Blangy and Epler Wood, 1992: 4).

Another source of potential assistance is tourist boards. Blangy and Epler Wood (1992: 4) suggest boards should allocate funds for all stages of the education process, through the generation, printing and distribution of local guidelines. Distribution of brochures and printed matter at tourist centres and on-site is an effective means of reaching the tourist. Tour guides could play an important role by briefing tourists on what is acceptable and unacceptable in the region being visited.

However, despite the often good intentions of tourists and some tour operators, it is apparent that 'ecotourism can damage the natural assets on which it rests. The outcome depends on how it is managed' (Lindberg, 1991: ix). Thus the implications for management are enormous. Managers must find a way to 'capitalize on its potential without jeopardizing the special features of natural areas' (Boo, 1990: xiv).

In order for ecotourism organizations to become aware of their place and role in ecotourism, it is important for each to be made aware of the differing needs of local communities while also aligning both these groups with national conservation/development strategies: 'designed to demonstrate to sectoral interests how they inter-relate with other sectors, thereby revealing new opportunities for conservation and development to work together' (McNeely and Thorsell, 1989). These different sectors include governments, private enterprise, local communities and organizations, non-governmental conservation organizations, and international institutions. If each sector has an understanding of where it fits within the broader framework of the tourism and conservation sectors then there is a better

chance of carefully designed tourism programmes. These would take protected areas as a focus for fostering host communities' values while providing education for visitors in relation to both conservation issues and the local community itself (Kutay, 1990: 38).

Crocker (cited in Encel and Encel, 1991: 150) maintains that participatory ecodevelopment is a means of confronting the deleterious effects of tourism. Participatory ecodevelopment encompasses cooperative, self-management (autogestion), co-management (cogestion) and solidarity (solidarism) elements. While it is recognized by most in developing nations that the old economic models do not work and benefit only the developed nations who end up controlling the economy, there are alternate models currently in operation in varying forms.

Sometimes the imperatives to respect nature, satisfy basic needs, and participate in self-government point in the same direction. Establishing a more just system of land tenure, pricing, credit, and technical assistance for small and poor farmers could reduce deforestation and environmentally unsound farming practices, as well as be a source of basic-needs satisfaction and communal self-determination. Santa Rosa National Park rightly prides itself on integrating the restoration of its dry tropical forest with the education and employment of local residents as 'eco-tour' guides, foresters, educators, and researchers. A proposed Peace Park on the Costa Rican–Nicaraguan border can protect the fragile regional peace as well as an endangered tropical ecosystem. (cited in Encel and Encel, 1991: 159)

Originally, in both ecotourism and biodiversity debates, conservation issues were foremost and the local community element was neglected. However, it has become increasingly obvious that biodiversity cannot be conserved without the involvement of local resident communities. While it is necessary to recognize national parks and protected areas as integral to biodiversity and ecotourism, ecotourism must also stress the importance of local human populations and tourist experiences.

Case Study   Partnerships: national parks and native peoples

The Sitka National Historical Park comprises 106 acres of spectacular scenery bordered by the mouth of the Indian River, Alaska. The park is said to embody one of the most successful partnerships between the native population and national park authorities. In the park, Native American cultures are central to the interpretive experience of visitors and the Tlingit Indians operate the Southeast Alaska Indian Cultural Centre in association with the National Park Service (NPS). Native artists practise their skills, with a focus on 'elders' and the cultural traditions they represent: 'Bringing them [the elders] together is insurance for where we Tlingit are going in the future.'

Such partnerships are evident in Glacier National Park, where native programmes include Slaish, Kootenai and Blackfeet (Indian) lecturers, drummers and dancers. Glacier's programmes began in 1980, funded by the Glacier Natural History Association and other private sources. Although it was initially difficult to find native interpreters there are enough natives participating in the programme to run a programme almost each day in July and August, and employ Blackfeet natives as summer rangers. Glacier's chief of interpretation stated.

'This needed to be native Americans interpreting their own culture when we romanticize about a native culture, we lose sight that it's a growing, living culture, not an artefact.'

An appreciation for living culture is evident in Canyon de Chelly National Monument in Arizona, where the Navajo still own the 83 840 acres. Except for walking the trail to White House Ruin, and following the north and south rim drives, no visitor enters Canyon de Chelly without a Navajo guide. One young guide (Hunter) began his employment in the park in construction before moving into interpretation, the switch a natural progression for him. Hunter states:

'My grandmother said.' 'It's not your mouth you learn with, but your other senses. That's why we have two of everything else – ears, eyes, nostrils, hands. Your mouth is for sharing, everything else you learn with. She never used the word 'teach'. It's sharing.'

The Navajo guides are living history themselves, from families that continue to pasture sheep and goats in the canyon after 500 years. The canyons provided Hunter with this metaphor to describe the interplay of visiting and native cultures:

People talk about bridging. But with a bridge, two cultures come half way and then pull. A river [however] comes from all directions, comes together and slows together. No pulling, but weaving. Naturally. We people come in all different colours. Look at a finished rug, how beautiful it is. We just have to weave our threads.'

Source: S. Bowman 'Parks in partnership', *National Parks*. January/February 1998, pp. 30–33

Tourism and tourism based on natural areas does not take place in isolation from local people. Tourism requires infrastructure and access, all which impact on local communities. In many cases the natural environment is used by local people for sustaining their livelihood. With the introduction of ecotourism it is found there is a better basis for conservation of the natural resource as there are direct benefits to be gained from an intact environment. These benefits can be seen by local communities thereby encouraging an awareness of the need to conserve within an economic framework. However, if development is dictated by forces outside these communities it is common to see overdevelopment and excessive economic leakage followed by high social impact. Resentment can also build, causing blatant harvesting or destruction of so-called protected natural resources.

Travel essentials

- Local communities need to be involved in all levels of ecotourism development from planning through to management. The planning process must take into account community involvement with an understanding of how local communities can be best approached, understood and integrated. Only then can ecotourism provide a sustainable economic base for rural development, but where local people have traditional means of sustainable self-sufficiency, tourism should only act as a supplementary source of income.
- The appropriateness of foreign ownership and operation of facilities should be carefully investigated in order to reduce conflict and resentment between local people and foreign operators. If there are likely to be limited long-term benefits to the local people, then this must be brought to the attention of these people and the operators.
- Ecotourism views the natural resource as home in a broad sense to all humans, but more so to the local inhabitants. Ecotourism itself is concerned with low impact tourism experiences that are purposely designed to have the least impact possible on both the physical environment and the local inhabitants.
- Ecotourists and ecotourism operators should be involved with the management of the natural resource, as well as positive devotees to the relationship between its management and the local inhabitants. This would incorporate supplying locals with some of the positive financial and other advantages of the tourism activity, and providing an avenue for local people to participate in the planning and tourism development decision making.
- Ecotourism raises the consciousness of hosts about wilderness protection and sustainable development. It provides both the locals and visitors with genuine non-forced interaction, which does not intrude thoughtlessly on the local lifestyle.
- Ecotourism provides the local community opportunity to expand its economic resource base as a replacement or complement to traditional economic bases such as agriculture and forestry.
- Ecotourism does not restrict the benefits of education and access of the natural resource to the local community, in providing avenues for employment, education and enjoyment within the natural environment.

7

Case studies: the local and the national

Case study 1: the local – Costa Rica, the Santa Elena Ecotourism Rainforest Reserve and Monteverde Cloud Forest Preserve

Introduction

The Santa Elena Rainforest Reserve (SERR) project is an ongoing community-based project that seeks to addresses the critical problematic between development and conservation in attempting to foster economic self-sufficiency and natural resource conservation among a low-income community. The project served to provide a diversification of the Santa Elena community's economic basis in providing an alternative to traditional industry bases like agriculture and forestry which had significant negative impacts on natural areas and the communities associated with these areas. This project was established with the objective of enabling the Santa Elena community, who are living in a marginal or environmentally threatened area, to take an active interest in the preservation of their natural resources by providing local incentives through direct and perceivable benefits.

Ecotourism has become a key component of Costa Rica's growing tourism industry, particularly for its potential as a much needed alternative means of economic return while providing a stimulus for conserving natural resources. This case study illustrates ecotourism's potential as an alternative strategy for development, particularly through the development process being actually led and controlled largely by the local

---

Costa Rica

Costa Rica is a Central American country, approximately 52 000 square kilometres in area, located on the isthmus of Latin America. It is bordered to the north by Nicaragua, to the east by the Caribbean Sea, to the south by Panama and to the west by the Pacific Ocean. It is an extremely varied country in terms of landscape and flora and fauna due in large part to its geography as it lies as a bridge between two continents, with species transition occurring between North and South America.

A series of volcanic mountain chains run from the Nicaraguan border in the north–west to the Panamanian border in the south-east, effectively dividing the country in two. In the centre of Costa Rica's mountainous highlands lies the Meseta Central. This central plain, generally between about 1000 metres and 1500 metres above sea level, forms the foundation for four of Costa Rica's five largest cities – including San José, the capital.

History and development

When the Spanish[1] arrived in Costa Rica a large proportion of the country was covered with a dense cloak of deciduous forest, lowland tropical rainforest and cloudforest, broken only by dispersed Indian settlements where corn, beans, cacao, cassava and cotton were cultivated in shifting plots in the forest (Solorzano *et al.* 1991).

Colonization attempts by the Spanish in the sixteenth century were hampered by indigenous resistance, diseases and the rugged tropical terrain. Settlements were established throughout Latin America in the seventeenth and eighteenth centuries, concerned primarily with trade within the ill-defined and disputed regions. Smuggling and piracy was rampant along the Caribbean coast of Costa Rica and Nicaragua throughout this period.

The indigenous population of Costa Rica suffered great losses during this time of social and cultural reformation. The Indians who survived the wars, slavery and diseases brought from Europe were incorporated into a form of Spanish culture.

Costa Rica obtained independence from Spain in 1822 at which time the intensive use of its natural resources commenced. Coffee growing came to dominate many landscapes – a mass export trade had been well under way by 1825 which in the following decades quickly grew to become a central factor in the local economy. The location and expansion of the coffee industry was concentrated within the fertile central valley. In the early 1900s banana companies began creating an additional major export commodity, which to this day provides valuable foreign income for Costa Rica. However, the steep countryside and heavy rainfall constrain agricultural and industry development – 60% of Costa Rica's territory is suitable only for forestry. Its agriculturally based economy precipitated an exponentially increasing rate of deforestation and soil erosion, with deforestation rates averaging more than 48 000 hectares per year between 1963 and 1973. Government incentives for cattle ranching buoyed the demand for land in Costa Rica by providing incentives for professional squatters to clear one parcel of land after another merely to on-sell their 'improvements' (Cruz *et al.*, 1992). The result of systematically clearing and selling land in this manner resulted in 10% of the farmers owning three-quarters of the agricultural land.

Until the late 1940s Costa Rica still had extensive tropical forests ranging from lowland rainforest to cloudforest. Within 30 years however, many of these forests had been lost (Boo, 1990) and forestry experts estimate that in less than 10 years the only exploitable forests remaining will be within parks and private reserves (Whelan, 1991). Continued deforestation has not only exacerbated soil erosion and increased siltation in rivers but has also had adverse impacts, both direct and indirect, on marine and coral communities off the coast, particularly along the Caribbean. Due to the increasing rate of natural resource degradation, biologists and conservationists began to lobby for the creation of a system of protected areas, culminating in the creation of the National Parks Service (NPS) in 1970.

---

[1] The first recorded European contact with Costa Rica was by the Spanish explorer Christopher Columbus who first landed near present-day Puerto Limon on 18 September 1502.

[2] Since 1988, the Ministry of Natural Resources has provided concessionary credit to small farmers throughout Costa Rica for reforestation (Donavan in Western and Wright, 1994: 2) and some attempts have been made to commence plantation forestry. However, existing forests are likely to be exhausted before plantation forests are ready for harvest (Whelan, 1991).

community in partnership with government sectors and international NGOs. In order to understand the 'local' position of ecotourism development this case study provides a context for an analysis of the sociopolitical realities of ecotourism at the community level. Tourism development is a prime consumer of valuable land resources and changes in land use often involve a transfer of power relationships. The reactions to these shifts within communities can vary greatly but the impacts on them and their often delicately balanced sociocultural relationships present problems for all those involved in the process of development alternatives. This case study highlights the different understandings that can emerge about what constitutes appropriate development for a community. The high levels of demand for nature tourism in Costa Rica provide an initial base for tourism development and this case study illustrates one particular way in which local communities, through cooperative parnerships, have initiated and controlled tourism through the creation of regional conservation area systems which attempt to integrate the generation of economic benefits with protected areas.

The concerns of local communities such as Santa Elena to tourism generally fall into a number of interrelated categories. The first is the lack of opportunities for involvement in decision-making relating to protected area management and tourism. The second arises from what these communities regard as inadequate responses from governments, the tourism industry and NGOs to assist them in controlling tourism and its benefits and impacts. The third relates to the lack of financial, social and vocational benefits flowing to these communities from projects that commercially exploit what they regard as their resources. The fourth relates to the need to establish better tools for evaluating sociocultural impacts and ensuring this is completed in conjunction with the more emphasized environmental impacts on the natural environments which are usually of more interest to outside investors and conservation groups.

Tourism and protected areas in Costa Rica

Costa Rica's diverse climate and topography, particularly within or adjacent to protected areas, support a wide range of plant and animal life, all of which are significant attractions for visitors.

In 1992, tourism became Costa Rica's largest industry, with over 500 000 international visitors (Bowermater, 1994: 136). Because developing countries have low gross domestic product and income per capita, high debt burdens and generally low standards of living they require economic activity, foreign exchange, employment and development or industry which is less consumptive of primary resources (Marsh in Britten and Clarke, 1987: 27). As a result of this, tourism is an attractive form of development and has become an important industry in the past decade.

Foreign tourism grew rapidly in the 1970s, a period when growth averaged 11.2% annually (Boo, 1990), and this growth has continued at about 5.7% into the 1990s (WTTC, 1993) – over 500 000 international visitors (Bowermater, 1994: 136). Tourism in Costa Rica is now the third highest source of foreign income, growing from ($US) $89.9 in the late 1980s to ($US) 193.3 in the late 1990s (Banco Central de Costa Rica, Principles estadisticas sobre). Presently it is estimated at ($US) 331 million (CIDA, 1995: 15) and it has an average annual growth rate of 25%.

Foreign exchange from tourism is seen as an important element for the economic recuperation of the country. Historically, the country has lacked the financial resources and infrastructure for tourism and the market has been limited because of the view of Latin America as unstable, having limited capacity, poor quality accommodation and localization.

As such, tourism development has predominantly been on a small scale; 93% of the country's hotels have less than 50 rooms (Rachoweicki, 1994: 12) and approximately three-quarters of all licensed tour agencies are owned by nationals and long-term foreign residents.

Costa Rican protected areas

Due to the increasing rate of natural resource degradation, biologists and conservationists began to lobby for the creation of a system of protected areas, culminating in the creation of the National Parks Service (NPS) in 1970. Planning for the parks system took place at a national level with the main priority being to preserve habitat. This approach, however, alienated many of the Costa Rican farmers, ranchers and loggers, along with 'park dwellers who were relocated and who previously had used the forests as hunting grounds or agricultural land' (Whelan, 1991). People forced to move off their land were offered compensation for their losses – many of which have not yet been paid. Many local residents have few alternative sources of income so that encroachment into the protected areas in some cases is essential to lifestyle with slash-and-burn agriculture, gold mining, poaching and other activities occurring within park boundaries (Rovinski, 1991). Failure to include local residents in planning national parks in Costa Rica has resulted in conflict (Kutay in West and Brechin, 1991: 118) between community and national park staff.

In 1986 the newly formed Ministry of Natural Resources took responsibility for the NPS from the Ministry of Agriculture. Alvaro Umana, then Minister of Natural Resources, began to promote a new concept to solve the conservation versus development dilemma: sustainable development (Rovinski, 1991). The protected areas that support this idea consist of over 55 protected units, such as national parks, national forests, wildlife refuges and Indian reserves and these areas cover about 18% (926 000 hectares) of the national territory (Boo, 1990).

Costa Rica's parks and protected areas have been developed, to a large extent, without adequate funding for infrastructure and management. Spending for parks (excluding acquisition) has remained at the same level for ten years despite inflation and costs associated with managing new parks (Whelan, 1991). This indicates just how inadequate funding has been. The government has, however, been supportive of the establishment of privately owned reserves for tourism and research. Unfortunately deforestation in the rest of Costa Rica continues at a non-sustainable rate, and forestry experts estimate that in less than ten years, the only exploitable forests remaining will be within the parks and private reserves (Whelan, 1991).

However, this tendency is changing as increasing foreign investment is focused on the country. One development project proposed for the Gulf of Papagayo includes plans for an accommodation capacity of 20 000 moderate to high priced hotel rooms. Comparing this to the existing stock of 15 000 moderate to high priced hotel rooms in the some price range suggests parallels with the unprecedented growth that has occurred in parts of Mexico and the Caribbean.

Costa Rica's national tourist board (Junta National de Turismo) was established in 1931, later replaced by the Costa Rican Tourist Board (ICT) in 1955. In 1986, the government continued the practice initiated in 1985 of increasing the tourism board's budget from central funds and also increased the tax on airfares from 5% to 8% to increase the board's funding (Boo, 1990). Coupled with a 3% tax on hotel accommodation, these taxes are intended to fund the board totally. The government further demonstrated its commitment to developing a tourism industry by passing the Tourism Investment Incentives Law in 1986. This piece of legislation encouraged private sector tourism investment through various concessionary measures and has provided for numerous tax exemptions for tourist-related enterprises (Harrison, 1992).

The challenge of creating a viable tourism industry in the midst of Costa Rica's current rate of natural resource depreciation has become an imperative due to the urgent need to address the problems of poverty and unemployment, sustainable rural development and natural resource preservation. The interconnectedness of these issues has important policy implications for Costa Rica's government and people.

Ecotourism had caught the imagination of the local Santa Elena community because of the revenue returns to the adjacent Monteverde Cloudforest Preserve (MCFP) and the community generating interest from the government and international organizations operating in the country. It was seen as a way to sustain the natural environment while still earning valuable income for the community. However, a focus on the high return potential generated by foreign tourists and an over-emphasis on scientific value has contributed to a perception of exclusion in the Santa Elena community.

The Santa Elena Ecotourism Rainforest Reserve (SERR)

With tourism to the adjacent MCFP increasing from 300 in 1973 40000 in 1989, a significant amount of income has been generated within the area. However, limited real benefits have accrued to the Santa Elena community. The Santa Elena Rainforest Reserve (SERR) was a direct community-based response to this situation in an attempt to provide stability for the community through an ecotourism project which would provide sustainable economic land use alternatives for the community, and which, it was hoped, would see real benefits being delivered to the community from tourism.

The Santa Elena community established the SERR on a parcel of land that had been presented to their high school by the Costa Rican government in 1983 on a 10-year lease, for students to

The Monteverde Cloud Forest Preserve (MCFP)

In 1973, private donations were used to set up the private Monteverde Cloud Forest Preserve, now operated by the Tropical Science Center in San Jose. The reserve straddles the continental divide in the Tilaran mountains, spans six life zones, and the quetzal, bell-bird and umbrella birds are some of the more unique inhabitants . . . jaguars, ocelots; macaws, ag'outis, and kinkajous roam among immense oak trees. In all, the area has about 600 tree species, 300 orchids and 200 ferns, 100 mammals, and more than 2000 flowering plants and over 500 different types of butterflies.

The 10500 hectare reserve is one of the most popular destinations in Costa Rica for ecotourists because of its cloud forest preserve. The number of tourists increased from about 300 in 1973 to nearly 13000 in 1987, and by 1994 Monteverde was drawing 15000 tourists per year. The reserve has had to limit numbers and became supportive of the establishment of the Santa Elena Rainforest Reserve in order to decrease pressure on itself.

Tourism earnings are now the second largest source of income for local residents after dairy production. The increase in tourism has increased pressure on the area, especially new tourist developments such as restaurants and hotels. The area is threatened by subsistence agriculture, logging and land speculation.

Scientists, tourists and ecotourists continued to come in growing numbers to the Monteverde area. However, this increased tourism to the Monteverde area left very few benefits being retained within the adjacent Santa Elena community, who saw a limited return from the developing ecotourism industry in their region.

conduct agricultural projects. The project grew out of a response to the issues that have confronted many Costa Rican communities as a result of deforestation due to systematic land clearing, chiefly for agriculture, and the endemic unemployment level which has necessitated a gradual exodus of people from rural areas to larger cities in search of work. The project was seen as a sound initiative but later, due to the difficulties of clearing the forest and because of severe climate, infertile soils and lack of resources, it was abandoned. The high school's board of directors acted as a lobby group, overcoming existing local laws and government legislation and the failure of the nearby Monteverde Cloud Forest Preserve (MCFP) effectively to contribute to their area. (There are numerous examples of ways in which the MCFP could have used their networks effectively to create scholarships for students to attend universities or work with visiting scientists; however, the focus was on conservation and research mainly for developed countries' scientists and interests.)

In 1990 the community and the high school made the decision to develop the school's land for ecotourism purposes. The major objectives included:

- addressing the school's problem of lack of financial resources;
- addressing deforestation, which historically has seen local forests depleted through rural families' need to clear land in order to derive income from dairy farming;
- providing Costa Rican and international students with a centre for practical rainforest study;
- providing job opportunities and economic benefits for the community through an ecotourism project that would enhance their lifestyle and demonstrate the socioeconomic potential of conserving the natural environment in their area;
- construction of an interpretation centre and nature trail to provide Costa Ricans and tourists alike with educational information on rainforest conservation;

The Santa Elena Rainforest Reserve

Over 310 hectares in size and with 50% of the reserve located within the Arenal National Reserve, the Santa Elena Rainforest Reserve is of unique conservation value. While it is a habitat for most of the flora and fauna also found in the MCFP, it also has some unique characteristics of its own. It is the home of the non-migrating quetzals and has views of volcano Arenal, Lake Arenal and the Gulf of Nicaragua. The majority of the reserve is comprised of primary (pristine) cloud forest. This makes up 256 ha or 83.1% of the 310 ha reserve.

- provision of a further tourist attraction in the area that would directly benefit the community;
- fostering a conservation ethic in the children of the high school and subsequently the community of Santa Elena.

Funds for the project were raised from the local community, Canadian high schools, private and public sector sponsors, and international development organizations such as the Canadian International Development Agency (CIDA) and Youth Challenge International (YCI). CIDA and YCI initially provided the material, equipment and staff necessary to develop and construct an interpretation centre and trails. The local and regional government authorities cooperated by directing national government funds into the building of a road to the reserve (access to which was previously restricted due to high rainfall, clay soils, and severe erosion in some sections).

Local tour operators were involved in the establishment of the SERR from an early stage. The larger operators were approached for donations to assist in the establishment of the reserve and the smaller operators were allowed to bring visitors to the site to encourage their support. Many of these operators volunteered to work on site and also encouraged their clients to make donations to the reserve.

User charges are levied on visitors in order to raise revenue for further protection and management. Access rights to specific individuals or operators have not yet been addressed. To restrict the level of access to an area the numbers of visitors must be controlled and this may be achieved in the future through the issuing of permits to operators.

The community is coordinating a regional plan and have initiated land zoning controls, which is essential to the future management of the area. The school board established the Santa Elena High School Rainforest Foundation to assist in advising the management of the reserve. It is made up of a range of organizations, the Tropical Science Centre, Youth Challenge International, the Municipality of Puntarenas, the Fathers' Association of the Santa Elena High School, the Administration Board of the High School, the Integral Development Association of Monteverde, the Volunteers, Investigation, and Environmental Development Association (VIDA).

The Foundation's goals are to:

- conserve the rainforest;
- manage the reserve and allocate profits to the high school;
- provide employment and income to the community;
- acquire more land to be protected in the reserve.

Employment in the Costa Rican tourism sector in 1989 represented only 5.3% of the national available labour but this figure has increased, along with ecotourism-based activities. The Santa Elena project focuses on employment for graduates from the school. A guide training programme was developed and implemented along with biology, English and hospitality added to the school curriculum.

As it is not directly controlled by the government, the reserve does not experience the problems Boo (1990: 32) identified in Costa Rica, where revenues generated by parks are often diverted to other sources such as hospitals, or as McNeely and Thorsell (1989: 31) found where development is often inappropriate. The revenue from this reserve can be directed into creating urban infrastructure as well as management operations and interpretation facilities, and with the ongoing support from the community the appropriate infrastructure can be developed. The local and regional government authorities have been cooperative here in supplying funds directed from the national government to build a road to the reserve, allowing vehicle access. The joint cooperation of the different levels of government represented a major step towards the successful operation of the reserve. Tourism can provide economic justification (Boo, 1990: xiv) to conserve areas and is therefore an attractive proposition for the government, as Cater (1987: 202–8) maintains it can stimulate employment, investment, modified land use and make a positive contribution to the balance of payments.

Conclusion

The SERR project raises the potential for change and answers some of the political and economic questions which are now being raised about sustainable development, particularly in developing nations such as Costa Rica. Originally, in both ecotourism and biodiversity debates, conservation issues were foremost and the local community element was neglected. However, it has become increasingly obvious that biodiversity cannot be conserved without the involvement of local resident communities. While it is necessary to recognize national parks and protected areas as integral to biodiversity and ecotourism, ecotourism must also stress the importance of concerns raised by local communities about protected area management, lack of opportunities for involvement, benefits and sociocultural impacts.

It is hoped the reserve can become a 'living classroom', with programmes for grade school, high school and university students, civic groups and tourists from Costs Rica and elsewhere. The start of this will be the local high school, where the reserve will become an integral arm of the traditional school system by teaching ecology and natural history in the park itself. The research programme's findings can be incorporated directly into the teaching effort, thus making education as important as the interpretation centre, trails and rainforest. Although oriented toward local residents, the park's educational system is also a rich resource for other Costa Ricans as well as international tourists.

The interpretation programmes will aim to inspire biology-related activities at the Santa Elena High School and visiting schools as well as a deeper interaction with tropical nature by students, teachers and parents. Although the primary aim of the education programme will be to expose the local community to natural history and thus enhance biological understanding, it is also crucial to the continued survival of the reserve that the programme generate an on-going populace that understands biology. Students will be running the reserve, the town and political systems in the future and when a decision is to be made about conservation, resource management or anything else, they will have an understanding of the biological process that is behind that decision.

Tourists will also benefit from the park's education programme. It offers a high level of interpretation of its many attractions and intellectual stimulation as a result of its research. In association with the Santa Elena township the reserve is able to offer living facilities and other tourist services in a coordinated manner through its planning commissions.

The Santa Elena Ecotourism Rainforest Reserve offers a unique insight into what a community can achieve: its formula is home-grown and has required only an initial input from Youth Challenge International to assist the community in starting, although it is hoped the relationship is on-going. It has been devised to match the particular biological, political, economic and social circumstances of the Santa Elena community, it provides no formulas for others' success but possibly an example to observe. The reserve evolved in a practical and pragmatic way, partly as the community's reaction to look for strategies to counter the problems experienced by the local community. It is a practical solution that essentially relies on the local community of Santa Elena.

Today, the Santa Elena Rainforest Reserve hosts 7000 visitors and generates (US) $40 000 annually for the community. Two residents have been hired in permanent paid management positions. The curriculum of the high school has been expanded to include English, biology and hospitality courses, boosting opportunities for graduates to work as guides within the reserve. The Rainforest Reserve also contributes to the protection of the large Arenal Freshwater Catchment by acting as a 'buffer zone' of protected land adjacent to core catchment areas.

In order to understand the role ecotourism played, it is important to examine the Santa Elena project as it demonstrates how it focused the community and allowed them to find ways of creating infrastructure for tourism; to understand sectoral interests and how they inter-relate with other sectors, thereby enabling them to discover an opportunity for conservation and development to work together for them. With the local community as the focus, different sectors – government, private enterprise, conservation and non-governmental organizations, and international institutions – could then reorientate their approach to conservation through tourism.

Case study 2:
the national – 'Issues in protected area policy in Australia'

Penelope J. Figgis

AM Vice President, Australian Conservation Foundation[3]

The national estate of protected areas are areas of immense ecological, cultural and aesthetic importance; they are also the core 'resource' of the ecotourism industry. The expansion, protection and management of these lands should therefore be a core concern of the industry. Indeed, the major motivation for conservationists in becoming stakeholders in the industry was the hope that the industry would be a partner in pursuing these aims. Some current policies, for example the National Forest Policy and National Reserve System, should increase the areas under conservation management in the near future. However, will these areas remain outstanding refuges of the natural world? Philosophical and political shifts both internationally and within Australia may place protected areas under increasing strain. One of the major strains is likely to be the combined impact of protected areas being seen as primarily resources for tourism and recreation and the retreat of government from core funding. This case study briefly scopes other pressures on protected areas such as the demands for 'multiple use' parks allowing extractive industries, the demands of the 'access' lobby and the aspirations of traditional people

for title and management of parks. While supporting cooperation with indigenous people, the reassertion of the primacy of the concept of protected areas as refuges of nature conservation is argued for here, lest they become severely compromised by human demands and commercial motives.

Introduction

In a few centuries humans have transformed, to some degree, virtually every corner of the earth. Natural lands are now isolates in a sea of humanity. Historically some of these areas were set aside as refuges from expanding human development as protected areas. Nature preservation, more recently called biodiversity conservation, scenic and cultural conservation and non-damaging forms of recreation were seen as the primary goals.

However, in the late twentieth century we are facing a major dilemma regarding protected natural areas. The pressures of our massive global population, combined with ever-expanding material consumption or, in contrast, ever-expanding survival desperation, encroach relentlessly on the natural world. This crisis makes conservation of nature both a global moral imperative – our species does not have the right to obliterate the rights of other living things – and a pragmatic policy necessary for the survival and well-being of humanity. While all lands must be managed to retain their biodiversity, protected areas, national parks and reserves remain essential refuges of nature and are 'the most cost effective solution to the problem of biodiversity maintenance' (Thackway, 1996). Yet at the very time when the need for such areas to exist, and indeed expand, seems imperative, the same forces which created the need for these refuges are now claiming them as legitimate areas for commerce or 'consumption' in various forms.

Australia, is no exception. Despite its vast spaces, 200 years of European settlement have

[3] This case study reproduces a paper presented at the Conference of the Ecotourism Association of Australia, Kangaroo Island 14–17 November 1996. Penelope Figgis thanks the Conservation Councils and Trusts of NSW, WA, SA, Tasmania, Queensland and the National Parks Association of NSW and Victoria for their responses to a questionnaire on directions in protected area policy. The responses were a major source.

had a well documented devastating impact on the rich biodiversity of the continent. The 7.8% currently in protected areas plays a vital role in maintaining communities; however, it falls far short of representing all the biogeographic regions or ecosystems (Thackway, 1996). In the scientific community there is consensus that the real need is for a very substantial increase in protected areas. Yet nationally, and in virtually every state, there are major shifts to undermining the primary *nature conservation* purpose of national parks and protected areas in favour of tourism and car-based recreation and even extractive industries. At the same time, core funding from government is, in general, declining, which compounds the pressures to generate income by encouraging commercial development.

This study endeavours to give a brief overview of the major forces shaping protected area policy and the arising issues which are likely to impact on protected areas over the coming decades. The salience of this topic to ecotourism is clear. Currently protected areas are the major resource of the nature tourism industry; the future of both is closely interwoven.

Current philosophical and political influences on protected area policy

The following section explores some of the current broad philosophical and political influences which are shaping attitudes and policy directions in protected areas both in Australia and internationally.

Anthropocentrism

Globally, protected area policy is strongly influenced by what is essentially a philosophical failure. Despite several decades of effort environmentalists have failed substantially to shift the anthropocentic notion that nature has value if it meets human needs, either producing a commodity or service, to a more 'ecocentric' view. The 'ecocentric' or 'deep green' environmental philosophy, which has a strong affinity with the world-views of many indigenous people, ascribes important, non-quantifiable intrinsic, scientific, aesthetic and spiritual values to nature conservation. It has not replaced the dominant paradigm. This philosophical 'way of seeing' leads, in its mildest form, to a strong emphasis on human needs being met in parks, and in its strongest form to opposition to the preservation of natural land in protected areas as valueless 'locking up' of land.

When nature conservation is accepted it is from a 'utilitarian' viewpoint; that is, as a means to ensure future supplies for human industry or supply a service to humans in the form of recreation or a tourism product. This attitude underlies the rejection of 'wilderness' or exclusion zones in protected areas – they are of limited human use, *ipso facto* of no value. The dominance of the attitude that nature exists to serve human material needs underlies most of the issues of maintaining nature in a highly populous and consumption-driven world.

Anti-'preservation'

The prevailing model of protected areas in Australia has been the non-inhabited, minimal interference park. Two very different streams in global thinking may affect the viability of this model in the future. In much of the world sheer numbers and pressing social needs are dictating that a human exclusion, 'fences and fines' approach to maintaining nature is simply not feasible (Wells and Brandon, 1992). This has led to a gradual shift to integrate the development needs of local communities into protected area management. The 'preservationist approach' is condemned in this context as requiring 'an essentially militaristic defence strategy and will almost always heighten conflict' (Machlis and Tichnell, 1985). In the Caracas Action Plan, the major strategy document to come out of the IVth World Congress on National Parks and Protected Areas in Venezuela in 1992, the human-needs orientation is unambiguous: 'Protected areas must be managed so that local communities, the nations involved, and the world community all benefit (IUCN, Caracas Action Plan, 1992). A related aspect of this debate is the increasing emphasis on off-park conservation initiatives in the clear recognition that isolated 'islands' of biodiversity are extremely vulnerable and possibly non-viable in the long term. While the profound imperatives behind such changes are unquestionable the movement has strengthened the human centred orientation of conservation and, in the case of 'off-park' categories such as multiple use biosphere reserves, could undermine the concept of a protected area.

While Australian conditions are, in the main, very different from the developing world, the move away from the 'nature's refuge' model is having its impact. One impetus arises from the efforts to address the rights of Aboriginal people to their lands and the perceived inappropriateness of the current model (see discussion of indigenous issues below). Generally the effect of the debate has been a move for land managers to be more accommodating to neighbouring communities, largely as a response to the hostility which putting ecological need before human needs seems to engender. There is also far more reference to the need to consult and cooperate with various 'stakeholders' (Thackway, 1996). While such moves seem little more than common sense, they can also be seen as leading to a watering down of pure nature protection as each stakeholder is, at least partly, accommodated.

A quote from Ron Arnold, leader of the 'wise use movement' in the USA, encapsulates the views of a virulent anti-preservation lobby. 'Let the private sector build attractive resorts in parks . . . restore wise resource use – prudent mining, salvage logging . . . hunting, fishing, snowmobile adventures in winter.' This very different movement is also part of the big picture for the future of protected areas – its concept of the purpose of protected areas is certainly a far cry from the concept of a refuge. 'Wise use' adherents range from the industries who would like access to resources on parks, such as the logging, grazing and mining industries, and the many forces – hunters, off-road vehicle enthusiasts – who are hostile to nature-centred management, who believe that parks should be pleasure grounds for unconstrained human recreation. This thinking, which has long had its equivalents in the UK, appears to be strengthening the hand of this access lobby in Australia through informal ties and networks (see below) (Bob Burton personal communication).

Economic rationalism/the retreat of government

The 1990s have seen the ideological victory of capitalism over socialism and with it a victory of a conservative form of capitalism that argues powerfully for market-based allocation of resources, competitiveness, small government and a powerful private sector. As a result, the legitimate role of government is shrinking; banking, insurance, health, education, energy, water, transport – all are being progressively removed from public ownership and control. Government agencies are being asked increasingly to run on a business rather than public interest model. The breadth of this shift has meant that no sphere of government is seen as immune from scrutiny in terms of a role for private sector, market-based management. Protected Area Agencies have found themselves pressured to be more 'commercial', 'customer focused' and to produce more of their revenue from the services provided by parks.

A basic tenet of this philosophy is the superiority of the private sector and a belief that because it is subject to market forces, it will deliver outcomes more efficiently. Protected areas have recently come under pressure from this force with arguments being mounted for a much greater role for the private sector in national parks. The ability of the profit-driven private sector adequately to protect non-quantifiable values and long-term public interest issues such as environmental protection and social equity has been central to the debate over economic rationalism and remains a major concern for environmentalists.

Unemployment pressures

While the need to conserve biodiversity has become increasingly urgent, the political setting for convincing governments to allocate land to nature conservation has become increasingly difficult. As Australia entered the prolonged recession of the early 1990s and unemployment dominated the political agenda, the 'jobs versus environment' dichotomy worked against allocation of lands to nature. Despite some improvement in the economy in the mid-1990s, rural unemployment remains an intransigent problem and the political issue remains that governments are reluctant to take any decision which might cause unemployment. It has become increasingly necessary for conservationists to add economic benefit and employment opportunities to their arguments for nature conservation. Tourism, as a non-extractive industry, is the obvious choice. However, placing a strong emphasis on the tourism importance of protected areas strengthens the trend to see them as an economic resource, rather than an ecological refuge, and weakens the case of environmentalists against inappropriate development.

Issues in Australian protected areas policy

This section explores the impacts of some of the 'big picture' trends identified above and identifies other protected area issues specific to Australia.

Positive trends

Theoretically, Australia's protected areas should expand considerably in the near future. In the lead-up to the 1996 Federal election, the Coalition endorsed the National Reserve System goals of a 'comprehensive, adequate and representative' reserve system of 15% for all Australian ecosystems. The National Reserve System Cooperative Program (NRSCP) now has the support

of all states and territories and a major framework for the identification of priority areas has been developed called the Interim Biogeographic Regionalization for Australia (IBRA). A substantial $80 million over four years has been allocated by the Federal government. The Comprehensive Regional Assessment of Forests process, which is part of the implementation of the National Forests Policy also, aims to bring 15% of forest types into the reserve system. There are also processes under way such as the Indigenous Protected Areas (IPA) programme that may significantly add to the conservation estate through the voluntary self-declaration of Aboriginal land as a protected area (Szabo, 1996).

While these processes seem to augur well, they are still subject to the political realities of the day, which, as sketched below, suggest a far more ambiguous attitude to protected areas. There are also concerns that the national concentration on scientifically representative areas may lead to an overemphasis on the strict biodiversity 'sample' value, whereas many areas have wilderness, aesthetic and cultural values quite apart from their 'representativeness'.

Influence of conservative governments

The political setting in Australia shifted considerably to the right during the 1980s. Labour governments moved away from public interest policies and closer to the market-driven 'economic rationalist' philosophy identified above. The acceptance of economic growth as the overriding fundamental goal of government was unquestioned. The 'new' federalism of the Intergovernmental Agreement on the Environment embodied the Commonwealth government's retreat from the major pro-environment interventions of the 1980s to the more 'cooperative' state's rights approach. This trend is deepening as the conservative parties have won government nationally and in every state except New South Wales (NSW).

All conservative governments have central philosophical planks which are hostile to protected areas. The conservative parties in

Australia have traditionally been strongly pro-development and generally very favourably disposed to the mining, tourism and rural lobbies. They have a strong commitment to state's rights which will mean increased devolution of responsibility to the states who are, in the main, less inclined to strong protective measures for the environment. Conservative governments are strongly influenced by their Coalition partners, the National Party, who reflect the anti-protected area views of much of their rural constituency.

There are also general biases in the conservative ranks against those groups who are associated with non-mainstream thinking, so-called 'politically correct' ideologies like feminism, environmentalism and Aboriginal rights are out of favour with conservatives who still represent vested interests, rather than public interest. This will strongly affect access and influence in the event of protected area disputes with the advocates for nature likely to be defeated.

The current Federal Coalition government has already shown every sign of pursuing policies deeply hostile to nature conservation. Among them:

● Removal of the 'three mines' uranium policy with a current proposal for new mines in Rudall River National Park (Kintyre) and Kakadu (Jabiluka).
● The approval of the biggest tourist development in Queensland's history at Oyster Point near Cardwell with no environmental impact study (EIS) undertaken. The development will have adverse impacts on the magnificent Hinchinbrook Island National Park, the safe haven of the Hinchinbrook Passage and the nearby islands of the World Heritage Great Barrier Reef Marine Park
● The Wet Tropics World Heritage Area of North Queensland is under threat from severe funding cuts.
● Expansion of the woodchipping industry in the face of majority community support for its phase out.

● Opposition to 'single use' land tenure which translates to a belief that parks should be either 'multiple use' or used first and protected later.
● Attempted downgrading of Commonwealth powers by removal of export controls on mineral exports (which protected Fraser Island, Shoalwater and Shelburne Bays).
● Giving an effective veto to states over World Heritage nominations.

Funding issues

The entire public sector in Australia is in a state of massive change reflecting the philosophical and political trends described above. National parks and reserves, perceived largely as an unproductive sector, have always been substantially poorly funded and staffed. However, in line with the general trend to cut government spending, core funding to land management agencies is generally being even further reduced at both national and state levels. This inevitably sets up a pressure to generate funds. Conserving biodiversity does not directly generate funds; providing for people frequently does. Hence tourism fees; entry, licences, concessionaires – governments and agencies increasingly see levies as the answer to budget cuts. However, this in turn generates pressures for more concessions to tourism interests in park management.

Some examples:

● In NSW the National Parks and Wildlife Service (NPWS) has supported a major expansion in Kosciusko National Parks. Part of the development involves private apartments which can be on-sold for profit. NPWS takes a substantial premium for approval, covering infrastructure, plus a return to the service.
● In Victoria a levy on four-wheel drive vehicle registrations helps to provide funds for track maintenance but it is claimed this leads to major pressures for the Parks Authority to accommodate the lobby's demands for tracks to stay open. (Colong Foundation Bulletin, January 1996).

Private sector involvement

The ideological commitment to small government and the lack of adequate resources for management, is also fuelling a substantial push in some states for a greater role for the private sector in managing national parks. In answer to questionnaires sent out by the author (P.J.F.), Queensland, and Victoria responded most strongly that privatization was an issue. The privatization debate ranges over a wide field, from the privatization of services within national parks, such as the delivery of parks maintenance, accommodation, food transport and tour services, to a far more radical approach where the government's role would retreat to setting standards and monitoring outcomes while the private sector provided all services. The need for private commercial accommodation in parks is especially stressed (Charters *et al.*, 1996). The prevailing philosophy of such proponents is deeply anthropocentric; a human demand, tourism growth, exists, therefore it must be met. However, their arguments for commercialization of parks is couched in terms of 'protecting' the parks through better management of the 'inevitable' demands.

In response to this push in Queensland, the Environment Minister, Brain Littleproud, has issued guidelines for commercial developments in national parks, which most observers see as preceding a major wave of proposals. 'Everyone should have the right to experience the wonders of Queensland's National Parks, but not everyone is able to "rough it" (Press Release, 30 June 1996). The Department of Environment is being encouraged to solicit commercial development inside national parks as a means of generating revenue to pay for improved management. Proposals have been received for developments on Fraser Island and inside Carnarvon National Park with Wallaman Falls, the highest falls in Australia, being suggested as an ideal site.

Nature tourism

It is ironic that while humanity has relentlessly decimated wildlife and wildlands we have simultaneously grown to value them more highly. Nature tourism is a growing sector of a huge global industry. Most of Australia's $26.7 billion tourism industry is based on protected areas. This creates the ultimate two-edged sword. On the one hand, it creates a powerful economic argument for the dedication and proper management of protected areas for their value as a 'tourism product'. On the other, it creates substantial pressures for tourism-centred management of protected areas where the interests of tourism prevail over nature conservation (Figgis, 1994).

The approach of this industry will be a central determinant of protected area policy. From a conservationist's viewpoint there are some worrying trends. A recent publication of the Ecotourism Association of Australia, the *Australian Ecotourism Guide*, cites some case studies of 'ecotourism'. Two of the studies are of Kingfisher Bay Resort on Fraser Island and the Kuranda Skyrail nears Cairns. The first is a major resort, catering for over 1000 staff and guests in a world heritage area built on a previously pristine site. The Skyrail is a major engineering work, a 7.5 km cableway necessitating some 70 towers through a World Heritage rainforest and the Barron Gorge National Park. The publication states, 'Skyrail is ecotourism at its model best.'

This trend for tourism developments in protected areas is one of the major threats identified by environmental groups around Australia in responses to the author. That such developments are aggressively promoted by their supporters as 'models' of good ecotourism and in the interests of good management ignores the fact that commercial development and the assumption that demand must be met will inevitably compromise ecological integrity. It completely distorts the idea of ecotourism as tourism that supports nature conservation. Proponents ignore the inevitable strengthening of the idea of parks as 'human playgrounds' which will follow the penetration of human commerce.

The momentum is directly related to the poor funding of many protected area agencies. Tourism facilities can generate funds and many land agencies are actively encouraging further use. Some examples:

- The Victoria Parks Service proposed major commercial development in Wilson's Promontory National Park, including a lodge for 150 people, a backpacker hostel and commercial lodges along walking tracks. While the hotel was dropped after massive public protest, the other developments are going ahead.
- A fanciful tunnel with a train to a viewing tower above a seal colony was seriously proposed as a 60 million dollar 'ecotourism' development for the Nobbies area of Phillip Island, Victoria. A 13 million dollar first stage has been approved.
- In Queensland in 1996 the Environment Minister issued guidelines for commercial developments in national parks which most observers see as preceding a major wave of proposals. The Department of Environment is being encouraged to solicit commercial development inside national parks as a means of generating revenue to pay for 'improved management'. Proposals have been received for developments on Fraser Island and inside Carnarvon National Park with Wallaman Falls, the highest falls in Australia being suggested as an ideal site. (Queensland Conservation Council)
- In NSW in the Warrumbungle National Park some nine development sites dispersed over 40 square kilometres are proposed to cater for overnight camping and cabins, despite a town, Coonabarabran, existing nearby. The accommodation will be run by private enterprise but will still generate funds for the service. In NSW, the Parks Service has supported a major 1000-bed expansion in Kosciusko National Parks to expand the existing ski resort in the Perisher Valley. Part of the development involves substantial commercial retail space and private apartments which can be on-sold for profit. Proposals also exist for Blue Cow Guthega and Smiggins Hole. NPWS will take a substantial premium for approval, covering infrastructure, plus a return to the service.

- The Tasmanian Parks Service has been promoting a 'wilderness development' site at Pumphouse Point in Lake St Clair National Park.
- In Victoria 285 ha of the Alpine National Park at Falls Creek has been excised from the park for a downhill ski run and tourist development. The land includes important areas of habitat for the endangered Mountain Pygmy possum (burramys). The decision was taken without any consultation with environment interests.

A second issue arises from the increasing dependence of parks authorities on tourism charges to meet budget shortfalls. There remains widespread concern in the environment movement that this creates an inexorable dynamic towards tourism-centred management (Figgis, 1994). Some current examples:

- The dramatic decision of the Commonwealth government in 1996 to raise the Great Barrier Reef tourism tax, the Environment Management Charge, from $1 to $6 immediately brought calls for greater representation of tourism interests in management.
- In mid-1996, work commenced in the Otway National Park in Victoria on an extension to the Great Ocean Walk which will involve cutting of tracks through pristine coastal environments. No prior consultation was conducted with conservation groups.
- In Western Australia the strict nature reserve status of Two Peoples Bay is being altered to allow for a tourism centre despite serious scientific concerns over impacts on the rare species found in the reserve.

'Multiple use' parks/extractive industry push

In Australia's federal system there are around sixty categories of protected areas (Pittock, 1996). Many of these categories do allow for some extractive use but the majority of Australia's national parks are IUCN categories I–III, which preclude mining, grazing and other extractive uses. However, as identified above, the global trend towards 'multiple use' is strengthening. 'Multiple use' is a concept which has been pushed for many years by those opposed to 'preservation'. It contends that land can be adequately conserved for ecological values while supporting other land uses. The Australian mining lobby has been particularly concerned that national parks 'sterilize' their resources and have argued hard for a regime which allows for exploration and mining. The concept is also supported by landowners who wish to use parks for seasonal or drought grazing and by many interests who object to, or do not share an ecocentric viewpoint. The multiple use approach has been explicitly endorsed by the Howard government with the Minister for Resources and Energy, Warwick Parer, telling a business conference 'We will reverse the trend to single land use which has led to unbalanced and ill-considered decisions which have unnecessarily constrained access to areas for exploration and development' (*AAP transcript, 3rd* July 1996). Such an approach could have massive ramifications on both the ecological and aesthetic integrity of our protected areas.

Some current manifestations of this trend:

- The most prominent example is the possibility that the uranium mine at Jabiluka, on a lease within Kakadu National Park, will go ahead under the Coalition's pro-uranium mining policy. While not technically on park land it will clearly affect park values.
- There are current proposals to degazette a 26 000 core area of Yumburrah National Park, an important remnant of the once extensive mallee in South Australia, to allow gold and uranium mining. The area is both remote and has high wilderness values.
- In Tasmania two separate acts have given the mining and logging interests virtual resource security. The industries must be compensated if the land is subsequently used for new reserves, making such moves highly unlikely.

- In Western Australia, the government has legislated to excise 386 ha of D'Entrecasteaux National Park to allow sand mining beside Lake Jasper. The park, in WA's southwest, contains magnificent coastal wetlands and is of immense cultural significance to Aboriginal people. This sets an precedent for the 21 other WA parks where exploration leases have been granted and the 100 conservation reserves where mining can occur at the discretion of the Minister.
- Vital remnants of Box and Ironbark forests in Victoria are being lost to gold mining. There are 470 active leases in these areas which conservationists have argued are in urgent need of protection.
- Rutile mining is proposed for the last undisturbed high dune on North Stradbroke Island, part of Queensland's Great Sandy Region. The island has already suffered immense damage from sand mining. This mining operation will clear over 50 ha of native vegetation and threaten Ibis Lagoon, one of the last undamaged perched freshwater lakes.

Access lobby

Over the past twenty years Australia has seen an increasingly vociferous public access lobby develop. The lobby is a loose amalgam of four-wheel drive enthusiasts, horse riders and hunters; many are from rural communities. Their philosophy is an acute form of the anthropocentricism outlined earlier. Their principal aims appear to be the maintenance of public access by road and track to all public lands and the prevention of wilderness declarations, as they claim a democratic 'right' to access every part of public land. The lobby constantly argue that existing parks are poorly managed. According to this lobby national parks are refuges for every enemy of rural Australia – feral animals, especially pasture-consuming kangaroos, and predators, foxes and dingoes, as well as weeds and wild fires. The massive fires which consumed New South Wales in January of 1994 concentrated this antipathy to parks and brought great pressure on parks services to attend to management and accommodate such concerns (NPWS, 1995).

While NSW has resisted their call for no new parks or wilderness areas and in fact made substantial new declarations, there has been considerable accommodation of the access lobby in return (National Parks Association, NSW):

- In NSW while honouring some wilderness promises the Carr government has seen fit to appease this group with upgrades or new tracks, including the Barraba Track through Kaputar National Park which was condemned as having 'serious and detrimental effects on the environment' by Carr when Minister for the Environment in the 1980s.
- The Public Land Users Alliance, a strongly anti-wilderness four-wheel drive group, has claimed that the effort to stop areas being fully protected is 'full on, this is war now' (Public Land Users Alliance, 1996).
- In Tasmania the fragile Cental Plateau sub-alpine areas, despite being in the World Heritage area, are substantially degraded by horse riding and four-wheel drive access.

Indigenous issues

The simple reality that Europeans did not settle an empty land but one inhabited by the indigenous people of Australia for tens of thousands of years, has been finally recognized in the Native Title Act. The ramifications for protected areas are likely to be one of the biggest issues to be worked out over the coming decades. An estimated 14% of Australia is currently owned by Aboriginal people, significantly over twice the areas currently in protected areas (Boden and Breckwoldt, 1995). Much of this land is in areas less modified by European settlement and therefore retaining high conservation value. Any truly comprehensive reserve system would need to include components of these lands. The lands under indigenous control could substantially increase under Native Title as many claims have been lodged over national parks, though none

has yet been granted. However, some states have voluntarily restored title to Aboriginal people and instituted joint management. There is considerable potential for such initiatives to be extended, particularly in areas of Australia where land claims are less likely to be granted.

However, complex issues arise from the environment movement's commitment to nature conservation and their commitment to social justice and recognition of Aboriginal rights. 'Wilderness' and 'national parks' are viewed with some hostility as European concepts which have either ignored Aboriginal rights or been used to usurp them. As a result, new forms other than traditional protected areas are being mooted as the way forward in reconciling the needs. Cooperative land use agreements or Regional Agreements are seen as a way for negotiating conservation agreements on Aboriginal land. Under the NRSCP, funds have been allocated to develop a Indigenous Protected Area Program to promote cooperative agreements with indigenous owners. However, some tension exists over the aspirations of many Aboriginal people to reclaim existing protected areas and generate an economic base from their lands. In a statement prepared at an Australian Nature Conservation Agency (ANCA) workshop in Alice Springs in 1994 indigenous delegates made quite clear that 'in any conservation partnership . . . indigenous cultural objectives . . . have priority over environmental issues'. The delegates also asserted their right to 'develop economic benefit from all Aboriginal and Torres Strait Islander lands (ANCA, 1995).

Widening conservation agenda

In the 1970s and 1980s while a few groups campaigned on essentially urban issues, the predominant issue of the Australian environment movement was nature conservation. The political demand was comparatively simple – conservationists campaigned *against* development and *for* the declaration of protected area status over the land. This was the essence of most of the great battles – the Little Desert, the

Colong Caves, Bungonia Gorge, the Franklin, the Great Barrier Reef, Fraser Island, the Daintree, Kakadu etc. However, in the 1990s the conservation agenda has exploded. Following the logic of the ecologically sustainable development, environmentalists' energies are now cast over every aspect of the environment – water, land use, contaminants, urban planning, transport etc. While the issues have proliferated, so have the processes. To a very real degree modern environmentalists are victims of their own success. For twenty years we have argued for public participation in transparent decision making processes – now we have literally thousands of processes requiring public input at any one time. For a still financially limited movement this effort is debilitating and stretches every individual, paid and unpaid, to the limit. The consequence for protected area policy is that there are less people within the movement focusing on policy shifts and threats than perhaps in the past and less resources to mount a strong defence of the integrity of the system.

Conclusion

Having pushed nature to the wall globally, hungry eyes are on what little remains. The fundamental problem of pervasive anthropocentrism remains; there is little if any recognition that other species than our own have rights, that they did not evolve purely to serve our needs. The emerging issues identified here make for a gloomy prognosis despite the general commitment to an enhanced National Reserve System. The Australian ecotourism industry has a choice: it can either decide to be part of the forces who are gathering to blur the integrity of the concept of a protected area, to increase commercialism in the small percentage of Australia set aside, or it can be part of the forces defending these precious areas. The industry can either regard protected areas as a resource for its use, to be shaped to the needs of the industry, or can regard its use of such areas as an immense privilege, and it should be the industry which adapts itself to the constraints necessary to protect these areas in perpetuity.

8

Marketing ecotourism: meeting and shaping expectations and demands

This chapter seeks to explore the relationship between ecotourism and marketing, both conceptually and practically. It examines the structure and nature of the tourism industry, and the implications of ecotourism's world-wide growth. Fundamental to understanding and evaluating the connection between ecotourism and marketing is the issue of supply- versus demand-driven marketing which we will examine in depth in moving towards an analysis of the strengths, weaknesses, opportunities and threats to ecotourism.

Pivotal to understanding the marketing relationship to ecotourism are the implications for protected areas, conservation and local communities. Ecotourism marketing has been surrounded by much confusion and controversy as it attempts to take into account the dual objectives of protected areas and local communities on the one hand and those of the tourism industry on the other. The marketing of tourism products is generally still associated by many people with a commercial enterprise selling the maximum level of product for short-term profit. However, in the 1990s social marketing and ecological marketing are now being acknowledged as important ele-

ments of a more holistic marketing perspective. These perspectives significantly challenge the somewhat archaic belief that all marketing must be demand-led (*cf.* Middleton, 1998).

Ecotourism's place in the tourism industry

Any definition or range of definitions of ecotourism must have relevance to its practical implementation, its working context – the tourism industry. What then is this thing called the 'tourism industry' and what are its characteristics? Stear *et al.* provide us with an initial definition:

> [a] collection of all collaborating firms and organizations which perform specific activities directed at satisfying leisure, pleasure and recreational needs. (1988: 1)

An industry can be considered a group of sellers of close substitute outputs who supply to a common group of buyers.

Case study Kruger National Park, South Africa

Kruger National Park is one of the top ten National Parks in the world and provides a destination site and services for tourists interested in the park's remarkable ecosystem, comprising more than 2000 different forms of plant life, 146 different types of mammals, more than 490 species of birds, 114 species of reptiles and 49 types of fish, and innumerable other forms of life (Middleton, 1998: 202). This park is of interest to a specific type of tourist that is catered for by a group of travel agents that will generally specialize in the area of nature-based tourism.

Case study Cradle Mountain Huts, South-Western Tasmania National Park, Australia

Cradle Mountain Huts provides accommodation for hikers as they trek the Cradle Mountain Track. Individual hikers however utilize products not only from the accommodation sector, but air and coach travel from the carrier sector, natural areas from the attractions sector, rangers and tour guides from the tour operator sector and so on. But it is these different products that are packaged together to form an ecotourism product.

The tourism industry does not produce close substitute products, as does the manufacturing industry, but it is comprised of sectors, each of which produces closely substitutable products. The tourism industry sectors include: accommodation, attractions, carrier, coordination, promotion and distribution, tour operators and wholesalers and miscellaneous groups (Stear *et al.*, 1988). Conceptualizing ecotourism as an amalgam of products incorporating a particular *style* of tourism, allows its relationship with the tourism industry to be understood. In this way ecotourism is not an industry per se but it does draw from products produced by the many sectors of the tourism industry.

Marketing ecotourism: supplying demand or demanding supply?

In order to gain an understanding of the market of ecotourism, it is important to examine exactly what marketing is. Marketing is neither a precise science nor is it an art but is chiefly 'concerned with research which is the foundation for organized planning'. It is primarily 'concerned with production and pricing and promotion and not least profits' (Jefferson and Lickorish, 1988: 27). Marketing is a component in a system of business activities: 'Designed to plan, price, promote and distribute want – satisfying products, services and ideas for the benefit of the target market – present and potential household consumers or industrial users, to achieve the organization's objectives' (Stanton *et al.*, 1992: 6).

The term 'organization's objectives' is critical here, as it leads us to the heart of the marketing and ecotourism debate. What should the primary objective of an ecotourism operator be – sustaining the environment of profitability? Can the two objectives be pursued successfully and simultaneously?

The tourism industry has been swift to capitalize on new forms of tourism and in some cases the principles and philosophy of ecotourism we have discussed have been lost in the rush to profit. Naturally, both private enterprise and governments are supportive of the tourism industry because of its present and potential economic benefits in the form of individual profit for firms which accrue to nation states in the form of Gross National Product (GNP).

There are numerous striking examples of opportunistic market responses to ecotourism.

The Environmental Management Industry Association of Australia (EMIAA) 1994 International Conference on Environmental Management and Technology for a Sustainable Tourism Industry brochure, called on professionals, scientists and academics world-wide to submit and present papers at its conference titled 'Tourism Ecodollars'. In an attempt to entice potential delegates to attend, the EMIAA brochure states: 'Tourism Ecodollars '94 will give you more ground-breaking, money-making insights into tourism towards 2000 than you could obtain from any other source.'

Another example includes Valentine's (1991a) account of his attendance at the 'Ecotourism and Small Business in the Pacific' conference held in Pohnpei, in the Federated States of Micronesia and staged by the United States Department of Commerce, Economic Development Administration (EDA):

> There were more bankers speaking than ecologists: [as] there were more developers . . . architects . . . governors . . . administrators . . . and . . . bureaucrats than ecologists.

> Despite the encouraging prospect of bankers speaking about 'ecotourism' in glowing terms, I came away with a distinct impression that there is an urgent need to put the ecology back into ecotourism. (1991a: 2)

Marketing ecotourism

Traditionally marketing can be defined as 'the development of products/services which are consistent with client needs, pricing, promoting, and distributing these products/services effectively' (National Park Service, 1984: 3). As indicated in the above definition, marketing is based on the 'four Ps' of product, place, price and promotion, with the emphasis on attracting, maintaining and expanding a customer base.

Theoretically, markets are places where buyers and sellers meet to engage in exchange. In the process of exchange prices are determined and quantities produced and this process hinges on the amount of demand for a particular product. Economists generally view demand as the desire and ability to consume certain quantities of goods at various prices over a certain period of time. The law of demand states that the quantity of a good or service is negatively related to its price. In other words, if everything is held constant consumers will purchase more of a good or service at a lower price than at a higher price. Tourism is no different in this respect. Tourism marketing is demand-led, that is to say if there is a demand for a certain product or service by consumers, it will be supplied and marketed by profit-maximizing organizations. This demand orientation determines that the 'requirements of the tourists are given highest priority and the destination area seeks to provide services to meet those requirements' (Ashworth and Goodall, 1990: 227). Examples of this can be seen in sectors such as transport and accommodation where new services are provided as a result of increased tourism demand for a destination. In Costa Rica a special bus service has been provided from San José to the now internationally renowned Monteverde Cloud Forest Preserve (see Chapter 7). However, because of its prohibitive price, it is used exclusively by tourists. The local bus service is a somewhat poorer and longer service in comparison.

Supply on the other hand refers to what firms are actually willing and able to produce and offer for sale at various prices over a period of time. The law of supply states that the quantity supplied of a good or service is usually a positive function of price. With all else held constant, suppliers usually will supply less of a good or service at a lower price. As we shall see, with the limited number of ecotourism 'destinations' prices will play an important role in controlling demand.

Supply-driven tourism places considerations other than profit at the centre of tourism products. Considerations such as the social impact of the tourism product on destination sites, the needs and wants of destination communities and the natural resource management of the supplier country and destination sites becomes central. The supply side nature of ecotourism means that the 'impact on the local natural resource base is more easily controlled than is the case with demand side tourism ... dangers of overload and cultural submersion and tourists exceeding biological carrying capacities may be thus minimized' (Lillywhite and Lillywhite, 1990: 92). This is imperative for ecotourism. To establish the best methods for marketing an ecotourism destination it is important to stress the necessity of marketing to be a holistic enterprise, working with community groups, indigenous and other private voluntary organization programmes.

Case study   Catlins Wildlife Trackers, South Dunedin, New Zealand: alternative response to increasing visitor demand

Catlin's Wildlife Trackers is a small-scale tour operation, offering two to three day in-depth guided tours of the Catlins area. The mission statement for the venture covers three areas for the operators:

● Personal – 'We see this venture as an opportunity to provide us as a family, with an income in an environment and doing activities that we enjoy, and allowing personal growth by mixing and sharing with others'

● For others – 'We wish to offer a recreational and educational service to people, particularly those interested in active involvement with the natural, aesthetic, historic and human environment of the south-east coast and Catlins Area'; and

● Conservation – 'We wish to highlight and share environmental values and to make a positive contribution to the protection of those values'.

The quality of the experience is assessed by the response from visitors who take up the tour. The experience itself is unique, with key aspects of the operation illustrating this fact. Management relies on home-grown and home-made foods, produced with only organic pesticides, rain water is collected on the roof of the 'home-stay' facility, solar heating panels supply hot water, all organic matter is recycled and, when necessary, local produce is used as much as possible.

Visitors themselves are actively encouraged to collect litter seen during day excursions, weed certain areas (under the direction of the guide), count bird numbers and record sightings – small, but significant contributions to the improvement and sustainability of the natural environment.

In 1991 visitation rates were relatively small, at 100 visitors. In 1994, this number had increased to 274. Although this rise had no visible and discernible effects on the environment, management needed to consider an alternative strategy in order to prevent increased demand from having detrimental effects on the physical environment. Since the quality of experience is not determined by rates of visitation, but by feedback from participants, the operators chose to offer a three-day excursion. Originally, all tours offered were on a two-day basis. The introduction of three-day tours provided potential consumers with an alternative, and has thus far been successful at limiting numbers based on supply.

Source: Mary Sutherland, Catlins Wildlife Trackers, South Dunedin, NZ: British Airways Tourism for Tomorrow Awards 1995

Ecological and social marketing

Ecological marketing differs from traditional marketing and relates very strongly to the marketing of ecotourism as it involves the marketing of products and services with positive ecological outcomes to environmentally concerned consumers. It would be naive to suggest that those organizations practising ecological marketing are not motivated by making a profit, but this is not their sole measure of success. Quantifiable and unquantifiable outcomes are equally pursued, such as long-term environmental protection and customer satisfaction. Profit determines the level of a product's viability, but is not the only measure of success.

It has been suggested that, for ecological marketing, 'the relationship between demand and supply' is the prime issue (Henion and Kinnear, 1976: 1). Ecological marketing questions the role of demand stimulation: if the product is environmentally harmful, demand stimulation is strongly discouraged (Henion and Kinnear, 1976). This is of fundamental importance to ecotourism: as a result of ecotourism growing at a much faster rate than mass tourism, more and more members of the travelling public are opting out of the traditional 'lie around the pool' holiday and are instead choosing a more experiential ecotourism product and 'These people are going to create a demand and this demand is going to be met as usual by supply' (Richardson, 1991: 245). The danger is that supply may be met, not by the small, environmentally concerned operators, but by mass tourism operators with little understanding, or concern about the environment.

Related to ecotourism and ecological marketing is social marketing. Social marketing is defined generally as the design, implementation and control of programmes which are able to influence the acceptability of social ideas and involving considerations of product planning, pricing, communication and market research (*cf.* Kotler and Andreasen, 1991). Put simply, it involves the application of marketing ideas and principles to promote a social cause, that is, to activities and ideas that have outcomes beyond simply the satisfaction of individual desires. However, social marketing in its strictest sense differs from ecotourism and ecological marketing in that it does not ordinarily have a monetary profit associated with it (Henion, 1975).

With these dimensions in mind, we would like to suggest a definition of ecotourism marketing:

The development of ecologically sustainable tourism products and the pricing, promotion and distribution of these products, so impact on the physical and cultural environments is minimized, while maintaining some level of profit commensurate with these objectives.

The 'greening' market

There is no doubt that the tourism marketplace is becoming 'greener'. Increasing concern for the environment and conservation issues is evidenced by the growing number of environmental organizations such as Greenpeace and the World Wildlife Fund for Nature (WWF). Indeed, it has been estimated that 85% of the industrialized world's citizens believe that the environment is the number one public issue (Wight, 1993).

With this in mind, it is becoming increasingly difficult to dismiss the 'greening' of the marketplace as a fad. With the increasing range and proliferation of new products in most markets, consumers are becoming more discerning about what they want and they are far more independent as well as curious about what is on offer to them. According to Jon Hutchinson, the Australian Tourism Commission's managing director, this is due to a backlash against the 1980s when 'people bought regardless of quality and regardless of standards. People are more interested in gaining value from what they do then in gathering status symbols. There seems to be a psychological change in tourists' (Collins, 1993: 7).

Ecotourism is very much in the growth stage of its business cycle and its popularity will continue to increase as 'issues associated with urban congestion and crowding, atmospheric pollution, increased leisure time, more flexible work options, work related stress and concern for the environment continue to develop' (Carter and Moore, 1991: 141). Not only are people increasingly receiving messages through the media about the fragility of our environment, but also about its beauty and uniqueness and the importance of keeping areas as pristine and unspoilt as possible for now and for generations to come.

The incorporation of environmental principles and responsible behaviour codes in developing sustainable ecotourism establishments and other ecotourism ventures is indicative of an increasing consumer challenge to traditional ethics, in a search for new alternatives to traditional tourism activity (Wight, 1993). As we have seen in Chapter 3, codes of practice have emerged to integrate the concepts of sustainability and stewardship for appropriate behaviour relative to site visitation. These, however, are most often in the form of 'Codes of Ethics' which concentrate on the activities of the consumer/ecotourist, rather than the operators themselves (Wight, 1993).

Marketing by ecotourism operators based on generating maximum demand for short-term profitability is defeatist. By exceeding the deemed carrying capacity of the venue, failing to reconcile facility management strategies with those of the adjacent natural environment, or attracting a clientele with little regard for the preservation and conservation of the environment, management risks degrading the resource on which visitation is founded. For many ecotourism operators, particularly those with a fixed asset (such as accommodation establishments) there is incentive to plan, develop and operate their business with ethical consideration for not only their venture, but for the surrounding areas which are subject to impacts from ecotourists. High capital investment in facilities and its associated risk is an incentive to provide a quality experience for prospective visitors, translated into long-term cash flow and profitability based on heightened satisfaction (Middleton, 1989).

Given the growth and changing nature of ecotourism, it would appear that in order to market successfully operators will have to refocus their approaches to planning and communication strategies. That is, success cannot be measured by the number of people who visit the operation, but consideration must be given as to the customers' levels of satisfaction and their likelihood of returning. The total experience, including the emotional wants of the guests, must be considered: not just their functional requirements. Methods to do this often take the form of feedback from clients through surveys and questionnaires or just by talking to them, which can give some indication as to the emotional benefits they gained from the experience.

Sustainability is a critical element of managing all aspects of the ecotourism venture. It is derived not only from repeat patronage, but preservation of the physical and social environments of the region utilized on which education and interpretation of the environment are dependent. Just as feedback from ecotourists themselves is essential in determining the success of the business (in terms other than monetary), impacts of the business venture itself must be ascertained. This is frequently carried out as an environmental impact assessment in the initial phases of development which provides a 'snapshot' of likely environmental effects and thus the planning of management regimes created to combat them.

Best practice (as discussed in Chapter 3) goes beyond appreciation of the natural environment and its associated flora, fauna, geography and ecology to encompass an understanding of social activities, economic impacts on the facilities and region and spatial expression of community values. This may be achieved through a marketing audit and an associated statement of strengths, weaknesses, opportunities and threats (SWOT). A marketing audit of relevant internal and external environments that potentially affect business is the first step toward making marketing efforts sustainable for ecotourism organizations.

The SWOT is an effective way to analyse the current status of ecotourism marketing and project the future threats and opportunities likely to impact the ecotourism suppliers and managers and ecotourists themselves. We will now discuss the product, pricing, promotion and distribution issues and the role they play in shaping consumer expectations and demands. It will be presented as a SWOT analysis and develop into a discussion of marketing issues as they relate to management and suggest ways to capitalize from existing trends and opportunities.

Strengths in marketing ecotourism

Effective market segmentation is a key to defining an appropriate user group for ecotourism. To market a genuine ecotourism venture, it is important to ensure the validity and legitimacy of the experience. Obtaining accurate statistics and a demographic and psychographic profile may go some way to doing this, by aligning perceived user wants with the product/service produced (see Chapter 9). Thus, promotion of the operation can utilize presently existing data on likely user groups and align this with the orientation of the organization, removing some uncertainty from the need to match consumer with producer.

Ecotourism is based on visitation and appreciation of the natural attributes of a region. Although this dictates a degree of stewardship in order to preserve the resource, it provides a low cost attraction on which ecotourism products may be developed and moulded. As a marketeer of a potential product/service, the natural attributes of the area are important to consider, including the geography, geology and the flora and fauna. The unique and varied nature of many protected natural areas provides an excellent basis for development of specialized services focusing on a limited geographic zone, which can be translated to an appropriate advertising campaign and areas for sustainable competitive advantage.

Ecotourists are very discerning and take time to educate themselves about a destination prior to departure. Therefore an active knowledge

base is a major factor in the tourist's decision making process. There are strong correlations between involvement and information sourcing, and receptivity to promotional stimuli. This means that careful market research into the form of advertising most likely to attract the consumer by heightened involvement is liable to have a profound effect in achieving response, and therefore producing a decision based on the characteristics of the target market.

Threats in marketing ecotourism

In the past few years, ecotourism has become a marketing buzzword and has been used to sell any number of products, the 'eco' tag no real indication of the quality of the product on offer. There has been a substantial increase in the quantity of products in this vein, a multitude of references abound to the 'ecotour', 'ecosafari' and 'ecotravel'. One reason for the increasing proliferation of the 'ecotourism' label is because of the general lack of understanding as to what ecotourism is. Some of the products being marketed are totally unrelated to ecotourism, yet it is this label which is being used to sell them. As a result many of the problems or negative trends which make ecotourism unsustainable relate to the fact that 'principles fundamental to ecotourism are not being incorporated into the conception, planning, design, development, operation or marketing of the product' (Wight, 1993). Inappropriate developments are taking place in sensitive locations and many private operators and sometimes even government agencies are latching on to the short-term economic benefits of ecotourism 'without giving due regard to the underlying principles of ecotourism' (Wight, 1993: 55). The Ecotourism Society summed up the problem by warning customers of dubious claims of eager travel marketeers who exploit the trend towards integrating environmental values into holiday choices, offering the general public a cafeteria style of holiday to an exotic location; you can choose from prepackaged holidays just like most other commercial products; they are selling the experience the same way as most commercial products.

Demand factors have been primarily focused on by ecotourism suppliers – either the government or industry – and they seem to be particularly interested in developing supply in response to the demand-driven market (Wight, 1993). As with other tourism segments, 'demand information is viewed as enabling greater numbers of visitors to be attracted,' as well as enabling more effective marketing (Wight, 1993: 56). However, this orientation is not compatible with ecotourism and is largely due to general confusion about what ecotourism actually is, due in large part to ecotourism's 'varying mix of so many different activities and experiences' (Wight, 1993: 57).

Rather than defining ecotourism in terms of products, it is more valuable to recognize that within ecotourism there are a number of experiences which may be supplied and demanded (Wight, 1993). These may vary according to the following supply and demand factors:

Supply factors
- the nature and resilience of the resource;
- the cultural or local community preferences;
- the types of accommodation, facilities and programmes (Wight, 1993).

Demand factors
- the types of activities and experiences encountered;
- degree of interest in natural or cultural resources;
- the degree of physical effort (Wight, 1993).

Negative consumer opinion may result from a product offering that does not satisfy their needs and expectations and simultaneously assumes the 'cover' of environmental responsibility. Additionally, an unethical operator may exceed carrying capacities to bolster revenue through attracting increasing numbers of consumers at a reduced price. Accreditation within the industry may go some way towards reducing instances of this scenario.

Opportunities in marketing ecotourism

There are numerous opportunities available to marketeers of ecotourism products/services that allow the goals of sustainability and profitability to be met simultaneously.

The proliferation of interest groups, particularly nature-based organizations, provides an opportunity for direct marketing. Targeting specific age groups and nature-based groups such as adventure seekers, educational institutions, bushwalkers, canyoners and scientific groups is an extremely effective method of attracting users with an ecocentric orientation. Advertising in publications accessed by these groups, directly mailing promotional material to such organizations and cause-related marketing are methods of utilizing the communication channels of most benefit to the ecotourism operator. Remember, 'ecotourism should not be geared towards the masses, but smaller groups of discerning visitors who will pay more for an authentic value-for-money experience' (Kerr, 1991: 250).

Developing an image of a destination, or an image of the experience, is crucial in maximizing involvement and influencing the decision making behaviour of the intended audience (Boele, 1993). The way in which people interact with a particular physical setting is predisposed by the existence of images by which the environment is organized (Ittlesen *et al.*, 1974). A study in 1994 examined the relationship between a traveller's motivation to visit a destination and the strength of image assigned to that place, finding that high motivation with poor image ratings contributed to the most unsatisfactory experience. However, high motivation and high image respondents were most likely to repeat their visit. Therefore the creation of a strong image that is a realistic reflection of the product is extremely beneficial.

In order to ensure the sustainability of the venture, and the area on which ecotourism is based, the managerial philosophy adopted should be holistic. Ecotourism operators aligning their managerial plans with those existing and carried out by reserve/protected area/

wilderness area management is an example. The recognition of the similarities that exist between the impacts that tourism generates and those produced through recreational use of specific environments facilitates a transfer of managerial strategies which mitigate the effects that visitors may have on any facility or surrounding region (Mercer, 1995). This can only result in an improvement in the product itself, possible cost advantages, and the opportunity to promote the nature of this strategy to entice 'hard core' ecotourists.

The utilization of an Ecotourism Opportunity Spectrum (similar to the Recreation Opportunity Spectrum discussed in Chapter 4) presents a long-term opportunity to further segment the ecotourism market based on the degree of authenticity of the ecotourism experience desired by the potential client.

The pattern of growth in ecotourism markets is both a challenge and an opportunity. The opportunity involves 'understanding and responding to market needs, preferences and expectations: the challenge is in keeping foremost the supply-oriented management perspective' (Wight, 1993: 62). Therefore matching the markets to products (supply), 'both with respect to type and location is imperative ... otherwise resource capability can become secondary to actual or perceived market demand' (Wight, 1993: 63).

Weaknesses in marketing ecotourism

Ecotourism marketing, as a relatively new form of promoting nature-based activity, displays a range of developmental weaknesses.

Ecotourism product marketing can be significantly improved through increasing analysis and study of carrying capacities and host communities prior to operation establishment; improved education and interpretive material; and a greater focus on providing a quality experience by value-added attributes to the product. Limitations on supply can only be beneficial in assisting this aim, by emphasizing quality over quantity: 'All organizations in nature tourism should emphasize quality product, rather than quantity, to keep the numbers of visitors at a manageable level to protect the environment' (Kerr, 1991: 252).

In a supply-led industry, carrying capacities must first be determined and then marketing strategies decided on, so these levels are reached, but not exceeded. This level must be developed in conjunction with local communities, as the socially responsible and environmentally viable goals of ecotourism 'cannot be fostered without a dialogue constructed and controlled along indigenous needs and in indigenous terms' (Craik, 1991: 80).

As we have seen in Chapter 5, education and interpretive material is a critical element of the ecotourism product. Ecotourists express a strong desire to learn about nature on ecotours. An effective way to satisfy this desire to learn is through the use of interpretation. Unfortunately, a satisfactory level of interpretive material is rarely provided for participants. As a result, marketeers miss out on being able to emphasize one of the key factors differentiating ecotourism from mass tourism – the educative component – and their marketing activities lose much of their appeal.

A high quality educative experience in limited supply does, by marketing standards, imply a high price. Price in marketing can be defined as the cost that the buyer must accept in order to obtain the product and includes money costs, opportunity costs, energy costs and psychic costs (*cf.* Kotler and Armstrong, 1993). The main issue, then, is to formulate a price so that ecotourism remains supply-rather than demand-driven.

There are three primary ways for ecotourism to grow and remain profitable:

- increasing the size of groups on an ecotour;
- the establishment of more ecotourism destinations;
- charging higher prices (Merschen, 1992).

The first two options impact negatively on the environment and host communities, as well as being demand-rather than supply-driven. However, price manipulation is an effective means of decreasing demand to a level that does not exceed the carrying capacity of a region. Increasing prices is not necessarily negative as 'consumers may impute high quality to a high-priced product and low quality to a low priced product' (Henion, 1975: 233), and the fact that ecotourism is a prestigious product can be emphasized in marketing activities.

If demand is still greater than supply after prices have been increased, other non-price measures, such as requiring consumers to attend pre-trip lectures, would further limit demand. Another system which could be used is 'the ballot system' whereby names are either drawn out of a hat or potential visitors placed on a waiting list. This system is currently working effectively at a number of national parks in the United States.

If prices are to be increased, ecotour operators should donate some of this additional revenue to environmental causes or social causes, such as the improvement of host community living conditions. Drawing the consumer's attention to this strategy would also benefit the operator as tourists travelling with ecotour operators appear to be 'especially satisfied that a certain percentage of their tour cost is being donated to conservation' (Boo, 1990: 41). This already occurs in Costa Rica, where money donated by tour operators is put back into rainforest preservation programmes (Masson, 1991).

Ecotourism marketing can also be improved significantly in the area of promotion. Promotion is the communication persuasion strategy and tactics that will make the product more familiar, acceptable and even desirable to the audience (Kotler and Armstrong, 1993). Central promotional issues that need to be addressed by ecotourism operators are:

- the selection of target markets or 'niches';
- joint marketing;
- effective selection of promotional methods such as direct mail and special interest magazines.

Many marketing theorists have emphasized the importance of a highly targeted marketing campaign as opposed to a strategy that attempts to appeal to a broad sweep of consumers. This involves obtaining data, such as demographic and psychograph profiles of the potential market segments (see Chapter 9) and aligning operations with the identified consumer group that corresponds best with the ideals of the specific venture.

Ecotourists are known to utilize a wide range of media to gain accurate in-depth information on a destination or area of interest to them. Information distributed in special interest magazines and direct mail rather than newspapers and radio advertising may be one method of reaching a target market. Direct mail offers a particularly effective strategy to promote ecotourism (Durst and Ingram, 1989; Ingram and Durst, 1989). Direct mail involves a selected person receiving promotional material about a product. Where ecotourism is concerned, direct mail is particularly effective for keeping in touch with previous customers and encouraging them to take another tour with the ecotourism operator. Overall it 'is probably the most effective medium out there' (Merschen, 1992).

Joint marketing strategies by groups of two or more ecotourism operators also offer an effective means to market an ecotourism product due to the efficient use of resources that may already be strained by the small size of ecotourism ventures, as joint marketing is more cost-efficient and enables greater numbers of a target audience to be reached. Vertical joint marketing is particularly effective, for example, where a tour operator, accommodation establishment and carrier join promotional efforts and link their services. Additionally, if ecotour operators work together in marketing, chances are they will work together in other areas, such as carrying capacity determination, which would produce beneficial effects for the environment and local populations impacted upon by ecotourism.

The final broad area where ecotourism marketing can be improved is in distribution, or 'place' where the customer is able to purchase an ecotour from. The poor results of many social campaigns can be attributed in part to their failure to suggest clear action outlets for those motivated to acquire the product (*cf.* Kotler and Andreasen, 1991). This is a regular occurrence with ecotourism: consumers motivated enough to enquire about ecotours at retail travel agents are often persuaded by these agents to choose a conventional tourism product (Richardson, 1991). (In a supply-led industry, however, this restriction in demand may not be entirely negative.)

Ecotourism operators should not distribute their tours through general travel agents. The tours should only be sold at ecotourism specializing travel agents (Boo, 1990), or directly by the operators themselves. This will thereby restrict supply and also increase the efficiency of the ecotourism operators' marketing efforts, as they will no longer have to waste time in their mostly futile bids to convince travel agents to market their tours. This will also enable the operators to exercise more control over the type of tourists that participate in a tour with the company ensuring, where possible, that tourists motivated by environmental concerns make up the majority of the group.

From the above SWOT analysis of the strengths, weaknesses, opportunities and threats to ecotourism, it is apparent that numerous aspects of its development need to be ensured to produce sound marketing and sustainable resource management in order to shape demand and expectations appropriately:

- Ecotourism requires sensitively developed tourist infrastructure. The tourism industry therefore must accept integrated planning and regulation. To date, tourism development has occurred incidentally to the urban, rural and foreshore development as in many countries there is no specific tourism zoning. Economic

development demands increasingly stringent environmental assessment techniques and reports to be included in applications for development, especially in countries where economic imperatives may take precedence over more qualitative aspects such as environmental, social and cultural significance of development.

- Ecotourism requires a supply-led tourism industry. For this to become a reality the industry must firstly define itself holistically and, secondly, agree to cooperate with and support a coordinating body or authority to make decisions about: number of operators, operating licences, ceiling numbers for tours, price structures and so forth. Structural considerations such as pricing, economies of scale, price yield management, and all other financial tools will have to be modified accordingly. The very philosophy of ecotourism calls on low volume tourism with high ticket prices per head. This tactic also negates the business philosophy of competitive pricing to win new customers either from the latent market or from competitors.

- The body responsible for making these decisions and policing industry activities needs to be a third party to the tourism industry. However, care must be taken in appointing a government department or commission to adopt such a role, as even the government is not impartial to its interests in tourism growth, because of the short-term revenue that tourism can create for a region, state or country, especially where foreign currency is concerned.

- Ecotourism requires the establishment of carrying capacities and strict monitoring of these. It is a task that no profit-motivated organization in the industry sees as its responsibility. The establishment of carrying capacities requires a comprehensive knowledge and expertise in the field of environmental, social and cultural assessment. The latter two are very difficult to measure, but a commendable starting point is with the host community, by identifying, in partnership with each community, what is of social and cultural importance. This task in itself requires a great deal of time to be invested in living with and learning from the community in order to establish these social and cultural carrying capacities. Monitoring is an essential component of carrying capacity management. It requires on-going financial and human resource commitment to monitor and evaluate impacts and changing relationships.

● Ecotourism relies on the environmentally sensitive behaviour and operations of ecotour operators and tourists, but the proponents of ecotourism may have placed undue faith in the notion that the behaviour of tourists, developers and other industry operators can be modified through education and awareness programmes (*cf*. Butler, 1990; Pigram, 1989; Wheeller, 1992). In recent years there has been a flood of 'codes of ethics' of 'charters' released by a variety of tourism industry groups and environmental organizations ranging from conservation groups (*cf*. World Wide Fund for Nature, Australian Conservation Foundation) to industry groups (cf. Australia Tourism Industry Association [ATIA], Pacific Asia Travel Association [PATA]). The benefits of raising awareness in this fashion have been tentatively acknowledged (Jarviluoma, 1992), but it remains to be seen whether this results in modified behaviour.

The optimal method to market ecotourism involves taking components of traditional, social and ecological marketing. Ecotourism is certainly a product which fits under the aegis of ecological marketing, as it 'serves to provide a remedy for environmental problems' (Henion and Kinnear, 1976); and also social marketing, as it attempts to further the social cause of environmental quality. It is believed that the 'four Ps' of traditional marketing are still relevant to ecotourism marketing. This is, Kotler and Andreasen (1991) suggest, because the more conditions of a social campaign resembled those of a product campaign, the more successful the cause. Therefore, the marketing of ecotourism

and thereby the marketing of environmental quality should utilize the key components of traditional marketing, specifically the 'four Ps'.

The most productive and cost-effective promotional method is word of mouth (Merschen, 1992). If an ecotourist is satisfied with their ecotourism experience they will effectively become an 'ambassador for the company', spreading the good word very effectively. Asking tour participants to list the names and addresses of friends whom they think would be interested in participating in an ecotour with the company is a means of networking through word of mouth. Also, if a tourist is satisfied with their ecotourism experience, they are more likely to go on a tour with the company again, thereby ensuring an appropriate user group mentality and reducing the need for the company to conduct additional promotion.

The primary marketing factors which may be assessed and altered to fit with the environmental objectives in marketing for ecotourism organizations are:

1 The target markets – the group of people at whom an agency specifically aims its marketing effort.
2 Positioning statements – how you want your target markets to view your agency and its 'product'.
3 Company objectives.
4 Marketing mix – product
– place (distribution)
– promotion
– price

Target marketing is an important procedure in marketing of ecotourism. Because ecotourism is specific in its philosophies, it is important to select target markets that are compatible with organizational goals and objectives. A small group of potential customers may be targeted who share one or more similar characteristics and who have certain similar ideas as to what they want from the ecotourism experience. Some of these preferences would be the desire to travel to relatively remote areas, for the purpose of studying a natural area and its culture, having minimum impact on the environment and with the expectation of gaining educational gratification, with the knowledge that they will return something to the local community.

When considering the target market a number of things need to be taken into account Firstly, socio-demographic characteristics, which include such things as age/family life cycle stage, sex, income, education and occupation. Secondly, it is necessary to consider behavioural characteristics. This is a very important stage in selecting target markets for ecotourism as it enables marketeers to decide what characteristics they will select people on. It includes considerations of:

- The benefits sought.
- The consumer's motivations; perceptions of the ecotourism 'product'.
- The level of skill – is it necessary for targets to have some basic levels of skill before embarking on an ecotourism experience?
- Psychographic profiles – a concept that explains consumers' attitudes, opinions and lifestyles.
- Behavioural characteristics, which are especially important in choosing target markets because they can later be used as criteria in selecting people for specific 'ecotours'. As a marketeer for an ecotourism destination it is important to be specific in selection as you want a certain type of person to participate who is compatible with agency goals and objectives.

Case study   Belize, Central America

Belize is a Central American country with a tourism development policy focused on ecotourism. Although the country is well known for its outstanding barrier reef with unique diving opportunities, the attraction of natural and cultural assets to ecotourists is quite recent. With an array of attractions

to tempt potential visitors, tourists and ecotourists have equally diverse expectations of the destination.

It is therefore important for ecotourism policy planners to define what is meant by ecotourism from a visitor perspective. Palacio and McCool (1997) attempted to achieve this aim by developing information about the tourism market based on a benefit segmentation assessment. The study found that within the category of nature-based visitors, there existed specific characteristics that distinguished four types of tourists as different from each other. These categories were 'Nature Escapists', 'Ecotourists', 'Comfortable Naturalists' and 'Passive Players'. Nature Escapists and Ecotourists reported the highest activity percentages, followed by Comfortable Naturalists, then Passive Players. Ecotourists recorded the highest interest in a desire to escape, learn about nature, health related activity participation and responded positively to the need for companionship and group cohesion.

The study noted that each segment required different facilities due to different rates of recreation participation and differences in trip characteristics – perhaps with the exception of Nature Escapists and Ecotourists, whose characteristics were very similar. Furthermore, promotional and product strategies for each segment would need to be altered slightly to align consumer preference with the product offering. The effective linking of environmental attributes to specific benefits for different nature-based tourists could be achieved through improved marketing efficiency. It may also help organizations determine the social, cultural and biophysical elements in greatest need of sustaining.

Source: V. Palacio and S. McCool, Identifying ecotourists in Belize through benefit segmentation: a preliminary analysis, *Journal of Sustainable Development*, 5(3), 1997, 234–244

Positioning is an important consideration when marketing an ecotourism destination. Positioning is what the marketeer 'wants the target market to think about the product, therefore positioning of the product must be consumer oriented' (Tonge and Myott, 1989: 168). Ecotourism marketeers need to differentiate their 'product' from mass tourism. Agency positioning objectives (for the area and product) would encompass everything that ecotourism stands for: sustainable development, minimal impact, local control, supply-driven, quality experiences and so on.

The marketing mix constitutes the core of an agency's marketing system. The identification of client groups and the marketing mix represents the combination of variables which the agency can control and manipulate to achieve desired outcomes. Once these decisions have been made, the 'service' is offered in the dynamic environment of the community: 'The dynamic nature of this external environment is comprised of a host of variables such as political and legal forces, economic considerations, technology and competition' (Crompton and Howard, 1980: 332). The agency cannot control these variables, therefore it must adapt to them.

At this point in determining the marketing mix, it could be suggested that the agency adopt a different strategy. Normally, the marketing mix activities are used to encourage potential customers to take advantage of the services offered or to increase their usage. Ecotourism, however, is one of those areas that is faced by the need to discourage demand for a service. For example, exceeding carrying capacities in a remote wilderness area may provide short-term satisfaction for some at the expense of overriding the ecotourism philosophy and maximizing public welfare and client group satisfaction over the long term. Because ecotourism is dealing with a 'scarce resource' the agency may use the marketing mix effectively for discouraging participation. This discouraging of demand has been termed 'demarketing': 'to emphasize that marketing may be used to decrease as well as increase the number of satisfied customers. Demarketing is

not a negative concept . . . a decrease in numbers can lead to an increase in clientele satisfaction, through preserving a higher quality experience' (Crompton and Howard, 1980: 333).

Methods of demarketing may include:

- Increasing prices; so they increase disproportionately as time spent in the ecotourism destination increases.
- Creating a queuing situation to increase the time and opportunity costs of the experience.
- Limiting the main promotional strategy to select and specialized media.
- Promoting the importance of the area through education of the public and the need to conserve the area through minimal impact and sustainable development.
- Promoting a range of alternative opportunities in surrounding areas which may satisfy needs and wants.
- Stressing the environmental degradation that could occur if too many people frequent the area.
- Stressing any restrictions or difficulties associated with travel to the area.

Product and distribution need to be looked at a little differently. In the case of ecotourism, the product is essentially an intangible which provides a set of want-satisfying benefits to a customer in an exchange. The ecotourism product is the place, region or area. Because an area is a non-renewable resource it is imperative that it be maintained in its original natural state. Ecotourism in its purest form aims to do this. Distribution is the 'channel structure' used to transfer products and services from an agency to its markets. Destination areas are usually remote and therefore less accessible. This part of the marketing mix, as with the 'product', is virtually impossible to alter.

Marketing is often seen as simply flogging a product to a mass market and therefore has negative connotations. From this discussion it is clear that through appropriate and stringent strategies, an agency can market a 'destination' in a way that complies with organizational goals and objectives and upholds the ecotourism philosophy. Through manipulation of the essential marketing mix factors, target markets, positioning statements and company objectives, marketing can be utilized as a tool for directing the future development of ecotourism within the boundaries of sustainable development. Effective promotion and communication strategies are one of the industry's best opportunities to shape consumer demand and expectations so they are reconciled with the product offered.

Ideally, ecotourism is a small scale, low key tourism, so as to minimize the impacts which may occur on destination environments. Methods of achieving this may mean imposing ceiling numbers which in turn suggest economically that prices charged per person will be somewhat higher than 'mainstream tourism', where economies of scale and competition help determine pricing structures within and between organizations operating within one destination. These objectives, however, are unlikely to be reached in light of the nature and characteristics of the tourism industry in its present operations.

The initial objectives of ecotourism in a new destination may be to remain low-key and small-scale but it is difficult to guarantee this once the tourism industry perceives a new product development opportunity and starts to market that opportunity (Griffin and Boele, 1993).

Suggested restrictions associated with sustainable development and ecotourism have included both qualitative and quantitative measures, including charging higher prices for access to tourist destinations and attractions. Indeed, restricting supply would automatically increase the price of tourism products, thereby reducing the opportunities for some prospective tourists. The question is whether this is consistent with the principle of equity, embodied in the concept of sustainability, one of the central tenets of ecotourism.

9

Could the 'real' ecotourist please stand up!

A new group of tourism clients has emerged who are demanding different activities, experiences and approaches to tourism from the industry: 'these are the ecotourists – people who require environmentally compatible recreational opportunities ... where nature rather than humanity predominates' (Kerr, 1991: 248). They are 'shrugging off the shackles of traditional tourism' in search of knowledge and experience. Their interest is not in 'lounging by hotel pools or hectic sightseeing schedules' (Collins, 1993:7). They are, however, 'interested in visiting wilderness, national parks, and tropical forests, and in viewing birds, mammals, trees and wildflowers', they want to 'experience new lifestyles and meet people with similar interests to themselves' and they want to see their travelling dollars contributing towards conservation and benefiting the local economy (Eagles *et al.*, 1992).

So far we have explored many dimensions of ecotourism: a tourism product; a solution to planning; its relation to local, regional, national and international politics; a strategy for sustainable development. However, this has told us little of what ecotourists are actually like. As we have seen there are an extremely diverse range of ecotourism experiences, ranging from those tourists wishing to learn about specific ecosystems or wildlife, those interested in experiencing indigenous cultures, some are adventure oriented and are interested in more rigorously active experiences, while still others may wish to volunteer aid and community assistance in developing nations.

This chapter explores the characteristics that differentiate ecotourists through an analysis of tourist motivation. We will examine demographic and psychographic characteristics, the needs of ecotourists, the images and attitudes ecotourists ascribe to a destination, and the influence of social, cultural and physical environments. We will also address the managerial implications for ecotourism operators that we initially realized in the preceding chapter, particularly in attempting to align a preferred consumer group with a product offering. By understanding the nature of the target market, ecotourism operators can alter marketing mix components according to the needs of an environmentally conscious consumer.

Understanding what characteristics differentiate ecotourists also has significant implications for managers and protected area agencies. As any person visiting the environment will impact on it in some way, industry and park management agencies require knowledge of ecotourist characteristics in order to manage, influence and control impacts. However, due to the nature of ecotourism as an activity, with a focus on sustaining the environment and education and interpretation, ecotourists differ in their needs and attitudes relative to other travellers. This chapter will attempt to provide a clear picture of the ecotourist.

Table 9.1   *Ecotourist profile*

Age	Income	Education	Gender	Country of origin
20–40 or 55+	$37 000–$60 000	Generally possessing tertiary qualifications	Roughly equally divided between sexes	United States, Canada, Germany, Sweden, Australia

Building a profile of the ecotourist

There are two primary groups of characteristics which will assist in exploring what features distinguish ecotourists. They are *demographic* and *psychographic* characteristics. Demographic segmentation involves defining the market by variables such as age, gender, life cycle stage, occupation, income and education. It is a quantitative analysis method whereas a psychographic profile is qualitative, analysing 'soft' data such as values, motivations and pre-established images of the ecotourist. Both forms of information are vital to ecotourism operators, not only as a one-off measurement, but as a continued body of information on the changing needs of their clients.

Through the compilation of demographic characteristics we can initially begin to build up an image of ecotourists. Table 9.1 illustrates what the profile of the average ecotourist looks like.

Ecotourists can be generally characterized as having higher than average incomes, largely holding tertiary qualifications and equally divided on the basis of males and females.[1] The US Travel and Data Centre study in 1992 indicated that ecotourists are 5% more likely to have an income above $40 000, and 13% more likely to have college qualifications than the population as a whole (Blamey, 1995a, 1995b). Wight (1996) further refined the market profile of ecotourist characteristics, differentiating general

consumers interested in ecotourism and experienced ecotourism travellers. Experienced ecotourism respondents were very highly educated, more so than general tourists interested in ecotourism, and tended to travel as couples (61%), limited family (15%) and some singles (13%), compared to general tourists who predominantly travelled as couples (59%), with 26% travelling as a family. However, the most notable difference emerged in expenditure – experienced ecotourists are willing to spend more than general tourists.[2] Similarly, a study undertaken in 1990, commissioned by the World Wildlife Fund, found that people interested in nature travel and in visiting fragile environments generally exhibit higher expenditure levels than the average tourist (although this additional expenditure may be in high leakage areas). '[Ecotourists] on average, would spend 8.5 per cent more for services and products provided by environmentally responsible suppliers' (Wight, 1994: 41: *cf.* Boo, 1991).

In terms of country of origin the majority of ecotourists are from relatively affluent Western nations such as the US, Germany, Sweden, Canada and Australia. The rapidly ageing populations of these nations and the shift of the 'baby boomers[3] into late middle age may prove to be a substantial demographic trend for leisure and tourism as a significant proportion of these

---

[1] *Cf.* Bates, 1991; Blamey, 1995a; Boo, 1991; Duff, 1993; Valentine, 1991a; Williams, 1990; Wight, 1996.

[2] For example, a survey by Pamela Wight on the differences in expenditure of the conventional tourist over an 'experienced ecotourist' found that that the ecotourist was inclined to spend more than the conventional tourist (Wight, 1996).

[3] The term used to refer to the generation born in the postwar boom between 1946 and 1964.

groups will have significant levels of available leisure time allied with relatively high levels of disposable income to spend on leisure services.

Along with these socioeconomic (demographic) characteristics are a range of attitudinal and behavioural patterns (psychographic characteristics) that significantly allow us to differentiate ecotourists.

Generally, ecotourists demonstrate the following eight psychographic characteristics:

1 Possession of an environmental ethic.
2 Willingness not to degrade the resource.
3 Focus on intrinsic rather than extrinsic motivation.
4 Biocentric rather than anthropocentric in orientation.
5 Aiming to benefit wildlife and the environment.
6 Striving for first hand experience with the natural environment.
7 Possessing an expectation of education and appreciation.
8 High cognitive and affective dimensions (Ballantine and Eagles, 1994).

Ecotourists possess a preference for small groups and personalized service (Duff, 1993) and tend to be outdoor enthusiasts and frequently travel as couples or individuals and are frequent and experienced travellers (*cf*. Williams, 1990; Wight, 1996; see also Boo, 1991). They are 'generally more accepting of conditions different from home than are other types of tourists' (Boo, 1991: 13). Luxury accommodation, food and nightlife are far less important to this group than living in local conditions, and sampling local customs and food. Due to their 'strong science orientation' and focus on study and learning, ecotourists are instead demanding of information and instruction on the destinations they visit (Eagles, 1992: 12).

A study of Canadian ecotourists, for example, found that they were interested in tropical forests, birds, lakes and streams, trees and wildflowers, mammals, mountains and oceans. These physical features were highly ranked by ecotourists when asked about their motiva-

tions. The same group regarded gambling, amusement parks, nightlife, big cities, watching sport, doing nothing, indoor sports, shopping and resort areas as the least enjoyable activities and attractions to visit while on holiday. The study also found that while ecotourists are interested in nature in its own right they enjoy personal development through physical activity, experiencing new and simpler lifestyles, meeting people of similar interests, seeing cultural activities, and buying local crafts (Eagles, 1992).

In this way ecotourism is more than a simple leisure activity. It is a style of travel that reflects and promotes a particular orientation to not only travel, but significant lifestyles, behaviours and philosophies:

> [Ecotourists are] expecting discovery and enlightenment from their ecotourism experience. Personal growth in emotional, spiritual, as well as intellectual terms appear to be expected outcomes from ecotourism travel for the majority of these travellers. (Williams, 1990: 84)

In painting a picture of the ecotourist we will now broaden our brief brushstrokes by examining tourist motivations which helps detail the differences that emerge for ecotourists as a specific market. Such an understanding assists tourism managers in making appropriate decisions that will lead to tourist satisfaction, maximization of positive experiences and minimization of negative experiences (Pearce, 1993). This analysis will be based on a model of tourist motivation developed by Small (1997) which illustrates the key factors of tourist motivation by pictorially demonstrating each of the factors in relation to one another (Figure 9.1).

Tourist needs, images, attitudes and the evaluation of needs and image are the primary focus of this model, with attention given to impacts of the physical, social and cultural environments. Reciprocal impacts exerted by the tourist (or ecotourist) on these same environments are indicated by the two-way flow arrow. The

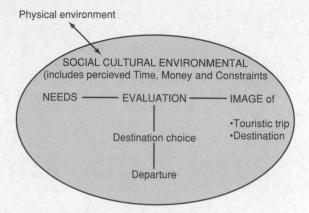

Physical environment

SOCIAL CULTURAL ENVIRONMENTAL
(includes percieved Time, Money and Constraints

NEEDS ——— EVALUATION ——— IMAGE of

•Touristic trip
•Destination

Destination choice

Departure

Figure 9.1   *A simple model of tourist motivation (adapted from Small, 1997)*

interplay of needs and images creates expectations, which differ for ecotourists relative to mainstream tourists. As sustainability is the focus of ecotourism, the impacts upon the environment will be critical in establishing whether ecotourism is viable with the present consumer base or whether operators need to define their market more stringently to achieve a match between environmental/social/cultural objectives, consumer needs/wants and profitability.

Tourist motivations

One way we can identify particular forms and styles of tourism is through an examination of what factors motivate tourists. 'Motivation is aroused when individuals think of certain activities that are potentially satisfaction producing. Since people act to satisfy their needs, motivation is thought to be the ultimate driving force that governs travel behaviour. Therefore, tourists' motivation should constitute the basis for marketing strategies' (Pyo *et al.*, 1989: 277). Motivational research is based on the early works of Dann (1981), who identified that 'push' and 'pull' factors are central in motivating tourists. Push motives are internal to the individ-

ual while pull motives are aroused by the destination. Push factors establish the desire for travel and pull factors explain actual destination choice (Bello and Etzel, 1985).

Crompton (1979) modified the push/pull model in identifying tourists' desire for pleasure and the desire for a break from routine. He identified nine motives in determining causal factors resulting in a tourist's departure. Push factors are motives concerned with the social and psychological status of the individual, while pull factors, on the other hand, are 'motives aroused by the destination rather than emerging exclusively from the traveller himself' (Crompton, 1990: 410).

He found seven primary push motives and two pull motives:

Push motives
● escape from perceived mundane environment;
● exploration and evaluation of self;
● relaxation;
● prestige;
● regression;
● enhancement of kinship relationships;
● facilitation of social interaction.

Pull motives
● novelty;
● education.

Crompton (1979) conceptualized motives as being located along a disequilibrium continuum. When disequilibrium arises due to a feeling of dissatisfaction in relation to one or more push factors, it can be rectified by a break in routine, thus restoring homeostasis (equilibrium) – that is, through travel. For Crompton (1979) the destination site is merely a medium through which motives are satisfied.

Significantly, Iso-Ahola (1983) found that the individual possessed an inclination to travel primarily for intrinsic rewards. Intrinsically motivated activities are engaged in for their own sake, rather than any external remuneration. The connection between intrinsic motivations and push and pull factors was made by

McGehee *et al.* (1996), who recognized that 'most of the push factors are intrinsic motivators'. It is important here to note that satisfaction for the ecotourist may come not only from the experience itself but from the external reward of having promoted environmental sound travel and having made a contribution to the destination region.

Push factors are strongly related to Maslow's hierarchy of needs (Uysal and Hagean, 1993). For Maslow actualization is the central driving force of human personality but before it can be pursued lower motivations such as hunger, shelter and safety (to name a few) must be satisfied first. Maslow grouped these needs into five levels:

1 *Physiological* – hunger, thirst, shelter, sex etc.
2 *Safety* – security, protection from physical and emotional harm.
3 *Social* – affection, belonging, acceptance, friendship.
4 *Esteem* – both internal (self respect, autonomy, achievement) and external (status, recognition, attention).
5 *Self-actualization*.

A tourist motivation framework developed by Pearce (Pearce, 1993; Pearce, 1988) and based on Maslow's hierarchy of needs provides an expansive framework to identify the needs that a tourist is fulfilling when travelling. A mainstream tourist is more concerned with fulfilling lower level needs of relationship, stimulation and relaxation where the ecotourist is more concerned with development and fulfilment, which includes self-education. If the focus of ecotourism is nature-based activity, often intrinsically aroused, with a degree of education and interpretation of the natural environment, it stands to reason that ecotourists are more focused on the self-actualization and higher level needs than basic needs identified at the base of Maslow's hierarchy, by the nature of the experience they seek. As Mayo and Jarvis note, intellectual needs can in some instances take precedence over some of the lower-order needs.

For example, 'curiosity, exploration, the desire to learn, the desire to understand these are sometimes pursued even at great cost to the individual's safety' (1981: 155).

Eagles (1991) also found that the motivations of an ecotourist and those of the general tourist differed in relation to intrinsic versus extrinsic motivations for travel. He found that the general tourist, in most cases liked to feel at home when away from home.

The results from this study align strongly with the 'push' and 'pull' factors which influence tourist motivation. This is not to say that pull factors alone provide enough stimulation for a trip departure, because despite the fact that pull factors are paramount for ecotourists, push factors still do (to varying degrees) influence the departure decision. The application of Crompton's (1979) theory illustrates that pull factors are necessarily ranked higher for ecotourists than mainstream tourists, based on their psychographic characteristics.

However, accurately gauging the motivations of ecotourists is difficult. To begin with, defining tourists' motivations using the push and pull model is more complex when applied to a specific market niche such as ecotourists, rather than mainstream travellers. The internal push motives of discovery, enlightenment and personal growth are important to ecotourists but features of a natural destination are more than simply pull motives to this group for ecotourists see physical locations as motivation in themselves. To describe this as a pull phenomenon is to overlook the importance of the natural environment as a motivator (Eagles, 1992).

The goals of ecotourism are to provide ecologically sound travel experiences that contribute to the natural, economic, social and cultural environments. The provision of tourism services is becoming central to local communities, particularly in a shift away from the dependence on extractive industries. A combination of ecotourist needs and the image they have of the destination pre-departure, creates expectations that an ecotourist assumes will be satisfied. By understanding ecotourist motivations the local community will be in a better position to meet these needs and expectations.

The tailoring of products using motivational research is important in any sector of tourism. Recognizing that motives of ecotourists differ is essential for tourism managers. Due to reduced numbers of tourists, the likelihood of reduced impacts and interest in an educative component, roles and rules for ecotourists may be redefined and shaped about the needs this market niche possesses, resulting in higher rates of satisfaction.

Research on visitor expectations was used in the ecologically sustainable management of whale shark tourism in Queensland. Swayed respondents felt regulations allowed divers to swim too near to whale sharks. Management used this research to modify guidelines, increasing the distance which enhanced protection of the species, while still offering a satisfying experience for ecotourists (Birtles *et al.*, 1995). This demonstrates a differing managerial response to the market based on their unique needs and characteristics.

Similarly a United States survey found that 45 per cent of US travellers felt that travel suppliers do not provide enough environmental protection training and support to employees. Respondents also felt that companies offered little educational content on environmental awareness and protection during tours. Familiarity with ecotourist motivations will help prevent such dissatisfactions and bring added environmental protection advantages. The ability of ecotourism operators to meet ecotourist needs will determine 'whether or not the destination is ultimately regarded as a viable and worthwhile ecotourism destination' (Wight, 1994: 47).

Tourism interactions

Tourist behaviour does not start at the time of travel, it exists before the tourist has left for the destination site and it is here that a major difference between ecotourists and mainstream tourists is evident. Not only does this include motivation, but also when the tourist first decides which destination to visit.

Social interactions involving tourists can take the form of tourist–peer group interaction, tourist–tourist interaction or tourist–host interaction. The first of these – tourist–peer group interactions – has a significant effect on destination choice. Social groups exert four kinds of effect in destination selection:

- direct persuasion to visit a certain destination;
- normative influence on a traveller's opinion of a destination;
- long-term socialization leading to conventional wisdom about a destination;
- social group members living in destination areas (Dann and Crompton, in Crompton, 1981).

Although each of these factors, to differing degrees, applies to the mainstream tourist, an ecotourist may not relate to any of these influences. For example, the ecotourist would be unlikely to visit a friend in a distant location and call it 'ecotourism'. In addition, the social group's opinion and persuasion is often of less significance for an ecotourist as they may well visit places that others do not necessarily know about.

Once a pre-departure decision has been made, the next significant 'phase' of social interaction is that which occurs at the destination site itself. For all people social interaction is fundamental: 'It has long been recognized that the interactive nature of social groups exerts a strong influence on an individual's behaviour' (Crompton, 1981: 551). In the case of mainstream tourists, the majority of social interaction occurs between members of the group of tourists. For ecotourism however – with a reduced group size and an emphasis on destination attributes – the focus of interaction is between the tourist and those encountered at the destination.

Ecotourists generally are likely to actively seek immersion in the local environment, rather than enforcing an artificial barrier between themselves and the host community. Cohen (1972: 167) refers to this as the 'environmental bubble' whereby the tourist is demarcated from the destination environment – such as resort facilities where recreation opportunities are enclosed largely within the resort.

In determining the qualitative and quantitative differences in social interaction that differentiate mainstream tourists from ecotourists, Cohen's (1972) typology of tourists serves to demonstrate that differences in interaction can be the result of a willingness or otherwise to venture beyond a tourist's comfort zone. Cohen's (1972) typology identifies four different types of tourists:

- the organized mass tourist;
- the individual mass tourist;
- the explorer;
- the drifter.

Each of these tourist types embodies unique characteristics that influence their likelihood to immerse themselves in the host culture, or alternatively, remain within the confines of their touring companions, thus minimizing discomfort or culture shock. Organized mass tourists and individual mass tourists never fully immerse themselves into an environment as familiarity is a fundamental concern for them. They tend to 'look' at the host from within the relative security afforded by their travelling companions. The individual mass tourist differs slightly from the organised tourist type in that their tours are not entirely pre-planned, however, both descriptions fit closely with a particular mode of tourist behaviour.

Explorers and drifters vary in the degree to which they communicate, immerse and learn from the host communities. The explorer is similar to the ecotourist in that they both travel individually and get 'off the beaten track'. They do leave the 'environmental bubble' yet, unlike the ecotourist, they often require comfortable accommodation with reliable transport. They travel primarily to interact with other cultures

but again, unlike the ecotourist, they are not necessarily motivated by the desire to experience the natural environment.

Cohen's (1972) final tourist type is the drifter. This tourist ventures furthest off the beaten track and wholly immerses themselves into a community's customs and culture, where novelty is of utmost importance and all familiarity disappears. The levels of social interaction with the host culture and environment are maximized by this form of tourist, particularly in comparison to the mass tourist (Cohen, 1972). Again this tourist type is similar to the ecotourist in that they are motivated by a desire for 'experiences' but they are not necessarily travelling principally to experience natural areas' scenery.

These differences in interaction between tourist types and the social environment can be contextualized broadly with reference to the notion of tourism 'authenticity'. MacCannell (1976) sees tourism as a modern functional substitute for the spiritual aspects of religion that have diminished in social significance as a result of the alienation of modern man from 'traditional' modes of life and therefore of perceiving the world. This shift from traditional institutional bonds has caused man to seek the 'real' life of others – that is, what are perceived as 'authentic' modes of life, cultures etc.

MacCannell proposed a continuum of tourist settings across six stages, each denoting a level of authenticity gained from specific tourist experiences. Stage One describes the social space that tourists attempt to overcome or penetrate, such as tourism facilities, institutional cultural sites etc. This 'front stage' often suffices for organized mass tourists, as it is constructed specifically for their benefit: 'Tourists commonly take guided tours of social establishments because they provide easy access to areas of the establishment ordinarily closed to outsiders' (1976: 98). At the furthest end of the continuum is Stage Six, which denotes the back region, where there is limited (if any) access to outsiders, a region where it is perceived that 'authentic' cultural representations take place (MacCannell, 1976).

Although MacCannell identifies that mainstream tourists experience 'staged authenticity' as a general rule, however he also recognizes that on occasions mainstream tourists do have intimate involvement with the social environment. Nevertheless, he also recognizes that often these authentic experiences happen by accident: 'The tourist is passive; he [sic] expects interesting things to happen to him' (Boorstin, in MacCannell, 1976: 104).

The constructed nature of the 'authentic' experience is often facilitated by the tour guide's instruction, mediated through the perceptions and choice of information conveyed. Boorstin recognizes the importance of the guide in influencing a tourist stating that 'a good guide, working in the correct context, provides a relatively safe and secure milieu for the tourist to collect those authentic experiences which fulfil the individual's motivation for travelling' (Pearce, 1984: 136).

The tour guide is important for tourist interaction with not only the social environment but also the natural environment. Tour guides are central to both mainstream tourism and ecotourism experiences, although their roles may differ significantly.

An ecotourist is generally likely to have obtained a detailed knowledge of the local environment pre-departure. However, ecotourists are not immune to inaccurate information given by the guide, as they also rely on the guide for information.

Not only is the information given by the guide important, but whether the tourist remembers the information is also important, as it will affect the tourist's behaviour: 'the tourist's own experience and knowledge; and the features of the setting at hand would appear to be a major requirement for promoting the tourist's memory and the recall of the setting' (Pearce, 1984: 143). This would imply that, in general, a heightened awareness of the environment for the ecotourist would result in a better retention of the information given by the guide regarding those environments. Therefore, the guide's role in influencing a tourist's behaviour

can be problematic. The mainstream tourist receives a 'mainstream' guide (by that is meant that the guide elaborates in less detail about specific sites and caters to the sightseeing needs of the mainstream tourist) while the ecotourist receives a more descriptive and environmentally aware guide to cater for their inherent interest. In addition, the ecotourist retains more of the guide's information about the environment than the mainstream tourist does, as the ecotourist has travelled with a specific interest in the topic of environment impact and interaction. Therefore, it seems inevitable that the ecotourist must behave differently to the mainstream tourist, as, in general, they have access to better and more detailed information. This information allows them to act more environmentally consciously. The mainstream tourist does not have the same opportunity to behave more like the ecotourist, because the nature of the information they receive does not assist in guiding their behaviour to be environmentally sensitive to the same degree.

Up to this point we have discussed the differences between the ecotourist and the mainstream tourist's interactions with their social and environmental surroundings. As we have seen, ecotourists generally have, and seek, an intimate understanding of the environment, which is not an essential factor for mainstream tourists. Therefore, it may seem obvious that the biggest differences between the behaviour of the ecotourist and the mainstream tourist lie in their interaction with the physical environment.

From the perspective of the physical environment, ecotourism and mainstream tourism play very different roles. The ecotourist ideally enters a destination in the 'discovery and emergence' stage of the 'tourism destination product life cycle' (Prosser, 1994: 23). This means that an ecotourist is an 'explorer' or someone who seeks the wilderness, or unspoilt areas, for the natural and cultural assets contained within the region before others have the chance to make a noticeable impact. In contrast, the mainstream tourist would be involved in a destination in all of the stages of the life cycle after the initial discovery and emergence stage.[4] However, the logical conclusion of placing ecotourism within the tourism destination product life cycle is the inevitable saturation and decline of an area through the emergence of mainstream tourism to the region once it is 'discovered'. Does it really matter then if ecotourists and mainstream tourists behave differently if the eventual outcome of an ecotourist entering a site is the eventual invasion of mass tourism, hence the region's destruction?

A tourist's attitude relates significantly to their behaviour towards the physical environment. It has been widely recognized that mainstream tourists generally tend to have a less environmentally conscious attitude when on holiday:

> When on holiday ... we may give little thought to whether such thought is socially or environmentally acceptable in our chosen destination, and indeed, if we are aware, we may rationalize that we have paid and they have taken our money, so we are entitled to take our holiday as we wish. (Prosser, 1994: 32)

Ecotourists, as we have seen, actively seek to minimize the impacts that they have on a destination. However, while the individual ecotourist may independently minimize their impacts, the management of the natural area to which they are travelling determines whether the impacts are minimized overall: 'Trekking tourists in the Nepalese Himalayas would almost without exception declare themselves to be eco-conscious or green, yet they too are pushing against the carrying capacity and hence the sustainability of the regional environment' (Prosser, 1994: 33). Therefore while the individual ecotourist may behave differently to the mainstream tourist in respect to the physical environment, the ecotourists, as a group, can potentially create similar impacts on the physical environment as a group of mainstream tourists.

As we have noted, mainstream tourists tend to visit established destinations, places where the physical environment has been developed to a considerable degree and tourism infrastructure is in place. Ecotourism, however, is often associated with travel to more remote and environmentally sensitive locations. The common thread which ties ecotourists and mainstream tourists is the behaviour of moving from one destination to another for new experiences. Mainstream tourists do not necessarily need to behave like an ecotourist in the respect of limiting impacts to the natural environment, as the physical environment is not as fragile as those areas often utilized by ecotourists (although the cultural and social environments may be as fragile).

One potential catalyst for difference in the behaviour of tourists is the perception that the individual has about what 'minimal impacts' actually are. Often people do not make changes to benefit the environment until they realize that it is damaged. However, the ecotourist is preventative in attempting to ameliorate impacts from the moment of initiating travel and by striving to leave the environment as they find it – an objective not always shared by the mainstream tourist: 'For every traveller prepared to meet the wilderness on its own terms, there exist hundreds of others who demand that it be modified for their use with the provision of surfaced roads, cafeterias, toilets, parking, picnic facilities and a range of other amenities' (Todd, 1989). This alone exemplifies the major difference in the behaviour of ecotourists and mainstream tourists towards the environment visited: ecotourist behaviour is determined according to the environment while the mainstream tourist adapts the environment to suit his or her usual behaviour.

Economic differences

Economic conditions are also fundamental to understanding the differences in behaviour

---

[4] These successive stages include 'growing popularity and fashion', 'saturation', 'fading fashion' and 'decline'.

between the ecotourist and the mainstream tourist. Economic based analysis of the destination region results in identification of a number of key differences in impacts (both direct and indirect) by ecotourists relative to mainstream tourists. A balance of economic impacts in any tourism region is dependent on the characteristics of the economy (e.g. size, level of development and linkages), the type of goods and services demanded (or supplied in the case of ecotourism), the type of tourism and ownership of services, infrastructure and superstructure. Due to the fact that the levels of development for ecotourism in the destination region are likely to be reduced relative to mainstream tourism, goods and services are produced in limited supply, based on the carrying capacity of the region, and ownership is more likely to be local.

Mainstream tourism often occurs in cities and towns, whereas ecotourism most often involves villages or smaller communities. Destination regions benefit from ecotourism, as the ecotourist minimizes cultural, social and physical impacts, while creating beneficial economic impacts, purchasing local goods and services. The ecotourist does not demand that local communities engage in extensive infrastructure development or changes in their normal cultural practices. Mainstream tourists, however, require that the products and services supplied 'must reach the required standards' of the tourist (Vellas and Becheral, 1995: 319). This is an example of the 'environmental bubble' whereby tourists need to recreate that which is found in their home country and determines the satisfaction of the tourism experience.

Similarly, the nature of ecotourism development – small scale with minimal social and environmental impacts – reduces the likelihood of economic leakages to external owners, operators and investors. Leakages are likely to be high if:

- the economy is small with a limited range of domestically produced goods and services;
- there is a high propensity to import goods and service provision;
- there is a low level of local ownership of tourist facilities;
- there is a high proportion of transient imported labour.

These are often characteristics of developing countries, whose adoption of ecotourism in some instances has reversed the high leakages dictated by the previous structuring of their tourism industries.

Case study   Ecuador

In Capirona, Ecuador, a community of 24 Quichua Indian families have chosen ecotourism as the most appropriate form of economic development. This community demonstrated a dependence on economic returns from crops (which had become insufficient), and sought ecotourism as a form of industry that directly benefits the community, whilst minimizing leakage. In economic terms, the venture has thus far been successful, however, impacts on neighbouring communities have yet to be gauged (Colvin, 1994).

Individuals' perception of the environment has a profound influence on how it is experienced: 'Both perceptual distortion and the expectations we bring to the environment affect the role we play in it. People develop selective and unique conceptions' (Ittelson *et al.*, 1974: 14). The expectations of a tourist therefore play a large part in the way a tourist behaves. They also determine if a destination will satisfy the tourist's needs, i.e. if the expectations meet the experience. Considering that ecotourists and mainstream tourists are motivated to travel by different desires it is understandable that tourists will hold different expectations, require the satisfaction of different experiences. An ecotourist is seeking education about a region along with the experience of both natural and cultural environments and may not be satisfied by the 'pseudo' events (Boorstin, 1972) that are dominating the tourist market. As we have seen, ecotourists will seek to educate themselves about the destination site prior to departure and will therefore have some knowledge about the destination. The mainstream tourist, however, 'seldom likes the authentic product of the foreign culture; he prefers his own provincial expectations' (Boorstin, 1972: 106). These expectations are often greater than the destination may provide and are often satisfied by a 'commodified' experience.

Service providers such as tour operators can manage the tourist and ensure satisfaction by providing a tour which fulfils the needs of the different tourist types. For a tour operator who is to provide the total ecotourist experience, the tour must enhance a genuine environmental experience whereby the tourist learns and communicates with the host environment.

The management of tourists is undertaken to control and influence tourist behaviour, thus seeking to minimize the impacts of tourism on communities and on the environments. This chapter has shown that ecotourists and mainstream tourists differ in their behaviour to a great extent so it stands to reason the management systems implemented for these two types of tourists will be vastly different. The difference in behaviour between the ecotourist and the mainstream tourist relates directly to the fact that the attitude and motivation for travelling is very different between the two groups. Ecotourists travel to experience natural environments, to educate themselves about these areas. Mainstream tourists on the other hand travel to satisfy leisure, pleasure and recreational needs. Therefore differing customer perceptions, needs, attitudes, levels of environmental stewardship and likely impacts must be considered by operators – both managers and marketers – natural area managers, and local communities when considering this market segment.

10

Ecotourism – a model for sustainable development

We currently live in a world dominated by rationalistic philosophies and practices, where 'good' decisions are deemed to be those that are able to identify and provide a tangible and measurable balance of benefits, adjudicated by cost–benefit ratios and statistical quantification. However, as we have seen, little, if any, accord is given to the underlying principles and values that underpin such evaluations. Whilst the Western world aspires to increasing ranges of low cost goods and efficiency of production and provision of services, it reaps large-scale unemployment patterns reflected in global trends and environmental debilitation in the form of atmospheric pollution, biodiversity decline, siltation, land degradation and global warming – which is beginning to have profound impacts on global weather patterns.

Just as wilderness and natural areas are in marked decline, both in terms of quality and quantity, demand for tourism to these areas is increasing markedly. However, tourism as an industry deserves significant criticism, not least because in many cases it contributes to the decline of natural areas. Tourism is dominated by developed Western countries with tourist marketers increasingly designing, planning and implementing tourism into developing countries. However, without inclusive processes that at the least utilize consultation with the host communities, or ideally where development of these projects is controlled by local communities, there is always the danger of imposing a cultural hegemony. Once established, cultural hegemony means that the values of the tourist culture not only encroach on and often destroy the host culture, but also reinforce the narrow perceptions and representations of these cultures through Western eyes.

The tourism industry often does not acknowledge that 'explicitly or implicitly, every debate on policy is a debate about values' (Stretton, 1976: 3–18), and yet decisions are made on approaches, projects and practices without considering the effect of values, especially their own, on their work. The transfer of methods, techniques and practices from mass tourism approaches to ecotourism practices without reassessment of their relevance or appropriateness has been problematic.

The analysis and outcomes are therefore likely to perpetuate the mode of practice rather than find appropriate alternatives. Ecotourism has often been defined and debated from within this frame, often as little more than a 'niche market'. However, as we have seen, ecotourism is one of many forms of 'alternative' tourism that are influenced by profound philosophic social and environmental shifts. Indeed they are all oriented by a change in current value systems.

Table 10.1 *Concerns of mass tourism and alternative paradigm (ecotourism) views*

Mass tourism	*Alternative tourism*
1 Management of 'evolutionary' change (survival of the fittest) within a Western rationalist approach based on existing economic principles	1 Radical change moving towards cooperatives and community based approaches outside of the existing tourism industry
2 Maintaining social order, existing tourism systems unquestioned	2 Transforming social systems, analysing structural conflicts and contradictions and including nature in the equation
3 Greater efficiency of current tourism systems, hence increased profitability	3 Creating more just and equitable systems that can step beyond the tourism system
4 Appearance of harmony, integration and cohesion of social groups involved in the tourism process	4 Contradictions between social ideals and reality, attempts to demonstrate this and alleviate it
5 Focus on ways to maintain cohesion and consensus	5 Ways to dismantle or change systems of domination
6 Solidarity	6 Emancipation
7 Identifying and meeting individual needs within existing social system	7 Current tourism systems incapable of equitably meeting basic human needs
8 Focused on actuality, discovering and understanding what is	8 Focused on potentiality: providing a vision of what could be

Source: Adapted from Maguire, 1987: 12

Despite claims to the contrary, ecotourism has not simply allowed the tourism industry significantly to expand in market scope. Its significance lies in its ability to offer alternative approaches to the industry's operational practices. These 'alternative' paradigms make possible an increase in the breadth and depth of understanding of the industry. Specific philosophical approaches such as ecocentrism and environmentalism, as we have seen, pose significant questions for the tourism industry in their challenge to the economic rationalist practices in tourism.

From an ecocentically informed perspective, ecotourism is not just an 'industry' or activity undertaken in the natural environment; it is intended to be an experience that an individual or group has that affects their attitudes, values and actions. Ecotourism then is as much about environmental education, the fostering of attitudes and behaviour that is conducive to maintaining natural environments, and empower-

ment of host communities, as it is about fostering a sustainable industry. Ecotourism can therefore be said to have three primary objectives: sustainability, conservation and empowerment of host communities. The unifying concern is one of living in harmony with nature and recognizing the intrinsic value in beings other than humans (Haywood, 1988). That is, it is concerned with the relationship between humanity and nature, with the intention of making that relationship more equitable.

In contrast to more conventional forms of tourism, ecotourism is unique in its ecocentric focus along with education, personal growth and other intrinsic values underlying travel motivation. Ecotourists tend to be highly focused on these intrinsic values and, unlike other tourist forms, they pursue these goals 'with high levels of physical and mental rigour' (Williams, 1990: 83). Many ecotourism activities combine physical activities such as trekking, cycling and kayaking with environmental awareness-raising pursuits. Experience of indigenous foods and customs occurs in close proximity to learning about native flora and fauna. Thus ecotourism activities focus on active appreciative endeavours (Swanson, 1992).

However, ecotourism should not only be concerned with identifying the target market of ecotourism and its level of satisfaction, but should also be concerned with understanding the range of experiences of all participants in ecotourism (host and guest) and explaining why these patterns of experience exist. It might also be concerned with identifying sites of oppression and possible processes to overcome such oppression. A wider focus in ecotourism will look for and question concepts such as globalization and anthropocentrism, which will limit the contribution of ecotourism. As such, it could examine the:

● ecotourist's experience;
● access to be an ecotourist;
● access to power and decision making in management of ecotourism;
● host's experience.

In exploring ecotourism the questions who participates, who makes decisions and who controls the structure of the ecotourist experience should be pursued. A changed focus would highlight and identify as one issue of concern the narrow socioeconomic group which constitutes the ecotourism 'market'. That is, the issue of equity of access. The issue is of concern not only because of the inherent imbalance of opportunity which reflects a system of oppression, but also because the issue needs to be addressed in order to fulfil the original agenda of ecotourism itself. Remember that ecotourism aspires to educating visitors about the value of natural environments, however without considering equity of access the current 'target market' will simply be 'preaching to the converted'. In addition, equity is an issue because ecotourism activities principally occur within publicly owned resources and according to current (but possibly changing) community views access should not be limited to elite groups.

As we have seen, ecotourism has great potential for its ability to be both a tool for conservation and sustainable development. Ecotourism appears to present us with one of the few activities where the link between economic development and conservation of natural areas is potentially clear and direct. However, these links have not led to the expected benefits for many communities or conservation groups, particularly in many cases because of the dominance of short-term profit-orientated goals. Clearly, where there has been innovation and new management practices which have separated ecotourism from mass tourism positive outcomes have occurred. Partnerships will be an important component of these innovations which can see ecotourism benefiting both parks and local communities. In a commodified market-place ecotourism also cannot exist without government regulation or strong delegation of management authority to the regional or local levels, otherwise ecotourism in most places won't differ from mass tourism. The challenge for ecotourism planners will be to establish regulations and incentives so that socio-economic benefits are generated, and appropriately distributed, from activities which are culturally and ecologically sustainable.

Unfortunately, however, government has also seen it as a panacea for development problems: a solution for lack of employment, foreign exchange, and capital for infrastructure. In formulating projects a lack of thought and direction has resulted, in many cases, in ecotourism not living up to expectations in terms of creating revenues for conservation or in creating alternative income sources for communities. It is regarded by many social scientists, and many tourists themselves, with increasing scepticism given the increasing documentation of its environmental record, cultural impact and the quality of jobs it has created. In a majority of countries, ecotourism has been promoted by government or industry without an overall strategy, effective protected area management plans, and without consultation or inclusion of local communities. While local communities do receive benefits from ecotourism, these benefits are most frequently in the form of seasonal or low-paying jobs. At the community level, ecotourism may generate increased revenues, provide for more infrastructure such as roads and electricity, or proceeds from ecotourism may be directed to community projects such as school construction, and health clinics, but this has to be clearly identified and specified in its development. Additionally it has to be made clear to these local communities that these benefits may be offset by interference in their daily lives and resultant cultural changes. When outside control or profit oriented segments of the local community dominate the decision-making process often the low-impact scale of ecotourism is exceeded and it takes on the characteristics of mass tourism, with increased traffic, pollution, sequestering of profits by outsiders and rising local prices all becoming significant problems. This model of development parallels that of developing countries' economies when dominated by a developed nation's agenda and the World Bank.

The effectiveness of ecotourism in the future will ultimately depend on who will benefit, as well as where, when and how it can be appropriately implemented: all of which is dependent on a wide range of actions which are underpinned by the philosophical approaches we have discussed in Chapter 2, particularly in relation to their implementation planning and management frameworks.

Underpinning this approach is a need for support from local communities, and to best investigate this support and involve these communities in an empowered way there is a need to use community development approaches. A community development approach advocates that change comes from within communities, not outside, and that power and decision making associated with that change should be community-driven and controlled. A recent initiative that would be relevant for ecotourism is community-based conservation (CBC) which arises from within the community (Western and

Wright, 1994: 1). A variety of terms have been used, such as joint management (Hill and Press, in Western and Wright, 1994: 499) and co-management (Brechin *et al.*, in West and Brechin, 1991: 5), all of which can be operationalized by organizations like the World Bank and the World Tourism Organization if they are willing to embrace the alternative paradigms offered through ecotourism. Ecotourism, from this perspective, is therefore concerned that communities retain and exercise control in ecotourism development and implementation. That is, from a community development perspective one of the central issues is equity of power between community, state, individual and corporate enterprise.

Developing tourism partnerships

Ecotourism has facilitated a major change in the relationship between host communities and tourism development. Since its recognition, there has been a movement away from developing a site or region without any consultation between local residents and development bodies. However, even now their needs and concerns are not often heard; but, ecotourism and other alternative forms of tourism have recognized that partnerships between local people, the private sector and government open up a range of opportunities not restricted to any one group. Most of these partnership arrangements are a recent development and are gaining acceptance because they make good economic sense and benefit all partners.

Some partnerships will be born of necessity, for example the need for local communities to market their destination to a wider audience with images that represent for them what they really are rather than what some marketeers would like to sell them as. Other linkages may result from a need for greater flexibility in management where areas of the natural environment are closed off to tourism only because of international conservation guidelines that have no relevance to the local community. These sorts of conflicts have led to the development of partnerships between governments and NGOs, where management is delegated to the NGO, who often can better act with the community in their interest. The Santa Elena Rainforest Reserve case study in Chapter 7 demonstrates how this might occur.

New ways of looking at partnerships between the government and the private sector have allowed the private sector to manage operations and run concessions in places where the government lacked the resources, capacity and investment, such as accommodation in national parks (see MacKinnon *et al.*, 1986). Interesting partnerships have started between governments and local people, such as at Uluru, in Australia, where joint management arrangements have created new approaches and more refined ways on interpreting the resource.

New mechanisms and arrangements are constantly being devised with an increasing number of partners, including many often not considered by more mainstream tourism organizations. With the global recognition of ecotourism international industry donors have come to play a role. For example, USAID (United States Aid Program) is promoting a tourism strategy called low-impact tourism (LIT). LIT focuses on establishing indigenous natural resource management through private sector initiatives and investment in rural village-based tourism business infrastructures. Rural communities would get a percentage of tourism revenues, employment benefits and improved infrastructure (Lillywhite, 1992) while international donors can provide water turbines or other technology-based infrastructure to markets that have not needed this before ecotourism came to these remote areas.

However, while bringing many partners to the table offers the strengths of the combined organizations, it can make coordination and decision making quite cumbersome. In such cases, ecotourism development may seem akin to a large integrated development project, with many of the difficulties that these projects face. Projects with fewer partners may be more manageable,

but may require high levels of coordination with other agencies. Ecotourism then provides the catalyst for the development of improving processes for decision making while giving an initial framework that may allow attempts to reach partnership agreements based on a shared vision.

Ecotourism, for example, would suggest that for equity to be established in say national parks and other conservation areas which are used extensively for tourism, there needs to be trust and respect between the traditional custodians of the land and the more recently arrived park management agencies. For this to happen, both parties must understand the other's culture in order to come to terms with each other's interpretation and perceptual view of any given situation. This understanding requires facilitation across a significant cultural divide. The role of culture in interpersonal dealings is more fully explained below:

Cultural learnings influence the perception of other people. Developing crosscultural understanding involves perceiving members of other cultural groups positively. By understanding the basic principles of person perception, and the natural effects of one's own cultural experience and learning on perceiving other people, unproductive explanations of crosscultural misunderstandings as prejudice or even just differences may be replaced with productive methods of avoiding misunderstandings and stimulating positive perceptions of other people. How we perceive other people affects how we behave towards them and how they, in turn, behave towards us. (Robinson, 1988: 49)

Placing external definitions and ways of life (such as tourism) on people and communities can affect the lives of those people in far-reaching ways (Schwartz and Jacobs, 1979). It is important then to acknowledge when working with marginalized sectors of society that we may already be dealing with stereotypes and misconceptions placed upon them by society in general

(Eckermann and Dowd, 1988). It is thus desirable to work with flexible models that are more open to allowing the expression of individual characteristics of a subject group. For example, in relation to the Australian Aborigines, their land and their cultures, Barlow makes four points:

> Aborigines have never had to define themselves, their cultures or their lands – that definition was made in the time before time when the great ancestral creative beings brought into existence land, people, and law. All other definitions have been made by people who are not Aborigines for their own reasons. People who are not Aborigines continue to define Aborigines, their cultures and their lands for their own reasons. These definitions are effectively imposed on Aborigines so that they are impelled to act in accordance with them. (Barlow, 1992: 57)

The underlying philosophies of ecotourism are significant to the manner in which it is examined and interpreted, and that these approaches take into consideration the original principles of ecotourism. There is a danger of losing the central ethical ideas that surround ecotourism without utilization of wider perspectives.

Ecotourism has offered the potential for the tourism industry to look towards alternative perspectives for tourism, when left as an assumed autonomous category it is in danger of becoming isolated through an economic rationalist focus devoid of any social experience. The very ambiguity of ecotourism lends itself to a theoretical and research approach that is itself about the use of alternative approaches.

We believe that ecotourism can offer a clearly defining philosophical approach; as shown in Chapter 2, and in doing this it has expanded tourism beyond an economic rationale; ecotourism is able to achieve environmental sustainability and its affiliated social goals. These goals include the minimization of damage to natural resources, education of ecotourists to conservation values, access of the tourism experience beyond a 'converted and elite' group, and the distribution of the rewards to local communities.

Ecotourism represents an alternative approach to tourism. That is the thinking around ecotourism is derived equally if not dominated by an alternative focus which will allow ecotourism to be placed outside of the current dominant framework and challenge contemporary tourism practices.

Ecotourism generates benefits for biodiversity conservation and can often succeed in meeting conditions which cannot be met in other activities. It often allows partnership where destinations can become competitive and the protected area authorities have the capacity and jurisdictional mandates to design, implement and manage sustainable ecotourism consistent with their protected area objectives through having a workable framework in ecotourism. In this case the cost reflects the true cost of tourism and site protection. Finally, there are mechanisms where revenues from fees can be allocated to the parks and can be applied toward priorities in overall biodiversity conservation in the country. These frameworks have been difficult to establish prior to the recognition of ecotourism.

Sustainable models and ecotourism

'Sustainable development' was a much talked about model for development in a policy context, debated at conferences such as the United Nations Conference of Environment and Development, Earth Summit, the International Union for Conservation of Nature and Natural Resources (IUCN) and the IVth World Congress on National Parks and Protected Areas. However, the mechanisms for local communities to participate only came about through the phenomenon of ecotourism. Local communities could learn about impacts, options and possibilities of ecotourism development, explore means for ownership of specific ecotourism ventures and consider strategies for ecotourism as compensation for restricted access to protected areas, including coordinated investments in local infrastructure and services that improve local quality of life and collection of local user fees from tourists which support local development initiatives.

Governments have found that it provides approaches to supplement ongoing activities by improving existing policy, including requiring the development of ecotourism strategies as components of government documents as well as clarifying the jurisdictional mandates and responsibilities of agencies involved in ecotourism planning and management. In addition, governments were able to justify developing pricing policies for use in protected area sites which reflect the social cost of operating and maintaining such areas and could decentralize responsibility for area-specific ecotourism, strategies and developments.

Additionally, many governments support the collection of user fees from tourists. However, in many cases these fees are often appropriated into general revenue rather than to maintaining and improving the quality of parks and protected areas by the development of facilities which are environmentally and culturally appropriate in scale construction and context. Similarly, broader principles also need to be adopted such as introducing sound environmental practices including waste reduction and recycling; and to explore joint ventures and partnerships with local communities, NGOs, and other organizations for ecotourism development. Additionally, the flow on benefit where the private sector can then see clear benefits on ground such as better facilities and are therefore implicitly introduced to the ideas of sustainable development.

NGOs and academic institutions who had supported the development of the tourism industry have found in ecotourism a mechanism with which to practise sustainability. In this context, they were able to have a clarified role in the industry, such as acting as intermediaries between the private sector and local interests in ecotourism development. Similarly, they could identify technologies and products that are produced or used locally and which are econom-

ically and environmentally sustainable in order to reduce waste, provide local groups with training, technical assistance and information necessary to participate in the benefits and employment opportunities from ecotourism; and collect information and monitor and evaluate ecotourism development.

This book has highlighted the complexity of using ecotourism as a tool for conservation and sustainable development. The explosion of interest in ecotourism as a funding source for conserving both biodiversity and cultural patrimony and as a strategy for generating socio-economic development has seen a mechanism for a movement of the tourism industry to become more aligned to the sustainable development models that underpin ecotourism. And with the demand for ecotourism steadily increasing, a trend that can be expected to continue its influence on the tourism industry and communities can only continue to promote sustainable models of development.

If ecotourism causes mass tourism to become more ecologically and culturally sensitive and less likely to bring negative impacts then it has made a major contribution to sustainability. This book has attempted to provide a means for the reader to evaluate how well ecotourism might live up to the expectation created for it. Case studies presented in the book cover a range of protected areas, cultures, types of ecotourism enterprises and management options and suggest we are moving toward more sustainable models. Where we have not lived up to expectations in terms of creating revenues for conservation or in creating alternative income sources to take pressure off protected areas or for local communities, they have at least begun to develop mechanisms that can become a potential avenue for conservation though ecotourism.

In learning about the impacts, potentials and possibilities of ecotourism development enables the creation of mechanisms to allow for every stakeholder's involvement in ecotourism planning and development. Sustainable models of development are not inherently designed to restrict, rather they allow for new ways of thinking that can, and should, achieve a range of objectives guided by a common interest. Ecotourism, as a sustainable development prac-tice, is a strategy for mapping and addressing new approaches to humanity's interaction with the environment for the twenty-first century.

Appendix I

Select glossary

Alternative tourism The common feature of 'alternative tourism' is the suggestion of an attitude diametrically opposed to what is characteristically viewed as mass tourism. Alternative tourism often is presented as existing in fundamental opposition by attempting to minimize the perceived negative environmental and socio-cultural impacts of people at leisure in the promotion of radically different approaches to tourism. Examples include ecotourism, green tourism, 'nature-oriented tourism', 'soft tourism' and 'defensive tourism'.

Anthropocentric Focuses on the human and the instrumental value of nature, regards humans as the central fact of the universe and therefore interprets everything in terms of humans and their values.

Areas of High Conservation Value Areas important at a regional or national level for the conservation of native fauna, flora, natural features or systems or sites of cultural significance.

Baseline study Assessment of the present situation in order to measure changes in that environment over time.

Best practice Involves seeking excellence, keeping in touch with innovations, avoiding waste and focusing on outcomes which are in the community interest. It involves managing change and continual improvement and in this way it encompasses all levels of an organization.

Biocentric Focuses on living things (different species and genetic variability) as the central point to the development of value systems as opposed to anthropocentricism which focuses on the human and the instrumental value of nature. See also **Ecocentric**.

Biodiversity The variety of different species and genetic variability among individuals within each species.

Biological diversity The variety of all life forms; the different plants, animals and microorganisms, the genes they contain and the ecosystems they form. It is usually considered at three levels: genetic diversity, species diversity and ecosystem diversity.

Bioregion A territory defined by a combination of biological, social and geographic criteria rather than by geopolitical considerations; generally, a system of related inter-connected ecosystems.

Built environment A reference to building, dwellings, structures, utilities, roads and services which enable people to live, work and play, circulate and communicate and fulfil a wide range of functions. The built environment of a place reveals its historical and spatial development, its past and present, and something of its social structure and conflicts.

Carrying capacity The level of visitor use an area can accommodate with high levels of satisfaction for visitors and few impacts on resources. Carrying capacity estimates are determined by many factors, environmental, social and managerial.

Code of conduct Guidelines for appropriate social, cultural and environmentally responsible behaviour. Codes of conduct are in no way binding on the industry or the individual.

Commodification   The production of commodities for exchange via the market as opposed to direct use by the producer. One form of commodified leisure today can be seen in specific forms of tourism, where travel to far distant and different places is marketed as 'paradise gained'. Tourism becomes a 'freely chosen' leisure activity to be consumed.

Community   see **Local community**

Community based tourism (CBT)   CBT is generally considered a privately offered set of hospitality services (and features), extended to visitors, by individuals, families, or a local community. A key objective of CBT is to establish direct personal/cultural exchange between host and guest in a balanced manner that enables a mutual understanding, solidarity and equality for those involved.

Conservation   The protection, maintenance, management, sustainable use, restoration and enhancement of the natural environment (ANZECC Task Force on Biological Diversity, 1993). The management of human use of the biosphere so that it may yield the greatest sustainable benefit to present generations while maintaining its potential to meet the needs and aspirations of future generations (National Conservation Strategy for Australia).

Conservationists   People who believe that resources should be used, managed, and protected so that they will not be degraded and unnecessarily wasted and will be available to present and future generations.

Constant attractions   Attributes that are widespread or have an intangible quality about them (eg. good weather, safety etc.).

Creative thinking   The act of redefining an issue by looking at it from a new perspective.

Decentralization   A conscious policy of locating or relocating some parts or the whole of an organization in outlying regions away from metropolitan areas with concomitant developments of infrastructure coupled with extensions of existing residential areas or the establishment of new towns. The policy may aim at the strengthening of specified regional administrative centres.

Deep ecology   The belief that the earth's resources should be sustained and protected not just for human beings but also for other species. People who believe in this philosophy tend to have a life-centred approach rather then a human-centred approach to managing and sustaining the earth's resources by working with nature, not wasting resources unnecessarily and interfering with nonhuman species to meet the needs of humans.

Demarketing   The term is used to emphasize that marketing may be used to decrease as well as increase the number of satisfied customers. It is used to decrease numbers so that an increase in clientele satisfaction can be increased, through preserving a higher quality experience.

Development   The modification of the biosphere and the application of human, financial, living and non-living resources to satisfy human needs and improve the quality of human life (World Conservation Strategy). The application of human, financial and physical resources to satisfy human needs and improve the quality of life: inevitably development involves modification of the biosphere and some aspects of development may detract from the quality of life locally, regionally, nationally or globally.

Ecocentrism   Focuses on the environment as the central point to the development of values systems as opposed to anthropocentricism which focuses on the human and the instrumental value of nature. See also **Biocentric**.

Ecologically sustainable development   Using, conserving and enhancing the community's resources so that ecological processes, on which life depends, are maintained and the total quality of life, now and in the future, can be increased (Ecologically Sustainable Development Working Groups, 1991).

Ecologically sustainable tourism   An activity that fosters environmental and cultural understanding, appreciation and conservation.

Ecosystem   A dynamic complex of plant, animal, fungal and micro-organism communities and the associated non-living environment interacting as an ecological unit.

Ecotourism   There is no general definition currently in circulation but any conception of it must involve travel to relatively undisturbed or uncontaminated natural areas with the objective of studying, admiring and enjoying the natural environment of that area. An important point is that the person who practises ecotourism has the opportunity of immersing him or herself in nature in a way that most people cannot enjoy in their routine, urban existences. As there is no strict consensus on a specific definition of ecotourism it had been suggested it also is responsible travel that conserves natural environments and sustains the well-being of local people.

Endangered species   Fauna and flora likely to become extinct due to direct exploitation by humans, intrusion into highly specialized habitats, threats from other species, interruption of the food chain, pollution or a combination of such factors.

Endemic tourism   Broadly defined as tourism which recognizes: (a) that each individual locality or community has its special character; and (b) that particular character or identity may well constitute its major attractiveness to tourists.

Environment   All aspects of the surroundings of human beings as individuals or in social groups (Commonwealth Environmental Protection (OP) Amendment No. 12, 1967).

Environmental economics   A recognized field of specialization in economic science. Environmental economics examines the costs and benefits of pollution control, and protection of the environment.

Environmental education   A concept ranging from media coverage of environmental issues to formal environmental education, its aims ranging from raising awareness to formal training.

Environmental impact assessment (EIA)   A method of analysis which attempts to predict the likely repercussions of a proposed major development upon the social and physical environment of the surrounding area.

Environmentalists   People who are primarily concerned with preventing pollution and degradation of the air, water, and soil. See **Conservationists**.

Ethics   What we believe to be right or wrong behaviour.

Ethics of 'nature'   Holds that non-human entities are of equal value with the human species. It is broadly intrinsic and ecocentric.

Ethic of 'use'   This is the normative or dominant mode of how human beings relate to nature: where nature is viewed predominantly as a set of resources which humanity is free to employ for its own distinct ends. It is an instrumental and anthropocentric view.

Infrastructure   The buildings or permanent installations associated with a site. Infrastructure for ecotourism is often developed in protected areas and usually involves a scaled down or minimal approach to physical development and change. Infrastructure such as boardwalks and viewing platforms can be used by resource managers to provide for visitor access to ecotourism destinations, while at the same time assisting the management of environmental impacts and the physical protection of natural resources.

Institutional planning Planning by institutional agencies and public bodies not central to the planning process, yet having significant implications for environmental planning. One of the functions of the central planning agency is to accommodate and coordinate proposals to enable the objectives of other agencies to be reconciled with overall planning objectives.

Integrated planning Planning process which takes into account the social and cultural priorities of host communities to shape tourism into a form appropriate for each locality.

Intergenerational equity Refers to a concept that the present generation should ensure that the health, diversity and productivity of the environment is maintained or enhanced for the benefit of future generations.

Internalization of environmental costs Internalization of environmental costs involves the creation of economic environments so that social and private views of economic efficiency coincide. It is concerned with structures, reporting mechanisms and tools to achieve this end.

Interpretation An educational activity which aims to reveal meanings and relationships through the use of original objects, first hand experience and illustrative media, rather than simply by communicating factual information.

Intragenerational equity Intragenerational equity concerns equity within a single generation. It concerns equity issues within nations and between nations. Inequity within a generation may involve failure to meet what might be widely regarded as basic environmental or social needs, or gross disparities between the environmental or social quality of life of individuals or groups.

Intrinsic value Is value that exists in its own right, for its own sake.

Land use zoning Land use zoning divides sections of land into areas based on their sensitivity and conservation values.

Limits of Acceptable Change (LAC) Is a model used to help establish the maximum 'damage' level for a resource that society is prepared to accept as custodian of resources for both present and future generations and to define the maximum level of use consistent with that damage level (RAC Coastal Zone Inquiry Information Paper No. 8, 1993).

Local community The concept of local community concerns a particularly constituted set of social relationships based on something which the individuals have in common – usually a common sense of identity (*cf.* Marshall, 1994: 73–76).

Management plan The process of the coordination and preparation of a document and the realization of a set of goals, within a protected area or local community or organization, that leads to some common directions.

Market demand How much of an economic good consumers are willing to buy at a particular price.

Market supply How much of an economic good consumers are willing and able to produce and sell at a particular price in a given period.

Mass tourism Mass tourism is generally seen as being an overarching term for tourism that is undertaken by the majority of travellers. This thesis, in exploring the specificity of a particular tourist experience in depth, may contribute towards an understanding of not only the significant divergences and convergences that exist between both mass tourism and alternative tourism, but also the subtle nuances that subtend these tourist experiences. Therefore, it is not simply a matter of differentiating, in a binary fashion, between a general category of mass tourism and the derivation of niche elements within it. Semiotically, in its structural sense, the appellation of 'alternative' logically implies an antithesis. It arises as the contrary to that which is seen as negative or detrimental about conventional tourism, so it is always a semantic inversion, which is found at all levels of discourse. In the domain of logic, an alternative is based on a dialectical paradigm that offers only two possibilities. Two contemporaneous terms are placed in mutual exclusion, with an 'excluded middle', that leaves a conclusion that is either one or the other. Therefore the terminology of alternative and mass tourism are mutually interdependent, each relying on a series of value-laden judgements that themselves structure the definitional content of the terms.

Micro-social   Macro- and micro-social are used in the context of sociology. The former generally examines the wider structures, interdependent social institutions, global and historical processes of social life, while the latter is more concerned with action, interaction and the construction of meaning. It is important, however, not to generalize too greatly as the relationship between social system and social actor is not always clearly distinguished (*cf.* Marshall, 1994: 298).

Motivations   The factors that determine a human's reasons for doing something, in the context of travel the reasons for someone to travel to a destination.

Multiple use   Principle of managing public land such as a national forest so it is used for a variety of purposes, such as timbering, mining, recreation, grazing, wildlife preservation, and soil and water conservation.

Natural   Existing in, or formed by nature; non-urban; also incorporates cultural aspects.

Performance standards   Standards employed in environmental planning which specify desired results and do not in themselves specify the methods by which performance criteria should be met.

Philosophy   The system of principles concerning all the conditions in which humans live and which influence their behaviour and development.

Precautionary principle   Where there are threats of serious or irreversible environmental damage, lack of full scientific certainty should not be used as a reason for postponing measures to prevent environmental degradation. In the application of the precautionary principle decisions should be guided by careful evaluation to avoid serious or irreversible damage to the environment and an assessment of the risk-weighted consequences of various options.

Protected areas   Defined in Article 2 of the International Convention on Biological Diversity as a geographically defined area which is designated or regulated and managed to achieve specific conservation. Protected area system characteristics are: *adequacy* – the ability of the reserve to maintain the ecological viability and integrity of populations, species and communities; *comprehensiveness* – the degree to which the full range of ecological communities and their biological diversity are incorporated within reserves; *representativeness* – the extent to which areas selected for inclusion in the national reserve system are capable of reflecting the known biological diversity and ecological patterns and processes of the ecological community or ecosystem concerned.

Recreation opportunity spectrum (ROS)   The basic assumption of ROS is that a quality recreational experience is assured by providing a diverse range of recreational opportunities, catering for various tastes and user group preferences. The ROS focuses on the setting in which recreation occurs. A recreation opportunity setting is the combination of physical, biological, social and managerial conditions that give value to a place. ROS has been described as a framework for presenting carrying capacities and managing recreational impacts. The ROS provides a systematic framework for looking at the actual distribution of opportunities and a procedure for assessing possible management actions.

Social impact assessment (SIA) An assessment of the impact on people and society of major development projects: social impact assessment is often a weak point in environmental impact assessments. Social impacts are defined as those changes in social relations between members of a community, society or institution, resulting from external change.

Stewardship An approach to the care of nature through its dominance by humans relying on predominantly economic value systems and the pre-eminence of technology (backed up by enormous advances in scientific understanding).

Strategic planning A dynamic and issue-orientated process to help the individual/organization take control of significant and desirable potential futures. Strategic planning is the process of deciding what the future of the operation should be, and what strategies should be followed in order to make that future happen.

Sustainability This is advanced through the magical transmutation of the term 'ecological sustainable development' into 'economically sustainable development' through the substitution of the letter E in the acronym 'ESD'. It is an indication of the latitude with which the concept of sustainability can be interpreted. Thus the concept of sustainability is both contested and deployed, often for profoundly different reasons.

Sustainable Able to be carried out without damaging the long-term health and integrity of natural and cultural environments.

Sustainable design Environmentally and culturally sensitive building design, where construction methods and materials have minimal impact on the environment.

Sustainable development Defined by the World Commission on Environment and Development (WCED) in 1987 as 'development that meets the needs of the present without compromising the ability of future generations to meet their own needs'. Environmental protection and management is central to sustainable development.

Sustainable yield The use of living resources at levels of harvesting and in ways that allow those resources to supply products and services indefinitely.

SWOT analysis SWOT is an assessment of the project/organization strengths and weaknesses and an analysis of the opportunities and threats that exist in the marketplace.

Technocentrism A belief system that supports the idea that the creation of new products and processes will be able to improve our chances of survival, comfort and quality of life before the depletion or destruction of renewable resources.

Tourism industry The collection of all collaborating firms and organizations which perform specific activities directed at satisfying leisure, pleasure and recreational needs (Stear *et al.*, 1988: 1).

Tourism optimization management model (TOMM) This model builds on the LAC system to incorporate a stronger political dimension and seeks to monitor and manage tourism in a way that seeks optimum sustainable performance, rather than maximum levels or carrying capacities. TOMM involves identifying strategic imperatives (such as policies and emerging issues), identifying community values, product characteristics, growth patterns, market trends and opportunities, positioning and branding, and alternative scenarios for tourism in a region, while seeking optimum conditions, indicators, acceptable ranges, monitoring techniques, benchmarks, annual performance and predicted performance having done this it can examine poor performance, and explore cause/effect relationships.

Tourists All visitors travelling for whatever purpose involving at least an overnight stay

40 km from their usual place of residence (World Tourism Organization).

User pays   The principle that management and maintenance costs for individual parts should be borne (either partially or fully) by those using them.

Utilitarian   A focus on the usefulness of nature in terms of human values rather than a focus on beauty or spirituality – practicality of nature's use by humans for material gain.

Visitor activity management process (VAMP)   The visitor activity management process relates to interpretation and visitor services. This framework involves the development of activity profiles which connect activities with the social and demographic characteristics of the participants, the activity setting requirements and trends affecting the activity. The VAMP framework is designed to operate in parallel with the natural resource management process.

Visitor impact management (VIM)   The visitor impact management process involves a combination of legislation/policy review, scientific problem identification (both social and natural) and analysis and professional. The principles of VIM are to identify unacceptable changes occurring as a result of visitor use and developing management strategies to keep visi-tor impacts within acceptable levels while integrating visitor impact management into existing agency planning, design and management processes. It attempts to do this based on the best scientific understanding and situational information available. While both LAC and VIM frameworks rely on indicators and standards as a means of defining impacts deemed unacceptable and place carrying capacities into a broader managerial context. VIM however, makes reference to planning and policy and includes identifying the probable causes of impacts, whereas LAC places more emphasis on defining opportunity classes.

Wilderness   Land that, together with its plant and animal communities, is in a state that has not been substantially modified by and is remote from the influences of European settlement or is capable of being restored to such a state, and is of sufficient size to make its maintenance in such a state feasible. A wilderness area is a large, substantially unmodified natural area (or capable of being restored to such a state). Such areas are managed to protect or enhance this relatively natural state, and also to provide opportunities for self-reliant recreation in a relatively unmodi-fied natural environment.

Zone of Opportunity   A geographic area that ideally encompasses an endemic core resource, as well as particular resources/attractions.

Bibliography

Allcock, A., Jones, B., Lane, S. and Grant, J. (1994) *National Ecotourism Strategy*, Australian Government Publishing Service: Canberra.

Ashworth, G. and Goodall, B. (1990) *Marketing in the Tourism Industry: the Promotion of Destination Regions*, Croom Helm: London.

AAP (Australian Associated Press) (1996) Transcript of Warwick Parer's address, 3 July, AAP: Sydney.

Australian Commonwealth Department of Tourism (1992) *A National Tourism Strategy*, Australian Government Publishing Service: Canberra.

ANCA (Australian Nature Conservation Agency) (1995) Transcript of a workshop in Alice Springs, Australian Nature Conservation Agency: Canberra.

Australian Tourism Industry Association (1990) *Environmental Guidelines For Tourist Developments*, Australian Government Publishing Service: Canberra.

Ballantine, J. and Eagles, P. (1994) Defining ecotourists, *Journal of Sustainable Tourism*, 2(4), 210–214.

Barlow, A. (1992) Land and country: Source, self and sustenance. In *Aboriginal Involvement in Parks and Protected Areas* (eds J. Birckhead, T. De Lacy and L. Smith), Australian Institute of Aboriginal and Torres Strait Islander Studies Report Series. Aboriginal Studies Press: Canberra.

Bates, B. (1991) Ecotourism – a case study of the lodges in Papua New Guinea. Paper presented at the PATA 40th Annual Conference, Bali, Indonesia, 10–13 April.

Bates, B. and Witter, D. (1992) Cultural tourism at Mutawintji – and beyond. In *Aboriginal involvement in parks and protected areas* (eds J. Birckhead, T. de Lacy and L. Smith), Australian Institute of Aboriginal and Torres Strait Islander Studies Report Series. Aboriginal Studies Press: Canberra.

Beaumont, B. (1997) Perceived crowding as an evaluation standard for determining social carrying capacity in tourism recreation areas: the case of Green Island, North Queensland. In *Tourism planning and policy in Australia and New Zealand: Cases, issues and practice* (eds C.M. Hall, J. Jenkins and G. Kearsley), Irwin Publishers: Sydney.

Beckmann, E. (1991) Environmental interpretation for education and management in Australian national parks and other protected areas. PhD thesis, University of New England.

Bello, D.C. and Etzel, M.J. (1985) The role of novelty in the pleasure travel experience, *Journal of Travel Research*, 24(1), 20–26.

Bilsen, F. (1987) Integrated tourism in Senegal: An alternative, *Tourism Recreation Research*, 13 (1), 19–23.

Birch, C. (1991) A titanic on a collision course, 21 C, Autumn, p. 82.

Birtles, A. and Sofield, T. (1996) Taking the next step. In *Ecotourism and nature-based tourism* (eds H. Richins, J. Richardson and A. Crabtree), Proceedings of the Ecotourism Association of Australia National Conference, Alice Springs, Ecotourism Association of Australia: Brisbane. pp. 15–22.

Birtles, A., Cahill, M., Valentine, P. and Davis, D. (1995) Incorporating research on visitor experiences into ecologically sustainable management of whale shark tourism. In *Ecotourism and Nature-based Tourism* (eds H. Richins, J. Richardson and A. Crabtree), Proceedings of the Ecotourism Association of Australia National Conference, Alice Springs, Ecotourism Association of Australia, Brisbane, 195–202.

Blamey, R.K. (1995a) *The nature of ecotourism*, Occasional Paper No. 21, Bureau of Tourism Research: Canberra.

Blamey, R. (1995b) Profiling the ecotourism market. In *Ecotourism and nature-based tourism: taking the next steps* (eds H. Richins, J. Richardson and A. Crabtree), Proceedings of the Ecotourism Association of Australia National Conference, Alice Springs, Ecotourism Association of Australia: Brisbane, pp. 1–8.

Blangy, S. and Epler-Wood, M. (1992) *Developing and implementing ecotourism guidelines for wild lands and neighbouring communities*, The Ecotourism Society: Vermont, USA.

Blangy, S. and Nielsen, T. (1993) Ecotourism and minimum impact policy, *Annals of Tourism Research*, 20(2), 357–360.

Boden, R. and Breckwoldt, R. (1995) *National reserves system cooperative program evaluation*, Australian National Conservation Authority: Canberra

Boele, N. (1993) Sustainability, tourism policy and the host community: an exploration of destination image assessment techniques. Bachelor of Arts (Leisure Studies) Honours Thesis, University of Technology, Sydney, Australia.

Boo, E. (1990) *Ecotourism: the potentials and pitfalls*, vols 1 and 2, World Wide Fund for Nature: Washington, DC.

Boo, E. (1991) Planning for ecotourism. *Parks*, 2 (3), 4–8.

Boorstin, D.J. (1972) From traveller to tourist: the lost art of travel. Chapter 3 in *The image: a guide to pseudo-events in America*, Atheneum: New York, pp. 77–117.

Bottrill, C.G. and Pearce, D.G. (1995) Ecotourism: towards a key elements approach to operationalising the concept, *Journal of Sustainable Tourism*, 3(1), 45–56.

Bowman, S. (1998) Parks in partnership, *National Parks*, January/February, pp. 30–33.

Bowermater, J. (1994) Can ecotourism save the planet?, *Condé Nast Traveller*, December, pp. 2–4.

Bragg, L. (1990) Ecotourism: a working definition, *Forum*, 2(2), 7–12.

Britten, S. and Clarke W.C. (eds) (1987) *Tourism in small developing countries*, University of the South Pacific: Suva.

Buckley R. and Pannell, J. (1990) Environmental impacts of tourism and recreation in national parks and conservation reserves, *Journal of Tourism Studies*, 1(1), 24–32.

Bunting, B. (1991) Nepal's Annapurna conservation area. In *Proceedings of the PATA 91 40th Annual Conference*, Bali, Indonesia, 12 April.

Burchett, C. (1992) A new direction in travel: Aboriginal tourism in Australia's Northern Territory. Paper presented at the Northern Territory Tourist Commission Environmental Conference – Expo 1992, April.

Busch, R. (1994) Ecotourism: responsibilities of the media. Paper presented at the 1994 World Congress on Adventure Travel and Ecotourism, Hobart, Tasmania, 7–10 November.

Butler, J.R. (1992) Ecotourism: its changing face and evolving philosophy. Paper presented at the International Union for Conservation of Nature and Natural Resources (IUCN), IVth World Congress on National Parks and Protected Areas, Caracas, Venezuela, 10–12 February.

Butler, R.W. (1990) Alternative tourism: pious hope or Trojan horse?, *Journal of Travel Research*, 3(1), 40–45.

Butler, R.W. (1980) The concept of a tourism area cycle of evolution: implications for management of resources, *Canadian Geographer*, 24(1), 5–12.

Butler, R.W. (1991) Tourism, environment and sustainable development, *Environmental Conservation*, 18(3), 201–209.

Butler, R.W. and Pearce, D. (1995) *Change in tourism: people, places and processes*, Routledge: London.

Calkin, J. (1997) *Sustainable tourism strategy for Tonga*, Calkin and Associaties: Sydney.

Cameron-Smith, B. (1977) Educate or regulate? Interpretation in national park management, *Australian Parks and Recreation*, Nov., pp. 34–37.

Carson, R. (1962) *Silent spring*, Penguin: London.

Carter, R.W. (1984) *A strategy for park interpretation*, Queensland National Parks and Wildlife Service: Queensland.

Carter, E. (1987) Tourism in the least developed countries, *Annals of Tourism Research*, 14, 202–206.

Carter, E. (1994) Introduction. In *Ecotourism: a sustainable option?* (eds E. Carter and G. Lowman) John Wiley and Sons: New York, pp. 3–17.

Carter, E. and Lowman, G. (eds) (1994) *Ecotourism: a sustainable option?* Wiley: New York.

Carter, F. and Moore, M. (1991) *Ecotourism in the 21st Century, First International Conference in Ecotourism*, 25–27 September, Brisbane, QLD.

Carter, R.W. (1979) *Interpretation: an approach to the conservation of the natural and cultural heritage of Australia*, Queensland National Parks and Wildlife Service: Queensland.

Ceballos-Lascurain, H. (n.d.) Faxed research notes from the author in 1987.

Ceballos-Lascurain, H. (1990) Tourism, ecotourism and protected areas. Paper presented at the 34th Working Session of the Commission of National Parks and Protected Areas, Perth, Australia, 26–27 November.

Ceballos-Lascurain, H. (1992) Tourism, ecotourism and protected areas: national parks and protected areas. In *Seminar proceedings of the International Union for Conservation of Nature and Natural Resources (IUCN) IVth World Congress on National Parks and Protected Areas*, Caracas, Venezuela, 10–12 February, pp. 84–89.

Ceballos-Lascurain, H. (1996) *Tourism, ecotourism and protected areas: the state of nature-based tourism around the world and guidelines for its development*. IUCN–The World Conservation Union: Gland, Switzerland, and Cambridge, UK.

Charters, T., Gabriel, M. and Prasser, S. (1996) *National Parks Private Sectors Role*. USQ Press: Toowoomba, Queensland.

Choegyal, L. (1991) Ecotourism in national parks and wildlife reserves. Paper presented at the PATA 40th Annual Conference, Bali, Indonesia, 10–13 April, pp. 93–102.

CIDA (Canadian International Development Agency) (1995) *Costa Rica – An Introduction*. Centre for Intercultural Training, Canadian International Development Agency: Ottawa.

Church, P.A. (1994) Protecting biological diversity: Jamica case study. USAID working paper 190. United States Agency for International Development: Washington, DC.

Clark, J. (1991) Carrying capacity and tourism in coastal and protected areas. Parks, 2(3): 13–17.

Clark, L. and Banford, D. (1991) Ecotourism potentials and pitfalls. In *The promotion of sustainable tourism development in Pacific island countries' seminar proceedings*, Regional seminar on the promotion of sustainable tourism development in Pacific island countries, Suva, Fiji, 18–22 November, pp. 56–63.

Clark, R. and Stankey, G. (1979) *The recreation opportunity spectrum: a framework for planning, management and research*, General Technical Report, Pacific North-West Forest and Range Experiment Station, US Department of Agriculture: Seattle.

Cockrell, D.E., Bange, S. and Roggenbuck, J.W. (1984) Normative influence through interpretive communication, *Journal of Environmental Education*, 15(4), pp. 20–26.

Cohen, E. (1972) Towards a sociology of international tourism, *Social Research*, 39(1), 164–182.

Cohen, J. and Richardson, J. (1995) Nature tourism vs. incompatible industries: megamarketing the ecological environment to ensure the economic future of nature tourism, *Travel and Tourism Marketing*, 4(2): 107–116.

Collins, C. (1993) Wraps come off the new age traveller, *The Australian*, 31 December.

Colong Foundation (1996) *Colong Foundation Bulletin*, January issue, Sydney.

Colvin, J. (1994) Capirona – a model of indigenous tourism, *Journal of Sustainable Development*, 2(3), 174–177.

Commonwealth Department of Tourism (1992) Forest ecotourism program, Commonwealth Department of Tourism, Australian Government Publishing Service: Canberra.

Commonwealth Department of Tourism (1994) *National ecotourism strategy*, Commonwealth Department of Tourism, Australian Government Publishing Service: Canberra.

Coppock, S.T. and Rogers, A.W. (1975) Too many Americans out in the wilderness, *Geographical Magazine*, 47(8): 508–513.

Cornelius, S.E. (1991) Wildlife conservation in Central America: will it survive the '90s? In *The Proceedings of the Trans 56th N.A. Wildlife and Natural Resource Conference*, 40–49.

Courtenay, J. (1996) Savannah Guides, Australia: British Airways Tourism for Tomorrow Awards 1996, Pacific Region (unpublished).

Cox, J. (1985) The resort concept: the good, the bad and the ugly. Keynote paper presented to National Conference on Tourism and Resort Development, Kuring-gai College of Advanced Education, Sydney, 4–11 November.

Craik, J. (1991) *Resorting to tourism: cultural policies for tourist development in Australia*, Allen & Unwin: Sydney.

Crompton, J.L. (1979) Motivations for pleasure vacations, *Annals of Tourism Research*, 3(1), 408–424.

Crompton, J.L. (1981) Dimensions of the social group role in pleasure vacations, *Annals of Tourism Research*, 8(4), 550–567.

Crompton, J.L. and Howard, D.R. (1980) Financing, managing and marketing. In *A strategy for tourism and sustainable developments* (ed. L. Cronin), Government of Canada: Ottawa, pp. 12–16.

Cruz, M, Meyer, C.A., Repetto, R. and Woodward, R. (1992) *Population Growth, Poverty and Environmental Stress: Frontier Migration in the Philippines and Costa Rica*. World Resources Institute: Washington DC.

Dann, G. (1981) Tourist motivation: an appraisal, *Annals of Tourism Research*, 4, 184–194.

Department of Tourism, Sport and Recreation (1994) Ecotourism adding value to tourism in natural areas: *a discussion book on nature based tourism in Tasmania*, Department of Tourism, Sport and Recreation: Hobart.

Dernoi, L.A. (1981) Alternative tourism: towards a new style in north-south relations, *International Journal of Tourism Management*, 2(4), 253–264.

Dernoi, L.A. (1988) Alternative or community based tourism. In *Tourism – a vital force for peace* (eds L. D'Amore and J. Jafari), L. D'Amore: Montreal.

Dowling, R. (1991) An ecotourism planning model. In *Ecotourism: incorporating the global classroom* (ed. B. Weiler), Bureau of Tourism Research: Sydney.

Dowling, R. (1992) An ecotourism planning model. In *Ecotourism: incorporating the global classroom* (ed. B. Weiler), Bureau of Tourism Research: Canberra, pp. 127–133.

Driver, B., Brown, P.J., Starkey, G.H. and Gregorie, T.G. (1987) The ROS planning system: evolution, basic concepts and research needed, *Leisure Sciences*, 9, 3.

Duff, L. (1993) Ecotourism in national parks, *National Parks Journal*, 37(3), 18–20.

Dunster, J. and Dunster, K. (1996) Dictionary of *natural resource management*, CAB International: UBC Press, Canada.

Durst, P. and Ingram, C. (1989) Nature-orientated tourism promotion by developing countries, Tourism Management, 26, 39–43.

EAA (Ecotourism Association of Australia) (1996) *National ecotourism accreditation program – application document*, EAA: Brisbane.

Eagles, P.F. (1992) The motivation of Canadian ecotourists. In *Ecotourism: incorporating the global classroom* (ed. B. Weiler), Bureau of Tourism Research: Canberra, pp. 12–17.

Eagles, P. (1994) Understanding the market for sustainable tourism, Paper presented at the National Recreation and Parks Association Annual Congress, Minneapolis, Minnesota, USA, 11–15 October.

Eagles, P.F.J., Ballantine, J.L. and Fennell, D.A. (1992) Marketing to the ecotourist: case studies from Kenya and Costa Rica. Paper presented at International Union for Conservation of Nature and Natural Resources (IUCN) IVth World Congress on National Parks and Protected Areas, Caracas, Venezuela, 10–12 February.

Eckermann, A.K. and Dowd, L.T. (1988) Structural violence and Aboriginal organisations in rural-urban Australia, *The Journal of Legal Pluralism and Unofficial Law*, **27**, 55–77.

Eckersley, R. (1992) *Environmentalism and political theory*. University College London Press: London.

Econsult Pty Ltd (1995) *National ecotourism strategy business development program report*, Commonwealth Department of Tourism: Melbourne.

Edward, S. (1992) The rape of the Himalayas, *The Guardian*, June.

Edwards, G. and Prineas, T. (1995) Plans, networks and lines: workshop on planning for networks of regional open space. The First International Urban Parks and Waterways Best Practice Conference, Melbourne 26 February – 1 March.

Eidsvik, H.K. (1980) National parks and other protected areas: some reflections on the past and prescriptions for the future. *Environmental Conservation*, 7(3), pp. 185–190.

Encel, J.R. and Encel, J.C. (1991) *Ethics of environmental development: global challenge and international response*. University of Arizona Press: Tucson.

ESDSC (Ecologically Sustainable Development Steering Committee) (1992) *Draft National Strategy for Ecologically Sustainable Development: A Discussion Book*, Australian Government Publishing Service: Canberra.

Evans-Smith, D. (1994) *National ecotourism strategy*. Commonwealth Department of Tourism: Australian Government Printing Service, Canberra.

Figgis, P. (1994) Tourism on fragile lands: the Australian experience. In *Proceedings of the world congress on ecotourism and adventure travel*, Hobart, Tasmania.

Fly, J. (1986) (unpub.) Nature, outdoor recreation and tourism: the basis for regional population growth in northern lower Michigan. PhD thesis, University of Michigan.

Forestell, P.H. (1990) Marine education and ocean tourism: replacing parasitism with symbiosis. In *Proceedings of the 1990 congress on coastal and marine tourism – a symposium and workshop on balancing conservation and economic development* (eds M.L. Miller, and J. Auyong), National Coastal Resources Research and Development Institute: Newport, OR.

Forestry Tasmania (1994) *Tourism in Tasmania's state forest: a discussion book*, Forestry Tasmania: Hobart.

Fox, W. (1990) *Towards a transpersonal ecology*. Shambhala: Boston.

Furze, B., De Lacy, T. and Birkhead, J. (1996) Culture, conservation, and biodiversity: the social dimension of linking local level development. John Wiley: Sydney.

Gabor, M.T. (1997) A millennium vision for tourism: a government perspective. In *Australian Tourism Conference Speakers' Papers*, 1–3 October 1997, Tourism Council Australia: Sydney.

Garcia-Ramon, M.D., Canoves, G. and Valdovinos, N. (1994) Farm tourism, gender and the environment in Spain, *Annals of Tourism Research*, 22, 267–287.

Gertsakis, J. (1995) Sustainable design for ecotourism deserves diversity. In *Ecotourism and nature-based tourism*: *taking the next steps* (eds H. Richins, J. Richardson and A. Crabtree), Proceedings of the Ecotourism Association of Australia National Conference, Alice Springs, Ecotourism Association of Australia: Brisbane.

Gilbert, D. (1984) Tourist product differentiation. Paper presented at *Tourism: managing for results conference*, University of Surrey, England, November.

Godfrey-Smith, W. (1980) The value of wilderness: a philosophical approach. In *Wilderness management in Australia* (eds R.W. Robertson, P. Helman and A. Davey), Proceedings of a symposium at the Canberra College of Advanced Education 19–23 July, Canberra College of Advanced Education: Canberra, pp. 56–71.

Goldfarb, G. (1989) *International ecotourism: a strategy for conservation and development*. The Osborn Centre for Economic Development, World Wildlife Fund – Conservation Foundation: Washington, DC.

Gonsalves, P.S. (1984) Tourism in India: an overview and from leisure to learning: a strategy for India. In *Alternative tourism*: *Report on the workshop on alternative tourism with a focus on Asia* (ed. P. Holden), Ecumenical Coalition on Third World Tourism: Bangkok.

Graefe, A.R., Kuss, F.R. and Vaske, J.J. (1990) *Visitor impact management: the planning framework*, vol. 2, National Parks and Conservation Association: Washington, DC.

Graham, R. (1990) Visitor management and Canada's National Park. In *Towards serving our visitors and managing our resources* (eds R. Graham and R. Lawrence), Proceedings of the First Canada/US Workshop on Visitor Management in Parks and Protected Areas, Waterloo, Ontario, Tourism Research and Education Centre, University of Waterloo and Canadian Parks Service, Environment Canada.

Graham, R., Nilsen, P. and Payne, R. (1987) Visitor activity planning and management: Canadian National Parks: marketing within a context of integration. In *Social science in natural resource management systems* (eds M. Millar, R. Gale and P. Brown), Westview Press: Boulder, CO, 149–166.

Graham, S. (1991) *Handle with care: a guide to responsible travel in developing countries*. Novel Press: Chicago.

Greenwood, D.J. (1989) Culture by the pound: an anthropological perspective on tourism as cultural commoditization. In *Hosts and guests: the anthropology of tourism* (ed. V.L. Smith), University of Pennsylvania Press: Philadelphia.

Griffin, T. and Boele, N. (1993) Alternative paths to sustainable tourism, *Annual Review of Travel*, 15–23.

Gunn, C.A. (1994) *Tourism planning: basics, concepts, cases*, Taylor and Francis: Washington, DC.

Hackett, M. (1992) Solving the ecotourism dilemma. In *Ecotourism: incorporating the global classroom* (ed. B. Weiler), Bureau of Tourism Research: Canberra, 207–211.

Hall, S. (1987) *The Fourth World: the Arctic and its Heritage*, Hodder and Stoughton: London.

Hall, C.M. (1991) *Introduction to tourism in Australia – challenges and opportunities*. Longman Cheshire: Melbourne, Australia.

Hall, C.M. (1994) 'Ecotourism in Australia, New Zealand and the South Pacific: appropriate tourism or new form of ecological imperialism?', In *Ecotourism: A Sustainable Option* (eds E. Cater and G. Lowman), Wiley and Sons: Chichester, 137–155.

Hall, C.M. and McArthur, S. (1996) *Heritage Management in Australia and New Zealand – The Human Dimension*, 2nd edn, Oxford University Press: Oxford.

Hall, C.M. and McArthur, S. (1998) *Integrated Heritage Management – Principles and Practice*, The Stationery Office: Norwich.

Hall, C.M., McArthur, S. and Spoelder, P. (1991) Ecotourism in Antarctica and adjacent sub-Antarctic Islands. In *Ecotourism: incorporating the global classroom* (ed. B. Weiler), Bureau of Tourism Research: Canberra.

Ham, S.H. (1992) *Environmental interpretation: a practical guide for people with big ideas and small budgets*, North American Press: Golden, COL.

Hardin, G. (1968) Tragedy of the commons, *Science*, 162, 1243–1248.

Harrison, D. (1992) *Tourism and the less developed countries*, Belhaven Press: London.

Hawkins, R. (1995) An action plan for travel and tourism, *Environment and Development*, 5 March, 3.

Haywood, K.M. (1988) Responsible and responsive tourism planning in the community, *Tourism Management*, 9(2), 105–118.

Healy, R.G. (1989) *Economic consideration in nature-oriented tourism: the case of tropical forest tourism*, Southeastern Center for Forest Economic Research: Durham, North Carolina.

Hedstram, E. (1992) Preservation or Profit? *National Parks*, **66**(1–2), USA, 18–29.

Henion, K. (1975) *Ecological marketing*, Grind Inc.: Columbus, OH.

Henion, K. and Kinnear, T. (1976) *Ecological marketing*, American Marketing Association: Chicago, USA.

Hill, D. (1993) Interpretation – a manager's perspective. In *Open to interpretation – ideas, feelings and actions* (eds S. Olsson and R. Saunders), Conference Papers of the Inaugural Conference of the Interpretation Australia Association, 16 and 17 November 1992, Interpretation Australia Association: Melbourne.

Holden, P. (ed.). (1984) *Alternative tourism: report on the workshop on alternative tourism with a focus on Asia*. Ecumenical Coalition on Third World Tourism: Bangkok.

Hore-Lacy, I. (1991) A mineral industry perspective on sustainable resource use, *The Australian Quarterly*, Summer.

Hultman, S.G. (1992) Why don't they come? Guided tours for campers. In *Proceedings of heritage interpretation international global congress, Honolulu*, University of Hawaii Sea Grant College Program: Hawaii.

Hvenegaard, L. (1994) Ecotourism: a status report and conceptual framework, *Journal of Tourism Studies*, 5(2), 24–34.

Ingram, D. and Durst, P. (1989) Nature-oriented tour operators: travel to developing countries, *Journal of Travel Research*, Fall, 11–15.

Inskeep, E. (1991) Environmental planning for tourism, *Annals of Tourism Research*, 14, 11–135.

Iso-Ahola, S.E. (1983) *Towards a social psychology of leisure and recreation*, Wm. C. Brown Company, Dubuque, Iowa.

Ittelson, W.H., Proshansky, H.M. and Rivilin, L.G. (1974) An introduction to environmental psychology. Holt, Rinehart & Winston: New York.

IUCN Interpretation Australia Association (1995) *Membership brochure*, Interpretation Australia Association: Collingwood, Victoria.

IUCN (International Union for the Conservation of Nature) (1985) *United Nations list of national parks and protected areas*. IUCN: Gland, Gstaad.

IUCN (International Union for the Conservation of Nature) (1992) *Caracas action plan*. IUCN: Gland, Gstaad.

IUCN (International Union for the Conservation of Nature) (1996) *Economic Assessment of Protected Areas: Guidelines for Their Assessment*. IUCN: Gland, Gstaad.

Jarviluoma, J. (1992) Alternative tourism and the evolution tourist areas, *Tourism Management*, March, 118–120.

Jefferson, A and Lickorish, L. (1988) *Marketing tourism: a practical guide*, Longman: Harlow, Essex.

Jenkins, O. and McArthur, S. (1996) Marketing protected areas, *Australian Parks and Recreation*, 32(4), 10–15.

Jenner, P. and Smith, C. (1991) *The tourism industry and the environment*. Condor, The Economist Intelligence Unit Special Report No. 2453: London.

Johnson, B. (1993) Breaking out of the tourist trap, *Cultural Survival Quarterly*, 14(1), 2–5.

Johnson, P. and Thomas, B. (eds) (1992) *Perspectives of tourism policy*. Mansell: London.

Jones, A. (1987) Green tourism, *Tourism Management*, 26, 354–356.

Joy, A. and Motzney, B. (1992) Ecotourism and ecotourists: preliminary thoughts on the new leisure traveller. In *Seminar proceedings of the AMA winter educator's conference*, American Marketing Association: Chicago, USA.

Kallen, C. (1990) *Tourism as a conservation tool*. Working Paper, Washington, DC: World Resources Institute.

Kenchington, R.A. (1990) Tourism in coastal and marine settings: the recreational perspective. In *Proceedings of the 1990 congress on coastal and marine tourism – a symposium and workshop on balancing conservation and economic development* (eds. M.L. Miller and J. Auyong), National Coastal Resources Research and Development Institute: Newport, OR.

Kerr, J. (1991) Making dollars and sense out of ecotourism/nature tourism, First International Conference in Ecotourism, Brisbane, 25–27 September.

Kinnaird, V. and Hall, D. (1994) *Tourism: a gender analysis*. John Wiley: Chichester.

Kotler, P. and Andreasen, A. (1991) *Strategic marketing for non-profit organisations*, Prentice-Hall: Englewood-Cliffs, NJ.

Kotler, P. and Armstrong, G. (1993) *Principles of marketing*, Prentice-Hall: Englewood-Cliffs, NJ.

Krippendorf, J. (1982) Towards new tourism politics, *Tourism Management*, 3, 135–148.

Krippendorf, J. (1987) *The holiday makers*. Heinemann: London.

Kusler, J. (n.d.) Protected areas approaches and ecotourism. (Unpublished.)

Kutay, K. (1990) Ecotourism: travel's new wave, *Vis a Vis*, July, pp. 4–80.

Lea, J.P. (1988) *Tourism and development in the third world*. Routledge: London.

Lea, J.P. (1993) Tourism development ethics in the third world, *Annals of Tourism Research*, 20, 701–715.

Lea, J.P. (1995) Tourism and the delivery of positive development, *Contours*, 17, 4–10.

Leopold, A. (1966) *A sand country almanac*. Ballantine: New York.

Lewis, W.S. (1980) *Interpreting for park visitors*, Eastern Acorn Press: USA.

Lillywhite, M. (1992) Low impact tourism: sustaining indigenous natural resource management and diversifying economic development. In *Proceedings of the 1991 world conference on adventure travel and ecotourism*, Colorado Springs, Colorado, 28–31 August, Englewood, CO: The Adventure Travel Society.

Lillywhite, M. and Lillywhite, L. (1990) Low impact tourism, coupling natural/cultural resource conservation economic development and the tourism industry. In *A Year in Transition*, Proceedings of the Fifth Annual Travel Review Conference, 1990, Washington, DC, 89–99.

Lindberg, K. (1991) Policies for maximising nature tourism's ecological and economic benefits. International Conservation Financing Project Working Paper, World Resources Institute: New York.

Lober, D. (1990) *Protecting a Costa Rican biological reserve forest: forest guards of Monteverde*. Yale University Press: New Haven, CT.

Locke, J. (1976) *An essay concerning human understanding*. Dent: London.

Lovelock, J. (1988) *The ages of GAIA*. Oxford University Press: Oxford.

Lucas, R. (1984) The role of regulations in recreation management. *Western Wildlands*; 9 (2), 6–10.

Lucas, R. and Stankey, G. (1988) *Shifting trends in wilderness recreational use*. United States Forest Service: Missoula, Montana.

Mader, V. (1988) Tourism and environment, *Annals of Tourism Research*, 15(2), 274–276.

MacCannell, D. (1976) *The tourist: a new theory of the leisure class*. Macmillan: London.

MacCannell, D. (1989) Introduction, special issue: semiotics of tourism, *Annals of Tourism Research*, 16, 1–6.

MacCannell, D. (1992) *Empty meeting grounds: the tourist papers*, Routledge: London.

Machlis, G. and Field, D. (1992) *On interpretation, sociology for interpreters of natural and cultural history*, Oregon State University Press: Corvallis.

Machlis, G. and Tichnell, D. (1985) *The state of the world's parks*, Westview Press, Boulder, CO.

Mackay, H. (1992) To tell a lie, *City Ethics*, Issue 7, 3.

MacKinnon, J., MacKinnon, K., Child, G. and Thorsell, J. (1986) *Managing protected areas in the tropics*. IUCN: Gland, Switzerland.

Maguire, P. (1987) *Doing participatory research: a feminist approach*, The Centre for International Education, University of Massachusetts: Amherst, USA.

Maguire, P. (1991) Ecotourism development policy in Belize. In *Seminar Proceedings, World Congress on Leisure and Tourism: Social and Environmental Change*, Sydney, Australia, 16–19 July.

Manidis Roberts (1994) *An investigation into a national ecotourism accreditation scheme*, Commonwealth Department of Tourism: Canberra.

Manidis Roberts (1997) *Tourism optimisation management model – final report*, Manidis Roberts Consultants: Sydney

Marriott, K. (1993) Pricing policy for user pays, *Australian Parks and Recreation*, **29**(3) 42–45.

Marsh, J. (n.d.) National parks in small developing countries, *Ambiguous Alternative*, pp. 25–37.

Marshall, G. (1994) The Concise Oxford Dictionary of Sociology, Oxford University Press

Mason, P. (1990) *Tourism: environment and development perspective*, World Wide Fund for Nature: Godalming, UK.

Mason, P. (1997) Tourism codes of conduct in the arctic and sub-arctic region, *Journal of Sustainable Development*, 5(2), 151–164.

Mason, D. (1991) 'Holidays to help the planet', *The Australian Magazine*, 21 February, 50–56.

Mathews, F. (1987) Conservation and the politics of deep ecology, *Social Alternatives*, 6(4), 37–41.

Mathews, F. (1993) When the planet sings to us, *Res Publica*, 2(1), 9–14.

Mathieson, A. and Wall, G. (1982) *Tourism: economic and social impacts*. Longman: London.

May, V. (1991) Tourism, environment and development, *Tourism Management*, 12(2), 112–118.

Mayo, E. and Jarvis, L. (1981) *The psychology of leisure travel*, CBI: Boston.

McArthur, S. (1990) *Friends by chance*, Tasmanian Department of Parks, Wildlife and Heritage and the Tasmanian Forestry Commission: Hobart, Tasmania.

McArthur, S. (1996) Interpretation in Australia – is it running on borrowed time?, *Australian Parks and Recreation*, 32(2), 33–36.

McArthur, S. (1997a) Introducing the national ecotourism accreditation program, *Australian Parks and Recreation* (Royal Australian Institute of Parks and Recreation, Canberra), 34(2), 11–13.

McArthur, S. (1997b) Beyond the limits of acceptable change – introducing TOMM. In *Proceedings of Tread Lightly on the World Conference*, Coffs Harbour, NSW.

McArthur, S. (1997c) Growth and jobs in Australia's ecotourism industry. In *Australian Ecotourism Guide 1997/98*, Ecotourism Association of Australia: Brisbane, 33–34,

McCool, S.F., Stankey, G.H. and Clark, R.N. (1984) Choosing recreation settings: processes, findings and research directions. In *Proceedings: symposium of recreation choice behaviour* (eds United States Department of Agriculture Forest Service), United States Forest Service: Missoula, Montana.

McCool, S.F. (1990) Limits of acceptable change: evolution and future. In *Towards serving our visitors and managing our resources* (eds R. Graham and R. Lawrence), Proceedings of the First Canada/US workshop on visitor management in parks and protected areas, Waterloo, Ontario, Tourism and Recreation Education Center, University of Waterloo, and Canadian Parks Service, Environment Canada, 185–193.

McCurdy, D. (1985) *Park management*, Southern Illinios University Press: Carbondale.

McGehee, N.G., Loker-Murphy, L. and Uysat, M. (1996) The Australian international travel market: motivations from a gendered perspective, *Journal of Tourism Studies*, 7(1), 45–57.

McIntyre, N. (1994) The concept of 'involvement' in recreation research. In *New viewpoints in Australian outdoor recreation research and planning* (ed. D. Mercer), Hepper Marriot: Melbourne.

McIntyre, G., Hetherington, A. and Inskeep E. (1993) *Preparing development plans*, Sustainable Tourism Development, WTO: Madrid.

McKercher, B. (1991a) The unrecognised threat to tourism: can tourism survive sustainability? In *Ecotourism: incorporating the global classroom* (ed. B. Weiler). Bureau of Tourism Research: Canberra.

McKercher, B. (1991b) Understanding tourism's impacts: six truths about tourism. In *Benefits and costs of tourism* (ed. P.J. Stanton), Institute of Industrial Economics: University of Newcastle, 63–74.

McNeely, J.A. and Thorsell, J. (1989) *Jungles, mountains and islands: how tourism can help conserve natural heritage*. IUCN: Gland, Switzerland.

Meganck, R., (1992) The Environmental Express – Trinidad and Tobago's mobile interpretation centre. In *Environmental Interpretation* (ed. S. Ham), North American Press: Golden, Colorado, 221–223.

Mercer, D. (1995) *A question of balance – natural resource conflict issues in Australia*, The Federation Press: Sydney

Merschen, A. (1992) 'Marketing techniques and critiques', in *Passport to marketing adventure travel and ecotourism as a sustainable economic, cultural and environmental resource*, World Congress on Adventure Travel and Ecotourism, 20–23 September, British Colombia: Canada.

Messer, J. and Mosley, G. (1980) *The value of national parks to the community: values and ways* of improving the contribution of Australian national parks to the community, Australian Conservation Foundation: Melbourne.

Middleton, V. (1989) *Marketing in travel and tourism*, Heinemann: Oxford.

Middleton, V. (1998) *Sustainable tourism: a marketing perspective*, Butterworth–Heinemann: Oxford.

Mieczkowski, Z. (1995) *Environmental issues of tourism and recreation*. University Press of America, Inc: Lantarn, Maryland.

Mitman Clarke, W. (1997) Insufficient funds, *National Parks*, July/August, 26–29.

Munn, C. (1991) *Macaw biology and ecotourism, or when a bird in the bush is worth two in the hand*. Smithsonian Press Inc: Washington, DC.

Murphy, P. (1985) *Tourism: a community approach*. Methuen: London.

Nash, R. (1989) *The right of nature*. Primavera Press, Sydney, Australia.

National Park Service (1984) *Marketing parks and recreation*, Venture: State College, CA.

NPWS (National Parks and Wildlife Service, (NSW) (1995) *A rural focus*, NPWS: Sydney.

Norris, R. (1994) 'Ecotourism in the national parks of Latin America', *National Parks* (United States), 68(1–2), 33–37.

NZTIF (New Zealand Tourist Industry Federation) (1991) Code of Environmental Principles for Tourism in New Zealand, Wellington, New Zealand.

O'Neill, M. (1991) Naturally attractive, *Pacific Monthly*, September, 25.

Palacio, V. and McCool, S. (1997) Identifying ecotourists in Belize through benefit segmentation: a preliminary analysis, *Journal of Sustainable Development*, 5(3), 234–244.

PATA Pacific Asia Travel Association (1992) *Endemic tourism: a profitable industry in a sustainable environment*, Pacific Asia Travel Association: Kings Cross, Sydney.

Payne, R. and Graham, R. (1993) Visitor planning and management. In *Parks and protected areas in Canada: planning and management* (eds P. Dearden and R. Rollins), Oxford University Press: Toronto.

Pearce, D. (1980) *Tourists in the South Pacific: the contribution of research to development and planning*, UNESCO Mana and Biosphere Report no. 6, National Commission for UNESCO: Christchurch, NZ.

Pearce, D. (1989) *Tourist development*. Longman: Hong Kong.

Pearce, P. (1984) Tourist–guide interaction, *Annals of Tourism Research*, 11(1), 129–146.

Pearce, P. (1988) *The Ulysses factor: evaluating visitors in tourist settings*. Springer – Verlag: New York.

Pearce, P. (1990) Social impact of tourism. In *The social cultural and environmental impacts of tourism* (ed. T. Griffin), NSW Tourism Commission: Sydney.

Pearce, P. (1993) Fundamentals of tourist motivation. In *Tourism research: critiques and challenges* (eds D. Pearce and R. Butler), Routledge: London, 113–134.

Pearce, P.L. and Moscardo, G.M. (1985) The relationship between traveller's career levels and the concept of authenticity, *Australian Journal of Psychology*, 37(2), 157–174.

Pearce, P.L. Moscardo, G.M. and Ross, G.F. (1996) *Tourism Community Relationships*, Pergamon, UK.

Peng, M. (1992) Nero's children. *New Internationalist*, April, 24–27.

Pepper, D. (1984) *The roots of modern environmentalism*. Croom Helm: Sydney.

Peterson, G.L., Driver B.L. and Gregory, R. (eds) (1988) *Amenity resource valuation: integrating economics with other disciplines*, Venture: State College, PA.

Pigram, J.J. (1989) Sustainable tourism – policy considerations, *Journal of Tourism Studies*, 1(2), 2–9.

Pinchot, G. (1910) *The fight for conservation*, Doubleday: New York.

Pittock, J. (1996) The state of the Australian protected areas system. Paper for CNPPA workshop, Sydney, June.

Prosser, G. (1986) The limits of acceptable change: and introduction to a framework for natural area planning, *Australian Parks and Recreation*, 22(2), 5–10.

Prosser, R. (1994) Societal change and the growth in alternative tourism. In *Ecotourism: a sustainable option?* (eds E. Carter and G. Lowman), John Wiley: New York.

Public Land Users Alliance (1996) *4x4* (May), Public Land Users Alliance: Sydney.

Pyo, S., Mihalik, B.J. and Uysal, M. (1989) Attraction attributes and motivations: a canonical correlation analysis, *Annals of Tourism Research*, 16(2), 277–282.

Rachowiecki, R. (1994) *Costa Rica – a travel survival kit*, 2nd edn, Lonely Planet Publications: Hawthorn, Victoria, Australia.

Richardson, J. (1991) The case for an ecotourism association. In *Ecotourism incorporating the global classroom* (ed. B. Weiler), Bureau of Tourism Research: Canberra.

Richardson, J. (1995) Strategic alliances. In *Ecotourism and nature-based tourism: taking the next steps* (eds H. Richins, J. Richardson and A. Crabtree), Proceedings of the Ecotourism Association of Australia National Conference, Alice Springs, Ecotourism Association of Australia: Brisbane.

Robinson, G. (1988) *Crosscultural understanding*, Prentice–Hall: Hemel Hempstead.

Roggenbuck, J.W. (1987) Park interpretation as a visitor management strategy. In *proceedings of the 60th international conference of the Royal Australian Institute of Parks and Recreation – Metropolitan prospectives in parks and recreation*, Royal Australian Institute of Parks and Recreation: Canberra.

Rovinski, Y. (1991) Private reserves, parks, and ecotourism in Costa Rica. In *Nature tourism: managing for the environment* (ed. T. Whelan). Island Press: Washington, DC, 39–57.

Runte, A. (1997) *National parks: the American experience*, University of Nebraska Press: Lincoln.

Sachs, W. (1995) *The development dictionary*, Zed Books: London.

Saglio, C. (1979) Tourism for discovery: a project in Lower Casemance, Senegal. In *Tourism passport to development? Perspectives on the social and cultural effects of tourism in developing countries* (ed. E. deKadt), Oxford University Press: New York.

Schwartz, H. and Jacobs, J. (1979) *Qualitative sociology: a method to the madness*, Free Press: New York.

Shackley, M. (1995) The future of gorilla tourism in Rwanda, *Journal of Sustainable Development*, 3(2), 61–72.

Sharpe, G.W. (1982) *Interpreting the environment*. John Wiley: New York.

Sheppard, D. (1987) Parks are for the people – or are they? Unpublished paper NSW National Parks and Wildlife Service: Sydney.

Shiva, V. (1989) *Staying alive: women ecology and development*, Zed Books: London.

Shurcliff, K. and Williams, A. (1992) Managing ecotourism in the Great Barrier Reef Marine Park – can we manage it together? In *Ecotourism: incorporating the global classroom* (ed. B. Weiler), Bureau of Tourism Research: Canberra, 178–183.

Simmons, M. and Harris, R. (1995) The great barrier marine park. In R. Harris and N. Leiper (eds), *Sustainable tourism: an Australian perspective*, Butterworth-Heinemann: Melbourne, 11–19.

Sinclair, M.T. (1991) The tourism industry and foreign exchange leakages in a developing country: the distribution of earnings from safari and beach tourism in Kenya. In *The tourism industry and international analysis* (eds M.T. Sinclair and M.J. Stabler), CAB International: Oxford, 185–204.

Sirakaya, E. and Uysal M. (1997) Can sanctions and rewards explain conformance behaviour of tour operators with ecotourism guidelines? *Journal of Sustainable Tourism*, 5(4), 322–332.

Small, J. (1997) A simple model of tourist motivation. Unpublished research paper, School of Leisure and Tourism Studies, University of Technology: Sydney.

Sofield, T.H.B. (1991) Sustainable ethnic tourism in the South Pacific: some principles, *Journal of Tourism Studies*, 2(1), 56–72.

Solorzano, R., de Camino, R., Woodward, R. and Tosi, J. (1991) *Accounts overdue: natural resource depreciation in Costa Rica*. World Resources Institute: Washington, DC.

Stankey, G.H. (1991) Conservation, recreation and tourism: the good, the bad and the ugly. In *Proceedings of the 1990 congress on coastal and marine tourism – a symposium and workshop on balancing conservation and economic development* (eds M.L. Miller and J. Auyan National Coastal Resources Research and Development Institute: Newport, OR.

Stankey, G. and McCool, S. (eds) (1985) *Proceedings – symposium on recreation choice behavior*. United States Forest Service general technical report INT-184. United States Department of Agriculture: Ogden, UT.

Stankey, G.H., Cole, D.N., Lucas, R.C., Peterson, M.E. and Frissell, S.S. (1985) *The limits of acceptable change (LAC) system for wilderness planning*. United States Forest Service general technical report INT-176. United States Department of Agriculture: Ogden, UT.

Stankey, G., McCool, S. and Stokes, G.L. (1990) Managing for appropriate wilderness conditions: the carrying capacity issue. In *Wilderness management* (eds J.C. Hendee, G.H. Stankey and R.C. Lucas), 2nd edn, Fulcrum Press: Golden, CO, 215–239.

Stanton, W.J., Miller, K.E. and Layton R.A. (1992) *Fundamentals of marketing*, McGraw–Hill: Sydney.

Stear, L., Buckley, G. and Stankey, G. (1988) Constructing a meaningful concept of 'tourism industry': some problems and implications for research and policy. In *Frontiers in Australian tourism: the search for new perspectives in policy development and research* (eds B. Faulkner and M. Fagence), Bureau of Tourism Research: Canberra.

Steele, P. (1995) Ecotourism: an economic analysis, *Journal of Sustainable Tourism*, 3(1), 29–44.

Stretton, H. (1976) *Capitalism, socialism and the environment*, Cambridge University Press: Cambridge.

Strom, A. (1980) Impressions of a developing conservation ethic 1870–1930. In *100 years of parks*, Australian Conservation Foundation: Melbourne.

Sutherland, M. (1995) British Airways Tourism for Catlins Wildlife Trackers – South Dunedin, NZ, 1995 Tomorrow Awards (unpublished).

Swanson, M.A. (1992) Ecotourism: embracing the new environmental paradigm. Paper presented at the International Union for Conservation of Nature and Natural Resources (IUCN) IVth World Congress on National Parks and Protected Areas, Caracas, Venezuela, 10–12 February.

Szabo, S.G. (1996) Indigenous protected areas: managing natural and cultural values – a two way street. Paper for CNPPA (IUCN Commission on National Parks and Protected Areas)

Taylor, G. (1990) Planning and managing visitor opportunities. In *Towards serving our visitors and managing our resources* (eds R. Graham and R. Lawrence), Proceedings of the First Canada/US workshop on visitor management in parks and protected areas, Waterloo, Ontario, Tourism Research and Education Centre, University of Waterloo and Canadian Parks Service, Environment Canada.

TCA (Tourism Council Australia) (1998) *Code of Sustainable Practice*, Tourism Council Australia: Sydney.

Teo, A. (1996) Managing Sakau Rainforest Lodge – Malaysia, British Airways Tourism for Tomorrow Awards 1996 Pacific Region (unpublished).

Thackway, R. (1996) The national reserve system – cowards a representative system of ecologically based reserves, paper for CNPPA workshop, Sydney, June.

Tilden, F. (1957) *Interpreting our heritage*, John Wiley: New York.

Tilden, J. (1977) *Interpreting our heritage*, 3rd edn, University of North Carolina Press: Chapel Hill.

Todd, G. (1989) Tourism and the environment. *Travel and Tourism Analyst* (Elu), 5, 68–86.

Tolhurst, C. (1994) Seeing red over green ruling 'with no teeth', *Traveltrade*, November, 16–29.

Tonge, R. and Myott, D. (1989) *How to plan, develop and market local and regional tourism*, Gull Publishing: Queensland, Australia.

Travis, A.S. (1985) The consequences of growing ecological consciousness, and changing socio-cultural needs, on tourism policy. Paper presented at the *Trends in Tourism Demand*, conference; AIEST, Bregenz, September.

Tubb, P. (1997) Victoria, British Airways Tourism for Tomorrow Awards 1997, Pacific Region (unpublished).

Turner, A. (1988) 100 years of national parks in NSW, 1879–1979: participation, pressure groups and policy. PhD thesis, Australian National University: Canberra.

Turner, L. and Ash. J. (1975) *The golden hordes: international tourism and the pleasure periphery*, Constable: London.

Uysal, M. and Hagean, L. A. R. (1993) Motivation of pleasure travel and tourism. In *Encyclopaedia of Hospitality and Tourism* (eds M. A. Kham, M. D. Olsen and V. Turgut), Van Nostrand Reihnhold, New York, 798–821.

Valentine, P.S. (1991a) Ecotourism and nature conservation: a definition with some recent development in Micronesia. In *Ecotourism: incorporating the global classroom* (ed. B. Weiler), Bureau of Tourism Research: Canberra.

Valentine, P.S. (1991b) Nature-based tourism: a review of prospects and problems. In *Proceedings of the 1990 congress on coastal and marine tourism – a symposium and workshop on balancing conservation and economic developments* (eds M.L. Miller and J. Auyong) National Coastal Resources Research and Development Institute: Newport, OR.

Vellas, F. and Becherel L. (1995) International Tourism: An Economic Perspective, Macmillan Business, London.

Vickland, K. (1989) New tourists want new destinations. *Travel and Tourism Executive Report*, 9: 1–4.

Wallace, G. (1992) Real ecotourism: assisting protected area managers and getting benefits to local people. Paper presented at the International Union for Conservation of Nature and Natural Resources, IVth World Congress on National Parks and Protected Areas, Caracas, Venezuela, 10–12 February.

Watson, A.E. (1989) Wilderness visitor management practices: a benchmark and an assessment of progress. In *Outdoor Recreation Benchmark: Proceedings of the National Outdoor Recreation Forum* (ed. A.E. Watson), 13–14 January, Tampa, FL.

Wearing, B.M. and Wearing, S.L. (1996) Refocusing the tourist experience: the flaneur and the chorister, *Leisure Studies*, 15, 229–243.

Wearing, S. and Gardiner, M. (1994) Outdoor adventure programs as a form of nature interpretation. Unpublished report, University of Technology Sydney, School of Leisure and Tourism.

Weiler, B. (ed.) (1992) Ecotourism: incorporating the global classroom. Bureau of Tourism Research: Canberra.

Weiler, B. and Johnson, T. (1991) Nature based tour operators. Are they environmentally friendly or are they faking it? In *The Proceedings of the Benefits and Costs of Tourism: Proceedings of a National Tourism Research Conference* (ed. J. Stanton), Marie Resort, Nelson Bay, 3–4 October, University of Newcastle: Newcastle, 115–126.

Weiler, B. and Hall, C. (eds) (1992) *Special interest tourism*, Belhaven Press: London.

Wells, M. (1993) Neglect of biological riches: the economics of nature tourism in Nepal, *Biodiversity and Conservation*, 2, 445–456.

Wells, M., Brandon, K. (with Hannah, L.) (1992) *People and parks: linking protected area management with local communities*, World Bank: Washington, DC.

Wescott, G. (1993) 'Loving our parks to death', *Habitat Australia*, 21(1), 1219.

West, P.C. and Brechin S.R. (eds) (1991) *Resident peoples and national parks: social dilemmas and strategies in international conservation*, University of Arizonia Press: Tucson, USA.

Western, D. and Wright, M.R. (eds) (1994) *Natural connections: perspectives in community-based conservation*, Island Press: Washington, DC.

Wheeller, B. (1992) Is progressive tourism appropriate? *Tourism Management*, 13(1), 104–105.

Whelan, T. (ed.) (1991) *Nature tourism – managing*

for the environment, Island Press: Washington, DC.

White, L. (1967) The historical roots of our ecologic crisis, *Science*, 155.

Wight, P. (1993) Ecotourism: ethics, or eco-sell? *Journal of Travel Research*, 31(3) 4–14.

Wight, P. (1994) Environmentally responsible marketing of tourism. In *Ecotourism: a sustainable option?* (eds E. Carter and G. Lowman), John Wiley: New York, 39–55.

Wight, P. (1996) North American ecotourists: market profile and trip characteristics, *Journal of Travel Research*, 34(4), 2–10.

Wild, C. (1994) Issues in ecotourism. In C.P. Cooper and A. Lockwood (eds), *Progress in tourism, recreation and hospitality management*, 6, John Wiley: Chichester.

Williams, P. (1990) Ecotourism management challenges. In *Fifth Annual Travel Review Conference Proceedings 1990: A Year of Transition*, Travel Review: Washington, DC.

World Bank (1992) *The World Bank and the environment*, World Bank: Washington, DC.

World Commission on Environment and Development (1987) *Our common future* (The Brundtland Commission Report) Australian edition, Oxford University Press: Melbourne.

World Conservation Monitoring Centre (1992) Global biodiversity – status of the earth's living resources, Chapman & Hall: London.

World Wide Fund for Nature (WWF) (1992) *Beyond the green horizon: a discussion paper on principles for sustainable tourism*, WWF (UK): Surrey.

WTO (World Tourism Organization) (1990) *Tourism to the year 2000*, WTO: Madrid.

WTO and UNEP (1992) *Guidelines: development of national parks and protected areas for tourism*, WTO/UNEP Joint Technical Report Series.

WTTC (World Travel and Tourism Council) (1993) *WTTC progress and priorities: travel and tourism*, WTTC: Madrid.

WTTC (World Travel and Tourism Council) (1992) Environmental Review, *Travel and Tourism* 2(2), September/October.

WTTC (1994) Travel and Tourism: A New Economic Perspective, WTTC: Madrid.

WTTC (1995) Travel and Tourism's Economic Perspectives. A special, report from WTTC, WTTC: Madrid.

Young, J. (1990) *Post Environmentalism*, Belhaven Press: London.

Young, J. (1991) *Sustaining the earth: the past, present and future of the green revolution*. NSW University Press: Sydney.

Yum, S.M. (1984) Case report on attempts at alternative tourism, Hong Kong. In *Alternative tourism: report on the workshop on alternative tourism with a focus on Asia*, (ed. P. Holden), Ecumenical Coalition on Third World Tourism: Bangkok.

Index